The Doctrine of Saint-Simon

STUDIES IN THE LIBERTARIAN
AND UTOPIAN TRADITION

The Doctrine of

Saint-Simon: An Exposition

First Year, 1828-1829

*Translated with notes and an introduction
by* Georg G. Iggers

SCHOCKEN BOOKS · NEW YORK

Contents

PREFACE TO THE SECOND EDITION

The present edition is a reproduction, unchanged except for minor corrections and the omission of a brief preface by G. D. H. Cole, of the edition first published by the Beacon Press in 1958. The introduction, too, remains unchanged. It contains in an abbreviated form the interpretation which I developed in my book *The Cult of Authority: The Political Philosophy of the Saint-Simonians* (The Hague, 1958; 2nd edn., 1970). In the essential points my further work since 1958, particularly my researches in the *Fonds Enfantin*, have confirmed the main lines of this interpretation. Rolf Peter Fehlbaum in his recent study, *Saint-Simon und die Saint-Simonisten* (Basel, 1970) has come to very similar conclusions.

On certain points, however, I would place the emphases differently today. The introduction in my opinion is correct in stressing the strongly authoritarian note in Saint-Simonian thought after 1828, a note which is for the most part absent in the writings of their master Henri de Saint-Simon, who had died in 1825. At least during the period 1828–1832, when Saint-Simonianism constituted an organized movement with a well-formulated doctrine, the central concern of the Saint-Simonians was to introduce order and organization into every aspect of life. Economic and scientific activity were to be subordinated to this aim. The authoritarian aspects of the Saint-Simonian vision of society did not derive from the fascination of the Saint-Simonians with science and rational planning, as F. A. Hayek suggested, but from an obsession with the ideals of order and authority and a deep suspicion of the scientific attitude and of critical inquiry. The interest of the authors of the *Doctrine of Saint-Simon* in the Catholic critics of the French Revolution, especially in Joseph de Maistre and F. R. de Lamennais, and their sympathy for the conservative position of these thinkers were not accidental but very central to their belief.

v

What makes the *Doctrine of Saint-Simon* so fascinating today is less the faith it expresses in the expansion of human control over nature through a more meaningful organization of society, than its deep discomfort with the quality of modern civilization, a discomfort which the Saint-Simonians shared with certain other conservative as well as socialist critics of emerging capitalist society in the early nineteenth century. They differed from the conservative critics in their condemnation of every form of inequality based on the privilege of birth or the private ownership of capital. But unlike most early socialists, including Karl Marx and Friedrich Engels, their aim was never to free the individual from external control in "an association, in which the free development of each is the condition for the free development of all." Rather, they sought to restore what they considered to be the normal condition of society in which a "legitimate" authority, one based on talent and performance, would govern in the common interest so that men would "lovingly return to obedience."

I would be much more careful today in using the term "totalitarianism" to describe the Saint-Simonian doctrine than I was in the original Introduction, not because the term does not describe the social philosophy espoused by the Saint-Simonians between 1828 and 1832 but because the term has been used in recent decades to refer to concrete political phenomena of the twentieth century. Such phenomena differ too profoundly in practice from the aims the Saint-Simonians wished to attain to permit reducing them to a common denominator. Yet the term "authoritarian" is insufficient to describe the Saint-Simonian social and political doctrine. What the Saint-Simonians preached in public in these four years—their private letters and discussions contained in the *Fonds Enfantin* reveal a much greater diversity of views—amounted to a totalitarian vision, a hope not merely to re-establish authority, as de Maistre and de Bonald sought to do, but to regulate and coordinate every aspect of life. Such control, to be sure, was to be effected mainly through persuasion, but the Saint-Simonians frankly admitted in the *Doctrine* and elsewhere, that they were willing to employ coercion where persuasion failed. It is questionable whether any of the European governments of the twentieth century can properly be called totalitarian. The studies of the Third Reich—for example, Helmut Heiger's monumental investigation in his book on Walter Frank of the Nazi attempts to coordinate the German historical profession—show, as do studies of the Soviet Union in its Stalinist phase, to what extent these regimes were marked by the arbitrary use of terror and inner conflicts of power. They contrast sharply with the Saint-Simonian conception of a well-integrated society centrally directed on the basis of defined principles. Fascists and Stalinist dictatorships can only in part be understood in terms of their doctrines; in part they develop in response to concrete political challenges, although their response to these challenges cannot be isolated from the mental and ideological patterns within which they operated.

The Saint-Simonians of the period 1828–1832 never found themselves in the possession of political power. Their doctrine remained a totalitarian fantasy. When certain of the Saint-Simonians, who in those years had participated in the formulation of the doctrine, later in the century found themselves in positions of economic power and to a limited extent even of political influence, the Saint-Simonian movement and its doctrine had long since disintegrated. What remained was a variety of ideas, some of which found their practical application, in a very different context, in such undertakings of the Second Empire as the consolidation of the French railroad system, the creation of the Crédit Mobilier as a modern-type investment bank, the construction of the Suez Canal, and the negotiation of the Chevalier-Cobden treaty lowering trade barriers between France and England. The direct relevance of Saint-Simonianism on later thought and practice has, I now believe, been overstated in the original Introduction. Yet the contribution of the Saint-Simonians to the intellectual climate of the nineteenth century, not only to its hope and its optimism but also to its doubts regarding the individualistic, libertarian, and democratic aspects of modern society, cannot be understressed.

One additional point of correction, more marginal to the central argument of the Introduction. I would today, on the basis of further reading, reformulate the discussion on pp. xviii and xix in which, as I now realize, I have stated the anti-individualistic and deterministic aspects of Hegel and Marx's thought somewhat too one-sidedly.

I would like to express my appreciation to the American Philosophical Society for a grant-in-aid which permitted me to use the Saint-Simonian papers in the *Bibliothèque de l'Arsenal* in Paris and to Prof. James L. Adams for the many instances of encouragement and advice he has offered me in my work over the years.

I also wish to thank the Librairie Marcel Rivière for permission to quote from the notes prepared by C. Bouglé and Elie Halévy for their edition of the *Doctrine de Saint-Simon: Exposition. Première Année, 1829* (Paris, 1924).

GEORG G. IGGERS

March 1972

INTRODUCTION

In the nineteenth century, the Saint-Simonians were viewed as socialists who reacted to contemporary disturbances in social organization, and to the impoverishment which resulted from the industrial revolution, with the humanitarian demand that a more just society be created which would apply human reason to resolve these disturbances. Until recently, the Saint-Simonians have been dismissed as ineffectual social reformers. But today they emerge as theorists of the modern totalitarian state whose doctrine subtly assisted in its establishment.

The Doctrine of Saint-Simon, the most decisive influence in the crystallization of the social philosophy of the Saint-Simonians (as distinct from that of their master, Henri de Saint-Simon), marked the most radical rejection of liberal and democratic institutions by any of the reform or revolutionary movements of the "Left" in the nineteenth century, not excluding Marxism. Indeed, the classification of anticapitalistic movements as left and right first ceases to make sense with the Saint-Simonians. Their doctrine integrates the conservative demand for order, hierarchial organization, and aristocracy with the socialist demand for equality of opportunity and social and economic planning in the interest of communal welfare. What emerges is the theory of a state which carried conservative and socialist ideas to their extreme to foreshadow the totalitarian mass state. The aim of Saint-Simonian doctrine was to stabilize the contemporary revolutionary situation which they viewed as the inevitable result of the inadequacy, in the technological age, of the feudal Christian social and intellectual order. The most spectacular, although not basic, expression of the current crisis was, of course, political. Born mostly around the turn of the century, the Saint-Simonians lived through the aftermath of the collapse of the old political order and the succession of the transient political regimes: the constitutional monarchy, Jacobinism, the Directory, the Consulate and the Empire, and the Restoration. Even in the

Restoration monarchy, the Saint-Simonians observed the continuation of the bitter struggle between the Catholic-legitimists
and the Revolutionary tradition on the eve of the Revolution
of 1830. The French Revolution had completed the destruction
of the organic social unity of France and intensified the division
of France into parties and classes. Yet the French Revolution,
the Saint-Simonians realized (as did de Maistre and Lamennais[1]),
had been neither a conspiracy nor a spontaneous uprising of the
masses in the name of liberty. The Revolution was the outcome
of a long development of inner decay, not only of the political
order but also of the entire outdated civilization. Nor could the
Revolution be considered to have ended with the fall of the
Bourbons or the establishment of responsible parliamentary
government; the 1830 Revolution could be successfully completed only after all vestiges of the medieval Christian-feudal
society had been destroyed, and also only after a new order had
been constructed. Parliamentary government, freedom of opinion, and the rights of men were all instruments of the historical
process in the destruction of an insufficient order, but as such
they were elements of crisis which would have to disappear with
the erection of a new social order. As in their political critique,
the Saint-Simonians' economic analysis appeared closer to that
of the conservative critics of capitalism than to that of the
socialists. What the Saint-Simonians considered to be the
economic crisis of the post-Revolutionary world was much more
closely related to the general revolutionary situation than to the
Industrial Revolution. In 1814, only two years before the appearance of Saint-Simon's *Industry,* only 15 steam engines were
in use in France, and in 1830 only 600. In 1843, France contained
only 5,000 mechanical looms, as compared with about 100,000
in England. The notable mechanization of French industry did
not come until later.

[1] Count Joseph Marie de Maistre (1753-1821) in works including the *Essai
sur le principe générateur des constitutions,* and *Du Pape,* and Hugues Félicité
de Lamennais (1782-1854) in the *Essai sur l'indifférence en matière de
religion,* were principal theoretical spokesmen of the Catholic ultra-conserva-
tive reaction, during the early Restoration, against the revolutionary spirit.
Lamennais was later to move radically to the left and become an advocate of
the reconciliation of Christianity with democracy and socialism.

The Saint-Simonians considered the current economic problems to be the results of the emergence of the laissez faire free-enterprise system. Just as the French Revolution had attacked the organic unity and the authority of the political order, so, the Saint-Simonians held, the economic revolution had destroyed the regulation of trade and industry which the ancient corporations exercised in the interest of society. The depressions of 1816 and 1825 especially impressed the Saint-Simonians with the danger of unbridled free enterprise. A conscious class struggle between industrial workers and capitalists was still unknown, and the Lyon riots occurred more than two years after the completion of the *First Year* of the *Doctrine of Saint-Simon. An Exposition.*

Just as the French Revolution appeared as an inevitable stage in the historical process once the old order failed to serve its organic function, the laissez faire economy was necessary to level the guild system once it failed to fulfill the changing needs of the times. The Saint-Simonians were economic determinists to the extent that they believed that history demonstrated the progressive decline of military activity and the constant growth of material production. The warlike, anti-industrial character of medieval feudalism and the otherworldliness of Christian doctrines, supports of the pre-Revolutionary order of privilege, were predestined to give way to values better adapted to production. Yet the economic, like the political crisis, could be solved only by the establishment of the Saint-Simonian order. While the Saint-Simonians stressed their sympathy for the working classes, they saw the basic critical characteristics of the laissez faire economy not in class struggle or exploitation but in the lack of social organization and the consequent predominance of individual over communal interest, which dominance, in turn, contributed to the serious plight of the masses and the degeneration of a "people" into an amorphous mass.

The deepest expression of the crisis of the time, however, the Saint-Simonians found in the intellectual realm. Incapable of admitting a pluralism of views, they considered the lack of intellectual unanimity as symptomatic of crisis. Like the Catholic Restoration thinkers, they saw the Revolution as the political aftermath of the forces unleashed by the Protestant Reformation and the subsequent intellectual revolution which gave birth to the skeptical spirit of eighteenth-century philosophy. The critical spirit of the *philosophes,* while basically destructive, was yet considered by both Saint-Simon and his disciples to fulfill a definite historical role, that of destroying an incomplete intellectual system which contained within itself its own germ of destruction. Yet unlike their master, Saint-Simon, the Saint-Simonians did not see the outcome of intellectual history in the triumph of "positive method" over theology; rather the intellectual revolution could not be terminated until a new intellectual synthesis had been created, which the "positive method" (because of its analytic character) could not offer. Just like political and economic individualism, freedom of conscience or free rational inquiry into the nature of things merely served a historical function, the destruction of the old order, and hence was "critical." The new intellectual order would require an "encyclopedia" in which all knowledge was systematically linked with *the fundamental ideas* and in which positive method and scientific inquiry would be restored to their proper place, that of technical tools in the service of a fundamental trans-rational faith. The revolution would be concluded only when this fundamental idea (with the technical aid of scientists, artists, and industrialists) would have found systematic application to every aspect of social life.

To expand upon a difference noted in the previous paragraph, the doctrine of the Saint-Simonians should not be equated with the social philosophy of Henri de Saint-Simon. The basic differences in the philosophies of master and disciples have not been recognized clearly enough and the Saint-Simonian doctrine has been identified by historians, including only recently Friedrich Hayek,[2] with the confidence of Saint-Simon in the efficiency of the positive sciences and industry as guides to the solution of the crisis of the age. Saint-Simonian doctrine goes a good deal further, makes a much sharper break with the faith in science and technology, and sees the solution in religio-political terms, in

[2] F. A. Hayek, *The Counter-Revolution of Science; Studies on the Abuse of Reason.* (Glencoe, Illinois: The Free Press, 1952).

ideological unanimity, and total social organization. This traditional confusion of the Saint-Simonian doctrine with the positivism and industrialism of Saint-Simon is especially misleading
to the English reader since it was the disciples' interpretation of
Saint-Simon, *The Doctrine of Saint-Simon*, rather than the writings of Saint-Simon, through which the political and social ideas
of Saint-Simon became known.

Saint-Simonianism must be understood within the framework of the three closely related intellectual traditions to which
it reacted and which it attempted to synthesize: the natural law
philosophy of the *philosophes*, Catholic Restoration traditionalism, and the philosophies of historically determined progress.
Despite the Saint-Simonian concern with economic and social
forces, and despite their approach to history from the standpoint
of the interrelation of social forces, their philosophy of history was
still basically idealistic: history was essentially the development
of the moral conception to perfection. Every civilization was the
concrete expression of an idea, and hence the student of the
contemporary crisis had to understand the fundamental ideas
at play. The Saint-Simonians saw opposed to each other two
mutually exclusive ideas—the conservative-authoritarian and the
liberal-humanitarian tradition—both with far-reaching political
and cultural implications but both insufficient and hence fated
to doom. Liberalism, in the form of "eighteenth-century philosophy," both the Saint-Simonians and the Catholic legitimists
agreed, had been the most important cause and the most powerful instrument of the Revolution. The basic premises of the
philosophy of the eighteenth century (represented for the Saint-
Simonians by Voltaire and the Encyclopedists) were the supremacy of a historical, immutable law of nature or reason over positively existing institutions; the possibility of the individual, by
rational processes of inquiry, to attain knowledge of this law; and
the ability of the rational individual through deliberate action
suddenly to transform the historical institutions according to a
rational plan. From this "metaphysics" of natural rights, as both
Saint-Simonians and Catholic traditionalists called it, derived the
belief that there existed an automatic harmony between the

actions of rational individuals and social welfare, "that ignorance, neglect, or contempt of human rights are the sole causes
of public misfortunes." [3]

The political expression of this philosophy was the liberal
idea of the state based upon a social contract. The classical
formulation of this concept is in Locke's *Second Treatise on
Civil Government,* written after the Glorious Revolution, but it
was not applied in French thought until after the middle of
the eighteenth century and the growing attack upon the absolute
monarchy. According to this theory, the sovereignty of the state,
rather than deriving from God, could only come from a social
contract among men born free with equal rights in nature, and
the state only existed for the protection of these basic rights of
man. The power of government should, hence, be strictly defined by a written constitutional law enacting the social contract,
and this power should be limited to the maintenance of civil
order and the execution of justice. In short, in Tom Paine's
words, a sharp distinction was to be drawn between the body
social and the body politic. The state was to be excluded from
the regulation of private life and social relationships except
where action on the part of citizens curtailed the rights of others.
The logical conclusion was that culture, economy, and religion
were to be the concern of private individuals, the result of voluntary associations rather than of coercion by the state. And the
state, moreover, was to be controlled by the representatives of
the parties to the social contract, even if the conclusion that all
men should be given the suffrage and full rights of citizenship
was generally not drawn by these thinkers who considered the
protection of property as the main function of government;
hence the state was the concern of the propertied classes only.
For the Saint-Simonians, the liberal-humanitarian idea of the
autonomy of the rational individual could never be a positive but
merely a negative force, a tool for the destruction of an imperfect
order, but basically an abnormal condition counter to human
nature.

Systematic conservative thought in France followed, rather
than preceded, the *philosophes'* attack on the old order. The

[3] *Declaration of the Rights of Man and of the Citizen.*

conservatism of the Old Regime had been largely unreflective. On the other hand the spirit of the medieval social order was expressed for the Saint-Simonians by the post-Revolutionary theocrats, the early nineteenth-century Catholic thinkers—Bonald, Ballanche,[4] Lamennais—but above all by de Maistre, who in defense of the modern Church and the modern monarchy expounded a unitary collectivism quite different from medieval particularism. The Christian-feudal, or perhaps more correctly the Catholic-Restoration legitimist idea, asserted the supremacy of historical forces over deliberate action, of society over the individual, and of collective faith over individual reason, and the need for authority and hierarchy. Deliberate action based upon abstract reason disturbed the harmony of society based on traditional forces and inevitably had to result in anarchy.

The Saint-Simonian conception of the "critical philosophy of the eighteenth century" and of the "defenders of the old order," as two clearly defined philosophic systems with clear political implications, mutually exclusive, was, of course, an oversimplification. The Saint-Simonians, despite their concern with social and economic forces, still saw ideas as the basic forces in history. Liberalism and conservatism to them were two logical systems of ideas rather than ideologies determined to any extent by political and economic interests or expediency. But were liberalism and conservatism mutually exclusive? For example, if not in his social philosophy, de Maistre in his method was strongly influenced by the growing empiricism of eighteenth-century philosophy, and he criticized the revolutionaries' doctrine of man and the historicity of the state of nature and the social contract for being abstractions unconfirmed by observation. Indeed the Saint-Simonians praised de Maistre for giving legitimacy a naturalistic and positivistic definition.[5] On the other hand, the sort of liberalism of the Restoration represented by Benjamin Constant (not to speak of the more conservative

    [4] Ballanche is, of course, in a class by himself among these Catholic thinkers in his attempt to reconcile Christianity with an idea of progress. See index for reference to Ballanche in text.
    [5] See Bouglé and Halévy's discussion in their edition of *Doctrine de Saint-Simon. Exposition. Première Année, 1829* (Paris: Marcel Rivière, 1924), pp. 122 f., n. 4, referred to in this translation in footnote 3 of Session I.

upper-bourgeois *doctrinaires* like Royer-Collard) differed sharply
from the radicalism of 1793: strongly influenced by counter-Revo-
lutionary historical thought, its ideal of government stemmed
from the English tradition rather than from the Revolution.
And the Revolution, far from effectively limiting the power of
government, had even in the *Declaration of the Rights of Man
and of the Citizen* enhanced the importance of the nation as an
integral organism. Throughout the eighteenth century, the natu-
ral-law conception upon which the contractual theory of government rested was being undermined by the *philosophes* themselves. By assuming the existence of certain universal human
rights which could be known by rational man at any point in
space and time, the natural-rights thinkers, in the Cartesian tradition, had implied a definite rejection of history and tradition
(held to be against human reason) as a guide to social and political truth. And yet Locke's epistemology in making knowledge
dependent upon sensory experiences stood in a definite sense in
contradiction to a priori natural law.

The replacement of Cartesianism by Lockean empiricism in
French thought in the course of the eighteenth century brought
with it an increasing relativism of values and in Helvétius and
Diderot, at least, a strong emphasis on environmental factors.
The rising belief in human perfectibility which up to Condorcet
was primarily a conviction in the inevitable development of man
toward greater rationality yet implied that man's understanding
of social truth was not independent of history. The Catholic
traditionalist philosophy, instead of constituting a complete re-
versal of eighteenth-century thought and a radical return to the
feudal-Christian Middle Ages, was deeply influenced by the increasing empiricism and incipient historicism of the eighteenth
century. Interestingly enough, de Maistre and Lamennais attacked the liberal theory of politics less from the standpoint of
dogma than of empiricism. The basic error of the Revolution,
they agreed with Burke, had been to look at the state in abstract
political and a-historical terms. The universal "natural rights"
of man, the postulation of a state of nature prior to the formation of political society, the theory of the contractual origin of
the state, were pure abstractions, fictions without empirical

foundation. The only source of knowledge concerning the nature of society was the empirical study of society itself. In terms of the latter, laws and institutions had to be understood within their historical setting; there were no rights of men but only rights of men within specific institutions. Society, rather than being the product of man created for the purpose of protecting his inalienable rights, coexisted with man as a condition for human existence. Social and political institutions were the outcome of age-old historical forces. The attempt to base government on certain abstract principles by revolutionary means was to misunderstand the very nature of society and history and to disturb social harmony. Change had to develop within the framework of traditional institutions. The true constitution could not be set down on a sheet of paper. Rather the pattern of forces within a society, the manner by which the society and its government functioned, formed a constitution.

Proceeding then from this empirical, anti-metaphysical analysis of society, the Catholic traditionalists derived an authoritarian conception of society. The neat distinction of pre-Revolutionary thinkers between the body social and the body politic was rejected. The state could not be understood apart from social and historical forces. Nor was the state a voluntary association of citizens which might be equated with voluntaristic associations of citizens in other spheres of social activity. The basic reality in social life was the society as an integral whole, as an organism rather than as a collection of basically independent and separable individuals. This view, it should be stressed, had not been entirely foreign to the French eighteenth-century thinkers or revolutionaries. In Rousseau's social contract, society, once formed by the surrender of all natural rights on the part of the members, had a "general will" superior to the interests of the individual. The revolutionaries had similarly conceived of the nation as a reality in which all sovereignty resided. Attempting to justify the Old Regime and the power of the Church, de Maistre and the other Catholic traditionalists drew the conclusion that society by its very nature demanded gradations in political and social importance. A society meant not only the interaction of all parts, but also unity—a common doctrine accepted by all its members

and a common governing authority. The scope of this authority
must be all-embracing and must stand beyond criticism. For de
Maistre and de Lamennais, the rule of the king must be absolute
in temporal matters, subject only to the spiritual rule of the Holy
Roman Church. The conception of the state and of the church
was, however, in de Maistre's case, rather modern-bureaucratic
than medieval. Without an existent authority in the intellectual
as well as the political life of society, error and dissent would
arise and lead to anarchy. The crisis of the modern age was one
of individualism in religion, reason, and politics; and the French
Revolution was the inevitable consequence of the Reformation
which engendered the critical philosophy of the eighteenth century.

A synthesis of the eighteenth-century myth of the rational
world and the rational individual, and the counterrevolutionary
traditionalism and collectivism, was provided to a certain extent
by the philosophies of progress. The origin of the philosophies
of human perfectibility lay, of course, in the rationalistic tradition of the seventeenth and eighteenth centuries. With the
"Quarrel of the Ancients and Moderns," the belief gained
strength that man progressed toward greater understanding with
time. Lessing, Kant, and Condorcet saw the history of the world
as the development of man toward perfection and rationality.
Yet this progress was still conceived by Condorcet (in the last
decade of the eighteenth century) as fundamentally intellectual.
The liberation of man from prejudice and superstition would
produce a society based upon reason. In the early nineteenth century, under the influence of the new traditional philosophies of
history, the philosophies of human perfectibility tended to de-
part from this emphasis on the individual and reason. For Hegel,
Saint-Simon, Comte, the Saint-Simonians, and later Marx, the
basic bearer of reason was not the rational individual but rather
a society or a social class. The individual and his reason were
merely the tools of the historical process. The final end of the
historical process was not as much the liberation of the human
mind from fear and its attainment of reason as the appearance of
a rationally organized society, an organization which inevitably
meant the subordination of the individual to society even if the

ultimate goal, as with Marx, might be the liberation of the individual from the state. In contrast to the view of the eighteenth-
century *philosophes,* the world was not yet organized in such a
rational fashion that there existed an automatic harmony between the enlightened actions of the individual and social and
individual interest. Rather, the history of the world marked the
gradual appearance of social harmony. This social harmony was
not achieved through the conscious and voluntary efforts of
rational individuals, but was instead the outcome of inner historical necessity. The world of the past was inevitably a world
of antagonism; the ultimate good revealed itself only in stages.
The very meaning of history was the achievement of this ultimate good. This philosophy of historically determined progress
toward an ultimate good for the sake of which the world existed
constituted a sort of secularized eschatology, and indeed we find
in medieval Catholic thought a foreshadowing of such a philosophy of history in Joachim de Floris,[6] studied by Lessing, who in
turn influenced the Saint-Simonians. Yet, the eschatological end
of human society was attained through the very conflict and imperfection which marked society: in Hegel, for example, through
the contradictory character of the ideas underlying the social
institutions; for Marx, by the development of a progressively
more simplified and universal class struggle; for the Saint-Simonians, through the alternation of progressively more comprehensive organic and critical epochs. For the Saint-Simonians, as we
shall see, this goal was the total organization and rationalization
of all human behavior within the framework of a hierarchy of
the able.

II

Claude Henri de Rouvroi, Comte de Saint-Simon, who was
born in 1760 and died in 1825, was in a sense the child of both
the Old Regime and the philosophy of the Enlightenment. Of

---

[6] Joachim de Floris (c. 1131-c. 1202) regarded history as divine revelation
in three stages, passing from the Age of the Father or Old Testament of
kings and patriarchs through the Age of the Son or New Testament of
freedmen and priests to the third and final era of friends and mystics living
without class distinction.

an ancient noble family, a relative of the Duc de Saint-Simon (the biographer of Louis XIV and the bitter aristocratic critic of royal absolutism), Henri de Saint-Simon, it is said, had d'Alembert as his preceptor. Already in his youth, Saint-Simon was deeply concerned with the need of applying reason and science to social organization and of furthering industrial development. Saint-Simon fought at the Battle of Yorktown for "industrial liberty," and in his early twenties he devised plans for the building of canals to join the Pacific and the Atlantic in Nicaragua and to link Madrid with the sea. Upon his return to France, he used his wealth to gather as his tutors the most eminent scientists of France. His soon-spent wealth was restored during the Revolution when he speculated in church lands, though he consequently almost lost his head under Robespierre. Once more he surrounded himself with the savants of the time, traveled to Germany and England, and unsuccessfully tried to marry Mme de Stael. Slowly his ideas on scientific methods, industrialism, and the application of science to social organization took systematic shape; and from 1802 onward, they appeared in a steady stream of pamphlets and books. Falling again poverty-stricken, Saint-Simon became dependent on the charity of a former servant. After 1810, he was surrounded by a following of young engineers from the Ecole Polytechnique, chief among whom were Augustin Thierry and Auguste Comte, who acted as his secretaries and collaborated in his writings. Apparently disappointed by his lack of success in persuading the rulers and the intelligentsia to support his proposal for social reconstruction, Saint-Simon attempted suicide in 1823. His last work, the *New Christianity*, with its religion of human brotherhood, appeared in the year of his death, 1825.[1]

Saint-Simon's thought between 1802 and 1825 was not constant; one can easily distinguish at least four phases which, although linked by the fundamental belief in the law of human

---

[1] A virtually unknown and today generally unavailable English edition of the *New Christianity* was published in 1834. None of Saint-Simon's works, until the publication of his *Selected Writings*, edited, translated, and introduced by F. M. Markham (New York: Macmillan 1953), has been available to English-speaking readers.

perfectibility inherent in history, were marked by differing, even if not contradictory, emphases.

The Genevan Letters appeared in 1802, only seven years after the posthumously published *Outline of a Historical View of the Progress of the Human Mind* of Condorcet, whom Saint-Simon acknowledged as one of the strongest influences on his own thought. In the *Letters of an Inhabitant of Geneva* and in his other early writings, Saint-Simon saw the perfection of scientific methodology as the basis of human progress. The history of the human mind was marked by the steady replacement of imagination by observational method, which led to man's increasing awareness of the basic lawfulness of the universe and which would lead with the ultimate attainment of an observational science of "social physiology" to the establishment of a "positive," scientifically ordered society. In the *Reorganization of European Society* of 1814, Saint-Simon, reacting to the political factors of the current crisis, advocated a confederation of Europe and the establishment of parliamentary governments. In the writings beginning with *Industry*, Saint-Simon, seeing in industry a force of at least equal importance with science, outlined the establishment of an "industrial regime." The history of man was seen to be marked by the constant decline of "parasitism" and the rise of peaceful industry. The past had been marked by the "feudal regime," the rule of the military aristocracy and its descendants, who had been consumers. But the future belonged to the producers. In most of Saint-Simon's writings the industrial regime was not to possess autocratic power. Instead, governmental powers were to pass into the hands of the most important merchants and manufacturers, the leaders of an "industrial" class which included all producers and owners as well as wage-workers. While society had obligations to the unemployed, Saint-Simon did not advocate social ownership of the economy. The leading industrialists would instead be able to render government at the lowest cost. The age had come when the government over men was to be replaced by the administration of things. In a last phase, Saint-Simon in the *New Christianity* called for a religion based upon brotherly love and concerned with achieving bliss on earth. The basic concern of religion was to be the speediest amelioration of the lot of the poor.

The basic concepts of Saint-Simon's philosophy found their way into the Saint-Simonian literature: the philosophy of progress, even if progress and social change were to be interpreted differently; the concern with industry and technology; the ardent pacifism; the stress on the duties of society towards the "poorest and most numerous class." Yet such basic elements of Saint-Simonian theory as the thoroughgoing authoritarianism, the abolition of inheritance, and the later feminism, although to a certain extent developments from Saint-Simon's writings, were not found in the master's work.

The term "Saint-Simonianism" refers here to the disciples of Saint-Simon. It must be made clear that Saint-Simonianism, while maintaining certain basic tenets, from its beginning until its dissolution, continuously underwent changes in others. Yet a basic unity existed in its attempt to put an end to what was regarded as the revolutionary situation of the age. Though I shall not discuss in detail the history of the movement, certain general phases in the development of Saint-Simonian thought should be distinguished. The Saint-Simonian school may be said to have begun with the publication (in 1825), shortly after the death of Saint-Simon, of the *Producteur. A Philosophical Journal of Industry, the Sciences, and the Fine Arts.* In this first phase, Saint-Simonianism did not constitute a systematic philosophy or a well-organized movement but rather, as Charléty has called it, a "state of mind." [2] Among the contributors to the journal—in addition to such later Saint-Simonians as Enfantin, Bazard, Laurent, and Rouen—were Blanqui, Buchez, and Auguste Comte, the one-time secretary of Saint-Simon, who had broken with the master two years earlier in disagreement with his religious emphasis. The contributors were linked by some basic views of the process of history and by a belief in the progressive character of science, industry, and art. History was viewed as a potentially "positive" science, and the possibility of a "positive" science of society ("social physics" or "social physiology") was

[2] Sébastien Charléty, *Histoire du Saint-Simonisme* (Paris: P. Hartmann, 1931), p. 31.

stressed. While Auguste Comte outlined his "positive philoso-phy," Bazard condemned the "principle of examination" and the rejection of religion as the major sources of the crisis of the age. While there was a strong collectivistic undertone in their philos-ophy of history as well as an implied antiliberalism, the early Saint-Simonians had no unified program for social reconstruc-tion. Enfantin envisaged the extension of credit to workers within the framework of private property and a free economy. Little attention was given to politics and religion, and the role of woman was not yet mentioned.

After the suspension of the *Producteur* in October, 1826, a close-knit organization of some of its contributors emerged: notably Enfantin, Bazard, and Buchez, and a number of engi-neering students from the Ecole Polytechnique. From the dis-cussions of this group arose a more precise formulation of Saint-Simonian theory, as well as a more definite organization—the *collège*. The theory was expounded in a series of public lectures held biweekly after December 17, 1828, and known as the *Doc-trine of Saint-Simon. An Exposition. First Year (1828-29)*.

Proceeding from its philosophy of history, the *Doctrine* took issue with the entire structure of contemporary European social organization and proposed a program for total social reorganiza-tion. Consciously going beyond the *Producteur* and even beyond Saint-Simon, the Saint-Simonians in the *Doctrine* systematically defined the nature of the crisis of modern civilization, attacked the right of inheritance, and formulated the need for the or-ganization of society under a "hierarchy of the able."

While this second phase of the Saint-Simonian movement had a general unity of thought, there emerged slowly a stronger religious and political emphasis which tended to subordinate the earlier scientific and industrial interest. Thus in the later "ses-sions" of the *Doctrine,* issue was taken with "positive method" in science; and in a second series of lectures, the *Second Year,* science and industry were clearly subordinated to politics and re-ligion in the hierarchy. This new emphasis led to the establish-ment of a hierarchically organized Saint-Simonian church with Enfantin and Bazard installed as the "fathers" of the "family" in late December, 1829. The doctrine was propagated through public "sermons" and "teachings" in Paris, by missions sent to the provinces and to Belgium, by pamphlets, and above all through the pages of the weekly *Organisateur* and the daily *Globe*. The *Globe* had been the famous liberal paper of the twenties and became Saint-Simonian in November, 1830, after the conversion of its manager, Pierre Leroux, to the new religion. In the *Globe,* the Saint-Simonians received their greatest degree of attention.

Between 1828 and 1832, the Saint-Simonians were to enlist as members several of the most important French and European social philosophers and artists of the nineteenth century, to become a highly controversial topic to the European intelligentsia and to attain, if not understanding, at least notoriety among the masses of French and German newspaper readers. Auguste Comte, the secretary of Saint-Simon until the latter's "religious phase" in the last two years of his life, rejected the Saint-Simonian movement because of its religious bias; nevertheless, he collaborated in 1825 and 1826 on the Saint-Simonian *Producteur* in which he outlined his "positive philosophy." The Saint-Simonian church foreshadowed the basic structure and philosophy of the Religion of Humanity of Comte in his later years. Buchez, the later Catholic socialist, was a member of the Saint-Simonian hierarchy. Heine and Franz Liszt repeatedly attended the Sunday meetings. Carlyle and Mill corresponded with the society. Sainte-Beuve and George Sand expressed their keen interest and approval, while Lamartine, Balzac, and Lamennais watched with mixed emotions. Stendhal, Benjamin Constant, and Fourier found the new philosophy sufficiently important to attack it. Even Goethe, while criticizing the Saint-Simonian collectivism to Eckermann, regularly received the *Globe.* In 1835, Heine dedicated *De l'Allemagne,* his essays on German philosophy and history, to Enfantin, and he pursued in them a basically Saint-Simonian method of treating history. The new religion claimed over 40,000 adherents by the middle of 1831 and was well known to every educated person in Europe. In the popular mind, the Saint-Simonians were wrongly held responsible for the 1831 Lyon uprisings.

The disintegration of this "second phase," during which

Saint-Simonianism was concerned primarily with social reorganization, was precipitated by the conflict within the movement on the question of woman. While there had been general agreement that woman, traditionally exploited like the worker, should be emancipated socially, a new orientation emerged under the leadership of Enfantin which increasingly emphasized the importance of the question of woman, finally advocated free love, and identified the outcome of history with the "emancipation" and "sanctification" of the flesh. This heightened feminism led to a schism, to the rupture of Bazard with the movement, the consequent departure of other members, and to legal persecutions after January, 1832. On April 20, 1832, the last issue of the *Globe* appeared, and the second phase of the movement's history may be said to have ended.

In the third phase characterized by heightened feminism and pantheistic religious thought after 1832, the concern with social and political problems lessened. The Saint-Simonians were now less interested in propagating the faith than in preparing for a more propitious time by the education of a hierarchy. They withdrew to a monastic life. The trials which resulted in the imprisonment of Enfantin further weakened the movement, which dissolved as an organized group after Enfantin's departure to Egypt in search of the "Woman Messiah." Later in the century, the Saint-Simonians were to be prominent in financial and industrial projects, such as the creation of the Crédit Mobilier, the extension of the French railroad net, and the construction of the Suez Canal.

To summarize: few movements in the intellectual history of nineteenth-century France have had as momentous and varied an impact on the development of social philosophy of that century as has Saint-Simonianism. The conception of society as an organic whole subject in all its aspects to social law, a view which they shared with Auguste Comte and Henri de Saint-Simon, was to dominate French sociological thought through Durkheim. The theory of regulation of the economy through a hierarchy of banks for the sake of eliminating competition, increasing efficiency, and bringing about a juster distribution of wages, was to be taken up both by socialist thinkers like Rodbertus, Lassalle,

and Louis Blanc, and by the founders of French corporation capitalism. Indeed, the Saint-Simonians under the Second Empire,
as noted above, were to be highly instrumental in the organization of the Crédit Mobilier, the forerunner of the trusts. The
advocacy of a literature which would portray social responsibility
found response in the "Young Germans," who were keenly interested in the movement, and in French mid-century realism.
Saint-Simonianism also advanced feminism and pacifism. As a
philosophy of history, in its conception of the critical character
of contemporary times and in its emphasis upon the establishment of a new aristocracy of labor, the doctrine appears to have
influenced the social philosophy of Thomas Carlyle.[3] And in a
more subtle way, the anti-liberalism of the *Doctrine* and especially of the *Globe,* the rejection of democracy, and the stress on
the need of order prepared for later authoritarian movements.

III

The opening chapter of the *Doctrine* describes modern society as being in a state of "permanent anarchy," in which social
ties are everywhere weakening. The task of the Saint-Simonians
is to offer a solution to the inner struggles of the society by bridg-
ing the struggle of the adherents "of the twofold religious and
political organization of the Middle Ages," and the revolutionary
"partisans of the new ideas." The crisis of the modern age, the
Saint-Simonians believe, is primarily one of authority and order.
The old order was overthrown when it was no longer legitimate,
which means, when it was no longer in harmony with the needs
of the time, but no new order has taken its place. For such a
new order to be established, a new philosophy of life, a general
doctrine, is required. A philosophy is not merely a collection
of abstract metaphysical ideas or isolated moral observations but
rather a conception which "embraces all modes of human activity
and which offers a solution to all social and individual prob-

---

[3] See the following studies: Hill Shine, *Carlyle and the Saint-Simonians.
The Conception of Historical Periodicity* (Baltimore: Johns Hopkins Press,
1941), and David Brooks Cofer, *Saint-Simonism in the Radicalism of Thomas
Carlyle* (Austin: Von Boeckmann-Jones Company, 1931).

lems." A philosophy is the fundamental belief of society. "There have therefore not been more philosophical doctrines worthy of the name than there have been general states of mankind."

Historical societies fall into two types: organic ones in which institutions and beliefs rest on a general doctrine; and critical ones, in which the doctrine of the previous epoch is rejected without its replacement by a new one. In the first stage of a critical period, there still exists a certain unity, a common action against the previous doctrine and institutions. In the second stage, to which the modern world belongs, the destruction of the old order has been virtually achieved, but the "critical" spirit has become deepened and has resulted in a complete lack of unity between and within the three general spheres of human and social activity—science, industry, and the fine arts. This lack of unity is essentially a lack of organization, which deficiency expresses itself in activity independent from social guidance. The modern crisis began in the fifteenth century, the *Doctrine* explained, with the appearance of the first reformers. The scientific crisis began with Bacon's method of analysis and the collection of observational data, and with the neglect of synthetic thinking which might lead to a comprehensive and systematic understanding of the world, including the realms of morality and politics. In the modern age, scientific research was carried on by individual, isolated scientists, rather than being co-ordinated by the state. In industry, the crisis expressed itself in the lack of coordination between science and technology, in the lack of regulation and organization of economic activity—in other words, in the prevalence of the laissez faire doctrine and the haphazard distribution of the means of production. Great art is possible only in thoroughly organized periods dominated by a great religious idea, the *Doctrine* asserts, evidently forgetting that Saint-Simon had considered individual freedom a prime prerequisite for artistic creativity.[1] The lack of unity, the inability of men to be free, independent of social guidance, has resulted in the

[1] Saint-Simon had written that great art was produced only in periods when the individual was relatively independent of the state and in which art and industry were the primary concerns of society as in the Athenian democracy or in seventeenth-century Holland. Cf. *Oeuvres de Saint-Simon et d'Enfantin* (Paris: E. Dentu, 1865-78), XXXIX, 224.

despondency of such romantics, as Byron and the Goethe of *Werther*.

The student of history must understand, the *Doctrine* maintains, that mankind is an organism subject to a strict law of development. The basic error of the historians of the past has been the failure to realize the interaction of all social action and the unity and lawfulness of human history. The most important fact in the development of human society is progress in the fundamental moral conception. This progress takes place through a process of contradiction in which the so-called critical periods destroy moral conceptions and their societies which, nevertheless, are progressively truer than previous societies insofar as they organize an increasing section of human activity. In the series of history to which the contemporary European world belongs, and which is alone important as a summary of preceding history, there have been two organic periods: the ancient polytheistic preclassical society; and the Christian medieval world, which came to an end with the emergence of the individualistic, critical philosophies, with Socrates and the Reformation, respectively. The Church of the Middle Ages constituted the most legitimate and organic society yet realized, through its establishment of an authoritarian, hierarchical institution on the basis of a doctrine, but the Church had to fall since its doctrine, which excluded the temporal realm from the hierarchy, was yet imperfect. The present crisis of individualism, rationalistic philosophy, and liberty had run its course, as witnessed by the collapse of the old order.

By what method is the lawfulness of history known and understood? The *Doctrine* proposes to demonstrate this principle by empirical data, because the rational temper of the critical age demands this type of proof. However, empirical knowledge can never establish general truths but can merely prove them once they have been discovered. This is the error of the positivists. Experience does not provide links between facts—only a will for order does. The links can be grasped only by the inspiration of the genius when the proper time in history has come; they are unattainable to the scientist following a definite "method." For that matter, in an organic period the individual scientist cannot question the validity of a unifying doctrine or dogma. All the special sciences are subordinated to the doctrine which systematizes them.

The end of the historical process is the achievement of "universal association, which is to say, the association of all men on the entire surface of the globe in all spheres of their relationships." This association, the *Doctrine* points out, is not merely a means; rather, at the same time, it is both means and the end. The expression of the lack of association or hierarchical organization is antagonism and progressive organization. In the direction of association the socio-political units of mankind expand from the family, through the city and nation, the Catholic Church or the association of several nations in a federation linked by a common belief, to a church embracing all men and all the modes of human existence. Antagonism and war, while inherently bad, have been means towards the attainment of the universal association. The world at the same time has been progressing to the unity of "doctrine and activity" within these units of organization. The basic driving force in the historical process is man's inherent need for unity and order.

Exploitation of man by man was the direct consequence of antagonism. The course of history, therefore, shows the steady decline of this type of exploitation and its replacement by the peaceful exploitation of the globe by all mankind and in the interest of all mankind. Slavery, which at first marked an advance in the humaneness of man over cannibalism, has ever since its inception undergone limitations in scope. Christianity—by its doctrine of the equal worth of man before God—helped to speed this process. The relationship of modern employer and wage worker constitutes the last and mildest form of slavery. But it is still slavery insofar as the worker, dependent entirely on the sale of his labor and unable to bargain effectively, is subject to the conditions set by the employer. "Today the entire mass of workers is exploited by the men whose property they utilize," and the manager, himself an exploiter, is exploited by the owner, even if to a lesser degree. The inheritance of misery imposed upon the "proletarians" is a form of slavery which expresses itself not only in material poverty but in the intellectual and moral retardation of the worker. This modern exploitation is based on the constitution of property and can be eliminated only by a transformation of property rights. The constitution of property, far from being immutable as some of the economists had implied, is subject to constant progressive change. The final step in the limitation of individual property right will be the transference of inheritance right from the individual to the state. This transfer does not mean the equal distribution of property or the democratic control of the funds of production by the workers themselves, for such a set-up would be counter to organic association, which implies a hierarchy of capacities. The *Doctrine* states: "In the organization of the future, each one will be classified according to his ability and remunerated according to his work. This indicates sufficiently the inequality of distribution."

The banks are the social institution through which order is to be re-established in the economy. They superseded the medieval corporations as an effective means of regulating industry and commerce in terms of social needs. The regulation of the economic life, far from running counter to basic human instincts, instead corresponds to the human need for order and to the consistent human preference for the state of society over isolation. Thus the transformation of freeholds to feudal fiefs could be explained not from economic motives, but merely from this desire for order. The banks will abolish "unlimited competition," the inevitable consequence of economic liberty. The entire economic life will fall under the regulation of the bank system. Unlike the existing banks, these banks will be organized hierarchically: specialized banks for industries and regions will be subordinated to a "unitary and directing bank," representating "the government in the material order," and the "depository of all the riches, of the total fund of production, of all the instruments of work; in brief, of everything which today composes the entire mass of individual properties." The budget of the bank would consist on the credit side of the totality of annual industrial production, on the debit side of the distribution of these products to secondary banks which in turn would have their own budgets. The task of the central and the secondary banks would be the distribution of the means of production and raw materials, the classification and direction of labor, and the appraisal of the value of work and its renumeration.

The aim of education is to bring the public conscience into accord with the organization of the social order. The primary school will be intended for the general education, which is all-comprehensive, including the arts, sciences, and industry; the primary school attempts to inculcate the future citizen with the basic values of the society. This education is, however, lifelong, and as pointed out elsewhere, will be presented to the adult public primarily through the arts, the main function of which will be the imaginative and symbolic expression of an ideological content. The rationalistic philosophy of education completely misunderstood the nature of man, in which reason is only one aspect, and through the emphasis on individual reason and conscience created the need within the liberal state of purely "repressive legislation." A moral system presupposes that the aim of the society is "loved, known, and concisely defined." The results of the social sciences must not be demonstrated but can be "presented to almost all men only in a dogmatic form." The task of special education is to classify the population in terms of its abilities, and to train the citizens technically as industrialists, scientists, or artists. A hierarchy of classes, destroyed by the Revolution, will thus be reconstructed, but a hierarchy based on talent rather than on birth. Legislation is essentially to be conceived as a means of education: "penal" or "repressive" legislation of the liberal state is to be replaced by "positive" legislation. The *Globe* elaborates that the prison in the future shall be a re-education center rather than a penitentiary.[2] Yet the positive legislation of the new society will govern all spheres of social and individual activity, as indicated by the proposed establishment of scientific and industrial courts, in addition to moral courts. The jury in the traditional liberal sense will be abolished since only natural superiors can judge. Lawyers too will disappear as unnecessary.

Yet the culmination of the organization of the future will be its religion. The *Doctrine* emphasizes that "society is to be organized according to a general idea (*prévoyance*) ceaselessly to

[2] *Globe,* September 13, 1831.

be guided in its entirety and in its details according to this idea."
Far from seeing the disappearance of religion, the future will witness the close identification of the political and social order with
religion, so that not only will religion dominate the political
order, but the political order in its entirety will be a religious
institution. The argument that religion is progressively being
replaced by science is invalid: the two are not mutually exclusive;
rather, science is merely an expression of religion. The irreligion
of the contemporary scientists is not the result of scientific discovery but is, instead, the consequence of the critical hypothesis
of the last three hundred years. Science always stands in need
of a general hypothesis which binds its observations—religion
alone can furnish one. Science, on the other hand, contributes
to the building of a complete religious conception by demonstrating the lawfulness of the world. In critical epochs, science must
needs be atheistic, since its function is the destruction of the faith
of the previous organic epoch. In organic epochs, however, science becomes systematic and dogmatic; every special science is
based on a hypothesis, and all sciences are direct deductions from
a general hypothesis or dogma. Implicitly in Session XIV, and
explicitly in Session XV, issue is taken with Comte's positivism.
The "law of the three stages" according to which science moves
from a theological through a metaphysical to a positive state
must, of course, be rejected. The history of science is not one of
methodological progress and of the replacement of religion by
sciences but is rather the process by which science progressively
gains a systematic understanding of the world. From the conception of the world as governed by many immediate causes, science
passes through the belief in a variety of laws to the understanding that there is one immutable law. The basic moving force in
scientific progress, as in all other human development, is the
"love of order (and) of unity." Yet the positive "method" of
observation must be closely examined and its limits defined. The
scientific impulse is only one aspect of man. The empirical scientist can gather observational data, but he cannot establish causal
relationships between them on the basis of observation. One
cannot reason about observed facts except by means of an idea
accepted beforehand. The presence of this idea must precede

reasoning. One can thus prove only theorems which one has posed. The discovery of a linking hypothesis is not open to empirical research but at the proper stage in the historical process, is revealed to be genius. The first step in scientific reasoning is thus "conception," or "invention," through nonmethodical revelation. Empirical observation and "method" constitute only the second step, that of "verifying" the first.

Religion, however, like philosophy, must not be conceived as an abstract theological or metaphysical system; for "religion, politics, and morals are merely different names for the same fact." The theology of any religion entails a philosophy of social organization. The history of religion parallels that of science: man conceives the world first in terms of innumerable, isolated causes, fetishism; later several causes are seen operative, polytheism; finally, all causes are reduced to one cause, monotheism. This development parallels the growth of human institutions from a plurality of political units, families or clans, at the time of fetishism; through the nation; to the international federation based upon a common social doctrine. Christianity—by its exclusion of matter from God's nature and by its separation of the sphere of Caesar and that of Christ—yet falls short of the final unitary association in which all will be a part of God, and all men in their activities will form parts of the universal association or church.

The ideas on religion are elaborated in the *Second Year* of the *Doctrine,* not here translated. Every theological or metaphysical belief must have a social basis and reference, or be in vain.[3] Politics rather than dealing merely with the prevention of violence on the part of the state embraces the entire social order: politics regulates all activity, "collective and individual," which is directed towards the "goal" of the society. Instead of being limited, the powers of government should be explained and expanded. As the *Organisateur* asserted in 1829, contemporaneously with the *Second Year:* "The individual, according to us, is free to the extent that social action masters him increasingly to aid in developing his special aptitude, to exercise his faculties fully, and to overcome the vicious inclinations which

[3] *Oeuvres de Saint-Simon et d'Enfantin,* XLII, 298.

would expose him to the vindictiveness of the laws and to infamy." [4] And elsewhere the Saint-Simonian preacher declares: "Freedom is the power given to each to develop his natural faculties with the support and under the direction of social paternity." [5] The true society, the *Second Year* explains, must be organized hierarchically. Where there is no hierarchy, there is no society but merely an aggregation of individuals. An organic society is the systematic expression of a religious conception. True religion is all-extensive: it does not recognize the separation of matter and spirit. While disliking to be identified with the theocracies of the past, the Saint-Simonians thus viewed religion in purely social and human terms as the instrument and the reality of social coherence. A threefold hierarchy was to rule all human activity, corresponding to the three modes of human activity.[6] A "general" or social priest was to head a religious hierarchy consisting of governors, educators, and artists. The function of the artist was to popularize the basic social doctrine for the public. Under the control of the "general priest" were the "priest of science" and the "priest of industry," each responsible for their respective hierarchies.

How the "general priest" was to be selected was made clear only in the *Globe*. The primary motor of social action was not to be found in written laws or rationally defined programs but in great men, in the "living symbols." [7] The great man differed from the Nietzschean "superman," for example, in his limited freedom; he was the servant of the people and the product and tool of history whose mission he carried out. The rule of the "great man" was not despotic, since the ruled, although not consulted, concurred with the decisions of the superior man. This view assumed, of course, that the great man would rule through charismatic appeal rather than through force, although the Saint-Simonian concern with the role of penology in the state constituted an admission that constraint would not disappear entirely. The great man, or genius, would not be chosen at the

[4] *Organisateur*, September 5, 1829.

[5] *Oeuvres de Saint-Simon et d'Enfantin*, XLIV, 90.

[6] For a discussion of the structure and function of the hierarchy, see the *Second Year*, beginning with Session X.

[7] *Globe*, March 23, 1832.

ballot box: he would reveal himself to be almost unanimously accepted by the people as their superior leader.

IV

It is indeed surprising how the interpretations of Saint-Simonian theory have led to one-sided identifications of the movement with industrialism, technocracy, scientism and positivism, and even with economic liberalism. The all-encompassing authoritarian character of the Saint-Simonian conception of the state, which brings the Saint-Simonianism of the *Doctrine* and the *Globe* in closer relation to the spirit of modern totalitarianism than to early nineteenth-century conservatism, liberalism, or socialism, has never been fully understood. This misunderstanding is partly due to an overly close identification of Saint-Simon and the post-1828 Saint-Simonians. Interestingly enough, most of the studies on Saint-Simonian thought are based on Enfantin's articles in the *Producteur* and on the first twelve chapters of the *Doctrine*. The last few chapters of the *Doctrine* and the *Second Year*, in which the religious theories of the Saint-Simonians were elaborated especially in relation to science and society, were generally disregarded as an expression of the religious-mystic phase of the Saint-Simonians. Similarly, the editorials of the *Globe*, devoted largely to the systematic rejection of parliamentary government and popular sovereignty and to the outline of the totally organized authoritarian state, have generally been neglected despite their impact on contemporaries. The students of Saint-Simonianism posed problems primarily in terms of the dominant intellectual and social movements of the nineteenth century concerning the position of the Saint-Simonians toward industrial organization, economic liberalism, proletarian socialism, economic determinism, pacifism and internationalism, scientism, and Comte.

The Saint-Simonians inherited from their master a great interest in industrial development and organization and in the application of science to social and industrial processes. The Saint-Simonians strove for the organization of industry and the economy in terms of the highest productive efficiency. Like

Saint-Simon, the Saint-Simonians believed that the feudal, war-like spirit of the past must yield to the production of the future, the exploitation of man by man to the exploitation of the globe.

The Saint-Simonians were strongly imbued with the myth of efficiency. To achieve maximum production, the economy must be organized for that purpose: the means of production must pass from the hands of the idle owners (entrusted with them through the accident of birth) to those men most able to administer them effectively. The function of the banks was only to extend credit or capital where it would be used most effectively by the best-fitted experts. The industrial hierarchy would also integrate scientific knowledge with industrial processes. From this point of view, the Saint-Simonian industrial organization is a technocracy. But at the same time, such critics as E. Halévy, Durkheim,[1] and Albert Salomon[2] did not understand that industrial efficiency was a secondary—not a primary—aim of the Saint-Simonian conception of society. For these critics, the economic theories of the *Doctrine* essentially foreshadowed the development of corporate capitalism. True, the influence of the Saint-Simonian writings in this direction is clear: such Saint-Simonians as the Péreire brothers and Chevalier, for example, later played an important role in the development of French capitalism. Yet the extension of the scope of industrial organization was understood by such writers as Bouglé and Halévy to take place ultimately outside the framework of the state. For Saint-Simon this view would be essentially true: the function of the state, which was to be administered in the interest of business and industry, was essentially limited to elementary regulation of competition, certain public projects like canals and roads, and the relief of the poor, functions revolutionary in the face of Adam Smith or J. B. Say;[3] the operation of the economy was fundamentally left in private hands. The iden-

[1] Emile Durkheim, *Le socialisme, sa définition, ses débuts: la doctrine saint-simonienne,* ed. by M. Mauss (Paris: F. Alcan, 1928).

[2] Albert Salomon, "Religion of Progress," *Social Research,* XIII (1946), 441-462.

[3] Jean Baptiste Say (1767-1832), economist and popularizer of Adam Smith's economic doctrines in France.

tification of the Saint-Simonians with this partial socialism rested in part on a misunderstanding of Saint-Simonian social philosophy, and in part on an inadequate reading of the elaboration of the theory of the banks in the *Second Year* and the *Globe*. The industrialism of the *Doctrine* is strictly subordinated to the general conception of society and the principle of association. Association for the Saint-Simonians means not the voluntary combination of efforts on the part of private individuals, but the formal organization of individual and social activity and their regulation through an authoritarian hierarchy. The absence of such formal organization is, for them, identical with anarchy and antagonism. The basic fault of the capitalistic economy of the early nineteenth century was, therefore, the lack of such a formal organization which would regulate all phases of economic life and integrate economic activity and organization with the total social welfare. Lack of economic regulation resulted in competition and consequent inefficiency and economic crises. The *Doctrine* appointed the state as the heir to all capital and identified the budget of the bank system with that of the state, thus clarifying the role of the state in the reorganized economy. The strictly hierarchical structure becomes especially clear in the *Second Year,* in which the entire economic sphere was subordinated to a chief "industrial priest," [4] and in the *Globe,* in which the future society was conceived as a sort of army in which each man would have a definite place and in which ration cards would replace money.[5] Yet production was not the primary aim of the Saint-Simonian society—this aim was order, the achievement of universal association. Industry corresponded, according to the Saint-Simonian sociology, to one of three faculties of man—force —which together with science was subordinated to the sentiments. In the political structure of the new society, the industrial hierarchy and the scientific hierarchy were to be strictly subordinated to what might be called the political and cultural hierarchy. The state—contrary to being ruled by technocrats— would rule the industrialists: the "general priest" would be su-

---

[4] *Oeuvres de Saint-Simon et d'Enfantin,* XLIII.
[5] *Globe,* September 31, 1831.

perior to the "industrial" priest and would regulate the economic organizations in terms of the ideology underlying the total social organization.

Less commonly, Saint-Simonianism has been misinterpreted as being a socialist movement in a proletarian, or an egalitarian sense. True, one of the main mottoes of the Saint-Simonians, adopted from Saint-Simon, was that of the "speediest amelioration of the moral, physical, and intellectual lot of the poorest and most numerous class." History marked the steady decline of exploitation; the wage worker of the day represented the latest stage of slavery. The foundation of slavery rested on the existing property rights. Yet exploitation was not to be replaced by equal distribution, nor private ownership of the means of production by workers' control. The aim of Saint-Simonian social policy was, rather, the destruction of arbitrary social and economic stratifications based on birth, and the replacement of the aristocracy of wealth by a natural aristocracy of talents. This program was made particularly clear in the *Second Year* and the *Globe*. A letter to the Chamber of Deputies in 1830 stated:

> The Saint-Simonians reject the equal division of property which in their eyes would constitute a greater violence and more revolting injustice than the unequal division originally effected by force of arms, by conquest.
>
> For they believe in the natural INEQUALITY of man, and consider that inequality as the very basis of association as the indispensable condition of SOCIAL ORDER.[6]

Rejecting the class struggle as a means to power, the Saint-Simonians considered the masses, as such, politically incompetent. The social revolution must come from above through the leadership of superior men. The new social structure in which the masses would be divided into a hierarchy of classes and ruled from above, in Saint-Simonian thinking, did not imply exploitation, since the naturally superior man could better understand the needs of the masses than the masses themselves.

---

[6] *Religion saint-simonienne. Lettre à M. le Président de la Chambre des députés* (Paris, 1830), p. 5.

Equality of opportunity would exist, as the positions in the hierarchy were open to talent. That this talent to govern constitutes a privilege of birth, as Durkheim pointed out, the Saint-Simonians did not consider; nor were they disturbed by the fact that the new upper classes or individuals would have much more complete power over the masses than the old owning classes. This natural inequality justified the inequality in renumeration implied by the formula, "From each according to his ability; to each ability according to its works."

Less justified than interpreting Saint-Simonian doctrine as "industrialism" or "technocracy" is to understand it as scientism or positivism. Saint-Simon had, in his early writings, urged that a science of politics be built on an empirical basis. But large sections of the *Doctrine* are devoted to a rejection of Comte's positivism and of the possibility of an empirical science of society as such. Hayek, who attempts to demonstrate that both modern positivism and modern socialism began as essentially "reactionary and authoritarian movements," [7] cites Saint-Simonianism as a prime example of the joining of positivism and authoritarian socialism. The Saint-Simonians, not Saint-Simon, influenced European thought, he comments, and Comte was the greatest Saint-Simonian. This analysis may be true if a careful distinction is made between the Saint-Simonianism of Comte and that of the "Saint-Simonian School." The belief in the possibility of a politics based on a positive science of society was voiced in the *Producteur,* shortly after the death of Saint-Simon, by Comte and Buchez, at a time when the Saint-Simonians did not yet present a systematization of economic efforts in terms of the creation of voluntary credit institutions and stock companies within the frame of an economy, free of state interference, governed by its own inherent laws. In the *Doctrine,* where the totally and hierarchically organized society was outlined, the use of the positive sciences as a primary tool to social truth is explicitly renounced. Positivism was considered as essentially an expression of the critical age of doubt, and the fundamental ideology of the authoritarian state is placed above rational or empirical inquiry.

[7] F. A. Hayek, *The Counter-Revolution of Science; Studies on the Abuse of Reason* (Glencoe, Illinois: The Free Press, 1952), p. 123.

Hayek states that with the appearance of the *Doctrine* and a number of articles by Enfantin, the development of ideas "of interest to us" comes to an end. But in the latter chapters of the *Doctrine* in particular, and in that periodical literature in which, according to Hayek, the "sentimental and mystic elements gained the upper hand over the ostensibly scientific and rational," [8] the authoritarian note was developed and the positive method de-emphasized. While Hayek's theory holds for Comte, it certainly does not hold for the Saint-Simonians proper. The organic epoch depended on the unconditional acceptance, by the members of the society, of the fundamental doctrine of society on the basis of faith. Individual reason was inherently analytic and hence destructive of social order. In contrast to the critical period, philosophic in spirit, the organic epoch was religious. True, for the Saint-Simonians as for Comte it was unbelievable that the universe was not governed by strict laws, and science for both meant not merely the application of an empirical method to the study of nature and society, but also the unveiling of this lawfulness. Yet, as we have seen, observation for the Saint-Simonians could only gather individual facts—inspiration was needed to understand the link. Thus science became basically esoteric: the primary truths of nature and life were not open to the scientist proceeding by an unbiased "method," but were revealed only to genius. The laboratory scientist could merely confirm the insights of the genius. Hence the direction of scientific research, rather than being left in the hands of scientists, would be entrusted to the genius-leaders of society. Science, like industry, formed only one aspect of human activity, and the scientist was strictly subordinated to the "general priest." It was he under whom the entire scientific enterprise was organized and who made clear the fundamental philosophy of society. Science was thus subordinated to ideology. This subordination did not mean that the scientist was relegated to an unimportant place in the hierarchy. But the scientist's work was considered not as a guide to truth but merely as technical or planning reason which would help to organize the state in terms of a basic philosophy.

[8] *Ibid.,* p. 152.

Science was to be applied to making possible the greatest systematization of social efforts.

The Saint-Simonians have conventionally been labeled "utopian socialists" by the historian of ideas and political and
economic theories. In this connection they have been linked to
a number of early nineteenth-century French social philosophers,
among whom Fourier and Proudhon appear most prominently.

Fourier and the Saint-Simonians were keenly and often
bitterly aware of each other, and the Saint-Simonians admitted
Fourier's influence on their conception of woman. Proudhon
later was to take sharp issue with the collectivism of the Saint-
Simonians. Buchez, Pierre Leroux, and Blanqui went through
the school of Saint-Simonianism, while Louis Blanc's views on
industrial organization, as well as Proudhon's theory of the reorganization of the banks, show possible Saint-Simonian influences. Certain similarities among the early nineteenth-century
French socialists are apparent at first sight, including the de-
emphasis of the class struggle (except, perhaps in the case of
Blanqui), the repudiation of violence, and the critique of the
existing capitalistic system as being not merely inefficient and
self-destructive, but also morally unjust. Yet basic differences
among these thinkers in regard to their conception of society and
their programs of social reorganization forbid our assigning any
great importance to the term "utopian socialism" as designating
an inclusive historical movement.

The Saint-Simonian conception of a totally organized society
in which the individual was strictly subordinated to the hierarchically structured collectivity was peculiar to, or at least extreme among, these thinkers. For Fourier, Victor Considérant,
and Proudhon,[9] the attainment of social justice was integrated
with a high degree of freedom for the individual from the state.
Proudhon's philosophy attempted to free the individual from the
state, while Fourier's phalange was a purely voluntary, co-operative organization. A large section of "utopian-socialist" thought,

_____

[9] See, however, J. Salwyn Schapiro's evaluation of Proudhon as a forerunner of Fascism in *Liberalism and the Challenge of Fascism* (New York:
McGraw-Hill, 1949).

xlii   INTRODUCTION

it may be said, fought as fervently against governmental coercion of the individual, as against the injustice of the capitalistic system. Even Louis Blanc, for whom the state initially was to play a definite role in organizing and supporting the *atelier national*,[10] thought that the intervention of the state, which was democratically organized on the basis of universal suffrage, should be limited to a specifically economic sphere, and only to one aspect of that. For Blanc, as for Fourier's *phalange,* the *ateliers* were to become voluntary "proprietary societies," which he contrasted with the Saint-Simonian "proprietary state."

The influence of the Catholic-Restoration traditionalists on their thought was freely admitted by the Saint-Simonians. Both shared in the view of society as an organic whole, and in the affirmation of authority and hierarchy. Yet the Saint-Simonian idea went far beyond that of the conservatives. The organic authoritarian idea was merged with modern rationalism: unlike the *philosophes,* the Saint-Simonians did not see in reason an epistemological tool open to every rational individual for the attainment of truth, but rather an instrument of total and systematic planning. To this view must be added the French revolutionary concern for the masses. Yet, by the complete identification of church and religion with society, Saint-Simonianism becomes essentially a secular Catholicism. The function of religion becomes purely social, that of a "social link"; and the church, which constitutes the government, therefore functions politically. The Saint-Simonian religion completed the totalitarian structure by the sanctification of the state, which thus became the concrete expression of the moral idea and of the divine will.

But of greater impact than these Catholic theoreticians was the impact of the Catholic conception of the Church. In order not to misunderstand the Saint-Simonian emphasis on religion as vague mysticism, one must realize that the Saint-Simonian conception of religion was essentially institutional, an extension and secularization of the Roman Catholic Church. The marks of the

[10] The "national workshops" conceived by Louis Blanc were to be co-operative groups of workmen financed in the first instance by public subscriptions and thereafter to be self-supporting. A short-lived attempt at establishing such workshops was made in 1848 by the Second Republic.

French-Catholic religious tradition, and of the centralistic-bureaucratic political tradition, are evident on almost every page of the *Doctrine*. The analysis of types of religious institutions in the literature of modern sociology of religion[11] may throw some light on the social implications of the Saint-Simonian conception of the church. The church, as analyzed in this literature as one type of religious institution, is an inclusive organization which assumes the faith of its members without expecting a special religious decision, as the sect does. In contrast to the sect, which is a voluntary association among other voluntary associations and often in conflict with the community, the Church strives to be coextensive with the community. While the sect sees the attainment of religious insight as the outcome of inner search and personal conversion, the church claims the possession of an objective truth which can be explicitly understood only by the select, while the many must be satisfied with an unquestioning implicit faith. Finally, the sect tends to be a democratic society of believers who share equally in the actions and responsibilities of the fellowship, while the church distinguishes between the professional religious and the laity, and establishes hierarchical, centralized control. The Saint-Simonians saw in the Catholic Church a pattern of autocracy applicable to the organization of society as a whole.

Saint-Simonian political thought has affinities with modern totalitarianism in both its conception of the scope of state power and of the inner organization of the state. In contrast to the Hegelian conception of the state, the Saint-Simonian, thoroughly centralistic, attempts through systematic rational planning and organization to link every phase of social and individual life to the state apparatus. In contrast to the autocracies of the past (for example, the monarchy of Louis XIV or that conceived by de Maistre), the Saint-Simonians attempted to link the masses with the autocratic state. The nucleus of the instruments by which the modern totalitarian state attempts to achieve this end —the ideology, the movement, the party, and the leader—were all found in Saint-Simonian theory. The ideology, the Saint-

[11] See Joachim Wach, *Church, Denomination and Sect* (Evanston, Illinois: Seabury-Western Theological Seminary, 1946).

Simonian theology, differed from ordinary political theories in
constituting not merely a theory of the state but a Weltan-
schauung which, like the Lenin–Stalin version of Marxism or
Nazi racial philosophy, was infallible and superseded empirical
knowledge. The Saint-Simonian theology, as noted, was a purely
secular philosophy of society. The Saint-Simonian Church re-
sembles the totalitarian party as an elite organization of men
subject to strict discipline, totally devoted to the ideology which
they apply to all phases of social life, to the arts, the sciences,
industry, and education. While the party is a closed group, it
still attempts to maintain its popular character by recruiting its
members from the ranks of the people. In practice, of course, the
Saint-Simonians failed utterly in creating a mass movement, and
despite their appeals to the workers they always remained a small
association of intellectuals. The real link of the people and the
state was represented by the leader, the "father" or "great man,"
"the living symbol" of the Saint-Simonian idea. The leader,
chosen not by ballot but by the spontaneous recognition of his
greatness by the masses, represented the state and its purpose
concretely, and while possessing absolute power, he still acted
both in the name of masses and with their approval. Parliament,
interestingly enough, was not abolished but transformed from a
"debating society" to a body which was to listen to government
experts and, like the Supreme Soviet or the Nazi Reichstag, to
vote its approval.[12]

Like the modern totalitarian state, the Saint-Simonians intended to control not only the political realm but all spheres of
cultural activity. All of society being encompassed by the Church,
the general priest or governors were to have thorough control
over the "moral, intellectual, and material" activities of man.
The scientific, like the industrial, hierarchy was to be strictly
controlled by the "general priesthood." Its task was not to explore the essence of the universe and of human nature but to
solve the problems posed for it. Thus the Saint-Simonian historian could no more challenge on empirical or logical grounds
the theory of the progressive decline of antagonism than a Soviet
economist can question the inevitable collapse of capitalist

[12] *Globe,* December 2, 1831.

economics. The artist, too, was to stand fully in the service of the state. As an arm of the government, he was to move the masses in accordance with Saint-Simonian ideas and governmental plans. Hannah Arendt sees in Enfantin a foreshadowing of the modern conception of propaganda.[13] In Barrault's *Aux Artistes*[14] and in the *Globe,* pure art was condemned. Good art was socially inspired and guided, art which described reality and stirred the masses to action. It was to be judged not by aesthetic criteria but in terms of ideological correctness. In contrast, Saint-Simon had believed that only in societies in which the individual was relatively free, like the Athenian democracy or seventeenth-century Holland, could great art arise. In libertarian societies art, when it did arise, was antisocial, frivolous, or if serious, satiric or in the mood of Romantic despair. Finally education, under thorough control of the state, was to direct the individual from birth to death in fulfilling his function in the organized society.

In their system of discipline, the Saint-Simonians also resembled modern totalitarianism. While the Saint-Simonians assumed the existence of an automatic harmony between individual conviction and the social doctrine in the organic society and explicitly condemned coercion, they reserved coercive means for "exceptional cases." Underlying this view is a theory of liberty which differs from the liberal conception of liberty as freedom of individual action from governmental restraint. Freedom, for the Saint-Simonians, was the development of one's potentialities with the aid of social guidance. The authoritarianism of the Saint-Simonian Church did not admit of any separate bodies or voluntary associations within its bosom, nor of divergences of opinion. Members of the Church-Society, unlike those of a sect, did not arrive at truth through subjective experience and individual search, but were confronted by an objective belief which they had to accept on faith. The Saint-Simonians thus found it necessary to establish scientific and industrial, as well as artistic courts.

[13] Hannah Arendt, *The Origin of Totalitarianism* (New York: Harcourt-Brace & Co.), p. 337.

[14] Emile Barrault, *Aux Artistes. Du passé et de l'avenir des beaux-arts. (Doctrine de Saint-Simon)* (Paris, 1830).

The prison was to be reformed from a penitentiary to a re-education center where, interestingly enough, intellectual criminals also received correction. Together with the broad definition of criminality came the abolition of the *Rechtsstaat*. The natural rights of man, as well as the institution of the jury and the written Roman law, were condemned as expressive of the individual's suspicion of the state in the critical stage. The accused would be judged by the institution of his natural superior.

In its negation of violence and terror, Saint-Simonianism differs sharply from modern Fascism and Communism. True, of course, the Saint-Simonian state always remained a theory. However, throughout the Saint-Simonian writings the basic purpose of the state remained human welfare: the amelioration of the moral, physical, and intellectual welfare of the poorest and the most numerous class. Authoritarianism was required in part for the efficient attainment of this goal, but even more so because it, rather than the libertarian form of government, was in accord with human nature: for man could be happy only in an organized, stable, unanimous society. For this reason, the philanthropists were scorned by the Saint-Simonians. But coercive power was never to be an end, only a means in exceptional cases. Despite the disciplinary powers they ascribed to the state, the Saint-Simonians were firmly convinced that in the perfect society, free of exploitation, individual volition would almost always be in accord with the demand of society. Similarly, the Saint-Simonian society was to be created not by violent revolution but by a gradual process of education, and by the co-operation of the upper classes and the masses.

Here the question arises as to whether one may compare the Saint-Simonian system to that of Soviet Russia. Actually several years ago the Academy of Science of the U.S.S.R. published the first Russian translation of the *First Year* of the *Doctrine*.[15] While V. P. Volgin explains in the introduction the practical failure of the Saint-Simonians as a result of their neglect "to value the proletariat as an active force and not only as a suffering

[15] *Izlozhenie ucheniya Sen-Simona*, translated by M. E. Landau, edited and commented by E. A. Zhelubovskoi (Moscow: Izdatel'stvo Akademii Nauk S.S.S.R., 1947). Introduction by V. P. Volgin. In 1948, the Academy of Science of the U.S.S.R. published the selected writings of Henri de Saint-Simon.

and exploited man," [16] he, unlike most Western critics of the last few decades, emphasizes not only the role of technology and large-scale organization in Saint-Simonian thought, but also the systematic rejection of democracy, even if he contrasts this "autocratism" negatively with Soviet "democracy." The great contribution of the Saint-Simonians to socialist thought, Volgin asserts, was their criticism of the egalitarianism of classical communism, their recognition of the need for competition, stratification, and inequality of renumeration in a socialist society.[17]

Ironically, the Saint-Simonians, imbued with the love of fellow man, did not realize the dangerous implications of their benevolent totalitarianism. Firmly believing in the goodness of the great leaders selected by historical destiny to guide the less able, they did not suspect that the philosopher-kings might deviate from the basic philosophy of the society, that of brotherly love. The Saint-Simonians thus proposed a political machinery in which the authority of the elite was all-extensive and unhampered by any effective controls. Since religion, morality, and society were fused in this system, religious ethics in the traditional Judaeo-Christian sense lost its position of independence and, consequently, the character of independent sanctions. Similarly, the hierarchy might not be appealed against on the grounds of natural rights or individual conscience. Saint-Simonianism, while attempting to abolish the exploitation of man, outlined a potential instrument for the most systematic despotism of man over man.

[16] *Ibid.*, p. 46.
[17] *Ibid.*, p. 38.

TRANSLATOR'S NOTE

This translation is based on the third, "revised and enlarged" edition of the *Doctrine de Saint-Simon. Exposition. Première Année. 1828-1829.*, published in Paris in 1831, which also served as the basis for the annotated edition of 1924 by C. Bouglé and Elie Halévy. In addition to notes of my own, I have utilized those explanatory notes of the Bouglé-Halévy edition, which in my opinion help the English reader to understand the text, or which are of particular interest to the historian of ideas.

Several persons deserve particular thanks for their assistance in the preparation of this translation: Professor James L. Adams for his guidance and advice in regard to both the Introduction and the translation; my wife, who carefully checked through the manuscript several times with me for accuracy of translation and correctness of style and who helped in many other ways; to Mr. J. B. Allin, Professor Bernard Knieger, and Professor Frank Manuel for reading the text of the translation and making extensive suggestions; to Professor G. D. H. Cole for writing the Preface and reading the Introduction; and to President M. L. Harris of Philander Smith College for providing extensive secretarial assistance.

GEORG G. IGGERS

October, 1957

On the Necessity of a New Social Doctrine

Gentlemen:

Considered as a whole, society presents at this time a spectacle of two opposing camps. In one are entrenched the few defenders of the dual religious and political organization of the Middle Ages; in the other are found those who, under the rather inappropriate designation of *partisans of the new ideas*,[1] have co-operated in or approved of the overthrow of the former structure. We have come to bring peace between these two armies by announcing a doctrine that inveighs not only against the horror of bloodshed but also against the horror of struggle, under whatever name the latter may be disguised—be it as *antagonism* between a spiritual and a temporal power, as *opposition* for the sake of political liberty, or as *competition* for the greatest welfare of all.[2] We do not believe in the eternal necessity of any of these engines of war. Nor do we acknowledge any natural law of civilized mankind that obliges and condemns it to commit suicide.

NOTE: Footnotes appearing in the third edition are indicated by asterisks. Translator's notes are marked by Arabic numerals. In the footnotes the critical annotations of the Bouglé-Halévy edition are referred to by a "B" followed by the number of the footnote in the 1924 edition.

[1] This expression was used by Ballanche in the *Essai sur les institutions sociales dans leurs rapports avec les idées nouvelles,* published in 1818, in which he attempts to reconcile (chapter 10, part II) what he calls *archéophiles* and *néophiles*. Cf. B1.

[2] "In bringing together these three terms—the first of which alludes to the religious, the second to the political, and the third to the economic problem —the Saint-Simonians mean to bring together the attitudes which they reject. They want to combat the same liberal ideas in all their manifestations which they held had been improperly modified by new ideas. The first sentence of the first session is therefore a declaration of war against the theorists of liberalism and of the philosophy of natural law even more than against the partisans of the past." B2.

We have no doubt that our doctrine will dominate the future more completely than the beliefs of antiquity ever dominated their epoch and more completely than Catholicism dominated the Middle Ages. More powerful than its predecessors, its benevolent influence will extend to the whole world. Its appearance will undoubtedly raise very strong aversion and its diffusion will meet with many obstacles. We are prepared to overcome the obstacles, and we are certain that sooner or later the aversion will disappear; for triumph is certain when one marches onward with humanity, and it is beyond the powers of any man to separate mankind from its law of perfectibility.

Having just emerged from a period full of disorder and confusion, we have seen the gulf close in which were swallowed up both the former beliefs and the former political powers that had ceased to be legitimate,[3] since they had ceased to be in harmony with the demands of the new society. It would seem that hearts, weary rather than content, should lovingly receive the law that will one day unite all of them. But the recent memory of a death struggle, and the revolutionary attitude which everyone feels obliged to assume, delay the day of this union. Our intractable state of mind and our distrustful hate and suspicion incessantly present us with the phantom of despotism. In a pattern of common beliefs and actions our pride can see nothing but a new yoke resembling the one which was just broken at the cost of so many tears and so much blood and sacrifice. To our eyes, dimmed by mistrust, anything that seems to re-establish order and unity appears as an attempt at retrogression (*rétrogradation*).[4]

[3] "Here the Saint-Simonians allude to the argumentation of the 'legitimists' who claim the hereditary right to rule over France for the older branch of the Bourbons. The Saint-Simonians praise Joseph de Maistre for having given legitimacy a naturalistic and positivistic formula. . . . But as for themselves, they can not accept the identification of legitimate and hereditary power. They founded legitimacy on the idea of adaptation to a changing and progressive historical reality. A power which is not 'in harmony with the times' is condemned by their philosophy of history." B4.

[4] "An allusion to the effect created by the doctrines of the theocratic school, particularly those of de Bonald. Saint-Simon praises him for having 'profoundly sensed the usefulness of systematic unity.' (*Introduction aux Travaux scientifiques du XIXe siècle; Oeuvres choisies de C. H. de Saint-Simon*, 1859, I, 211.) But this does not mean that he wants to return, like de Bonald and

This permanent anarchy, this universal weakening of social ties, in the midst of which mankind is struggling, seems to frighten some thinkers, but the majority of them, dominated by incomplete scientific ideas, believe that sufficient facts have not yet been ascertained nor enough observations collected for the formulation of a general doctrine. For us, the problem is solved. We have looked beyond the narrow circle of the present, and in penetrating the past we have seen ourselves encumbered and besieged by facts. From then on we had no longer any doubt that the time has come when a new conception is to embrace and explain the detailed work, work accumulated for so many years. We present this conception today with the confidence implanted by profound conviction. If it is false, if it is only one empty system added to so many others, it will not awaken any sympathy and will leave the masses submerged in egoism. But if it is true, if it is the fertile spring from which our children's children shall draw a happiness denied us, then the sympathetic impulse it will arouse in all hearts will be the testimony of its legitimacy.

Its value, however, must not be judged by the effect it can immediately produce on the most enlightened minds, for in the present general state of mind there is an obstacle to its popularity, namely the disdainful suspicion against any sort of general idea inspired by the narrow habits acquired by study in specialized fields. Philosophic doctrines are generally considered impotent: they are thought of as simple gymnastic exercises of the intellect, and the multitude of philosophies which appear, they say, in all epochs, is enumerated as proof of their sterility. In this point of view there is both truth and error. Before going on, it will be important to distinguish among them.

Powerless, certainly, are the dreams of spiritualism and materialism, which in every critical epoch appear basically the same, even if in different forms. Sterile indeed are moralists' aphorisms which have never produced one act of devotion or given society one honest man. But collections of maxims, of

his disciples, to beliefs which in the light of scientific progress are out of date.

"Saint-Simon himself used the expression *rétrograde* starting with the *Lettres d'un Habitant de Génève* and in the same sense. . . . (*Oeuvres de Saint-Simon et d'Enfantin*, XV, 15.)" B5.

judgments and detached moral observations, or systems about the play of the intellectual faculties, their essence and products, are not philosophic conceptions. This term can be attributed only to thought which embraces all modes of human activity and which offers a solution to all social and individual problems. It is sufficient to say that there have been no more philosophic doctrines worthy of the name than there have been general states of mankind, but the phenomenon of an orderly social order has occurred only twice in the series[5] of civilization to which we belong and which forms an uninterrupted chain extending to our own time,* namely in antiquity and in the Middle Ages. The new general state which we proclaim for the future will form the third link in this chain; it will not be identical with its predecessors but will offer striking analogies to them with respect to order and unity. It will follow upon the various periods of the crisis that has been disturbing us for three centuries; it will appear finally as a consequence of the law of the development of mankind.

This law, revealed to the genius of Saint-Simon and verified by him in a long historical series, shows us two distinct and alternating states of society. In the one which we shall call the organic state all the events of human activity are classified, foreseen, and arranged according to a general theory; the goal of all social action is closely defined. In the other, which we shall call the critical state, all communion of thought, all collective action, and all co-ordination has ceased, and society appears as a mere agglomeration of isolated individuals fighting one another.[6]

[5] "In the first half of the nineteenth century the expression *series* seemed destined to a great philosophic future. The organization proposed by Fourier, a 'serial mechanism,' rests on the discovery that the world is divided into series. Similarly Proudhon seeks in his *Création de l'ordre* to discover series everywhere or to deduce the 'law of series.' Saint-Simon had used the expression in his *Mémoire sur la Science de l'Homme* (*Oeuvres choisies*, II, 52)." B10.

* We shall state further on which historical period we have subjected to observation; we shall also explain why we have neglected preceding events.

[6] The idea that contemporary society is passing through a crisis out of which it can emerge only with the aid of a principle of organization appears throughout the works of Saint-Simon. But he did not draw the rigorously antirationalistic and antilibertarian conclusions which the Saint-Simonians did. Cf. B11.

Each of these states has occupied two periods in history. There was an organic era preceding that Greek era which is called the philosophic era, and which we shall term more exactly the critical epoch. Later a new doctrine was formulated which went through its different phases of elaboration and improvement and finally established its political power over all of the Occident. The constitution of the Church began a new organic epoch which ceased in the fifteenth century, at the moment when the reformers exhibited the first signs of the critique which has continued until our time.

Critical epochs present two distinct periods. During the first there is collective action which, while limited in the beginning to the most sympathetic men, soon spreads to the masses. Its goal, premeditated by some and instinctive in others, is the destruction of the established order, but only of an order which has aroused distaste in all. The accumulated rancor finally erupts, and soon there remains of the former institution nothing but ruins to testify that there has once been a harmonic society. The second period takes in the interval separating the destruction of the former order from the construction of the new order. At this stage, the anarchy has ceased to be violent but has grown deeper; a complete divergence of feeling, reasoning and action exists.

This is the state of uncertainty in which we are suspended, and the apostles of liberty have not been able to calm or temper it. They choose to consider as final that bastard system of guarantees improvised to respond to the critical and revolutionary needs of the last century. They present as an expression of the last stage of social perfection those "Declarations of the Rights of Man and of the Citizen" and all constitutions for which they serve as the basis. They assure us that it is for this great conquest (how absurdly small) that the world has been in travail for several centuries. If one calls the general uneasiness to their attention, they reassuringly answer that these disturbances have only passing and accidental causes. They regard the struggle of these people and of their leaders as a condition of human nature; they make the ultimate discovery that society has nothing further to hope now that *mistrust has been regulated by law.*[7] In support of modern theories, they cite the rapid development of the sciences and the important place taken by industry; and if they maintain a modest silence on that aspect of man's being which alone can speak to his heart and stir his emotions, if they say nothing about the fine arts, it is because they consider them merely as a relaxation, as a series of pleasant notes and fleeting impressions aiming to charm the leisure moments of ostentatious and burdensome idleness.

Let us cast a rapid glance at the sciences, at industry, and at the fine arts and see whether these three great organs of society, considered as a collective being, perform their functions with that ease and above all with that harmony which maintains health and vigor in the social body and facilitates the developments to which it is susceptible. We shall then be better able to appreciate the influence of the present general state of mind on the individual and on social relations.

The Sciences

Our century is imbued with a holy awe of the great scientific progress it has seen. It complacently points to the great number of its scientists; and if it condescends to preserve even the slightest memory of the past, it is only to contrast shadow with light, and sleep with waking, and thus to pay itself greater homage. Let us examine the evidence as briefly as possible to see whether this claim of superiority is as well founded as one might believe at first sight.

The work of science is divided into two branches: the perfecting of theories and their application. Let us first note in a general way that the majority of scientists neglects the first branch for the sake of the second. As for the very small number of scientists who work directly for the advancement of science,

---

[7] "Bentham proposes (*Constitutional Code,* Book I, chap. 9) as a political rule to 'minimize confidence' and elsewhere to 'maximize distrust and suspicion.' This is what he calls the *control-maximization principle,* diametrically opposed to the fundamental principle of the Saint-Simonians according to which it is necessary to generalize and regularize 'confidence' or 'credit.'" B15.

they all follow the road opened by Bacon at the end of the sixteenth century. They pile experiment upon experiment; they dissect nature in its entirety; they enrich science by new details; they add more or less curious facts to those previously observed. Almost all of them are engaged in verification.* Almost all of them are armed with microscopes lest the smallest phenomena escape their vigilant investigation. But what scientists classify and co-ordinate these disorderly heaps of riches? Where are those who establish order among the fruits of this abundant harvest? A few sheaves are to be seen here and there; but they are scattered on the wide field of science, and for over a century no great theoretical view has been produced.** If one asks what tie unites celestial and molecular attraction, or what general concept of the order of phenomena rules over the researches of scientists, or if, according to the division assumed, they have as their aim the study of inorganic or organic bodies, not only will such questions remain unanswered, but there will not even be any anxiety about searching for an answer. Work has been divided and subdivided, a very wise policy without doubt, but one that has broken the link that bound all work together and gave it a common direction. From that time on, every science, while congratulating itself on its liberation, has followed its own road. Since the former unifying concept was no longer satisfactory in the light of modern discoveries, the conclusion was that the scientist should devote himself exclusively to observational research, and build isolated columns instead of constructing an orderly edifice.

It will be said, however, that there are academies which recruit men who have demonstrated their great ability through their discoveries. One might therefore believe that the field of science is exploited by the academies in the most extensive and fitting manner. Academies undoubtedly exist whose members possess great knowledge; each one masters one science, and some even master several. This is not the place to investigate whether

* We shall later have occasion to say more concerning the great importance we attach to verification by facts, but at the same time we shall show that this is only one part of the scientist's work.

** Newton died in 1727. Berzelius's and Davy's Law seems to have been verified only for inorganic bodies.

the clique spirit which has entered the societies has not more than once determined an election; this is one of the contemporary evils which we shall not try to discuss here. About the groups of scientists, however, we shall say the same thing which we have said about the sciences themselves: there is no comprehensive view to bring about harmony among their endeavors.

The members composing the academies meet in the same hall; but, having no idea in common, they undertake no common work. They all wear the same garb, but the instruction alone represents some sort of unity, for basically there is no sympathy uniting the scientists. Each one devotes himself on his own to quite useful and certainly quite interesting research but does so without troubling himself as to whether or not a neighboring science might be able to enlighten his research.* Some physicists are abandoning the explanation of Newton for that of Huyghens, and the physics section alone is, so to say, concerned with this change. As for the moral and political sciences, they are not even represented at our Institute. The result of this vicious organization of scientific groups, this absence of an intellectual hierarchy, is that the most respectable academy does not believe that it has a sufficiently sanctioned mission to ascertain the state of acquisitions made, and of acquisitions to be made, to pose important problems to be solved, or to evaluate the results that have been obtained and the efforts that have been demanded, in short to direct the entire operation in a rapid and orderly fashion with perfection as the aim. It can easily propose a few mediocre prizes in order to obtain the solution of some questions; but if the public does not respond to this call, the problem is postponed indefinitely, and the step, although described as necessary by the programs, remains to be taken.**

* One of the most striking examples of this sort is offered by chemistry. A large number of human and animal parts are analyzed in the absence of any physiological view, and it is certain that this work, long, laborious and often loathsome, can in its isolation produce only imperfect results. We cite this example only as one among many.

** The Academy of the Sciences has finally arrived at the point to which its vicious organization had to lead it. Since scientific discoveries have been produced for a long time outside the Academy, it now no longer dares to guide the scientists, to direct them into roads in which new progress ought to be made. The Academy really handed in its resignation at the moment

Such are the various causes to which we must attribute the sterility of our academies. The idea behind their founding was much more to offer a reward and a haven to men who pursued a scientific career with great distinction than to create working associations destined to organize and centralize all scientific efforts. Thus having been deprived of any principle of action, without authority to distribute work and to judge its products, the academies obtain nothing but virtually insignificant results, even when these academies are composed of men of the greatest ability. What else can one expect, when they are constituted almost exclusively of scientists dedicated to detailed work and above all to practice?

What is occurring under our eyes is the consequence of the lack of order we have just pointed out. In the absence of any official inventory of ascertained discoveries, the isolated scientists daily run the risk that they may be repeating experiments already made by others. If they were acquainted with other experiments, they would be spared efforts often as laborious as they are useless, and it would be easier for them to obtain means for forging ahead. Let us add here that their security is not complete. They are haunted by the work of a competitor. Possibly someone else is gleaning the same field and may, as the saying goes, "get there first." The scientist has to hide himself and conduct in haste and isolation work requiring deliberation and demanding aid from the association. In brief, on all sides there may easily be seen the inconveniences that result from an organization that turns away from the perfecting of scientific theories to the pursuit of individual endeavors. The Academy no longer commands progress; it is satisfied to record it.

We have said that the majority of scientists are dedicated to practice. When the scientist's existence is no longer assured by social foresight, he contemplates the abandonment of all purely theoretical work; for if he is to dedicate himself to such work, the accident of birth must at the same time produce and provide income and high ability, two conditions very seldom fulfilled.

---

when it no longer feared to unveil its impotence by offering prizes for the best scientific accounts without indicating to the competitors a definite object or a question to be solved.

The government indeed rewards the scientists at times, but being as incompetent as it can possibly be, it tries to utilize them in schools, on faculties, in arsenals, and so on, thus always depriving them of precious time for theoretical research by exacting practical work. There remain then only the great and noble resources of the sinecures; but who would want to buy the advantage of working in peace at such a price? What superior mind would consent to being provided for by a function which he did not fulfill when he felt qualified for titles with real responsibilities? Why must the insulting word favor intervene where the word justice should express the whole idea? Moreover, in return for a favor, a power foreign to science demands complete political and moral submission from the scientist, reduced to the role of solicitor, and he must choose between his love for science, that is to say, for the progress of human intelligence, and his love for himself.

It will be said, however, that there is ground for the belief that society finds ample compensations for the inconveniences which we have pointed out: scientists, obliged to devote themselves to applied work for their livelihood, have undoubtedly made miraculous strides in that field. This opinion is voiced, of course; but if one tries to verify it by the facts, it will generally be found that some duties are badly carried out, and one will find no miraculous advances anywhere. Disgust and boredom are intermingled in work which one does not like. Life is wasted in regrets, and superior abilities are extinguished after having rendered society only a small part of the services they could have offered. Suppose that a capable engineer is called upon to find the cubic area of a highway and pave it. Probably a subordinate would perform the routine work better, enabling the engineer to be assigned to a more important task that might otherwise not be accomplished. Since we are talking about application, is it not evident that the first and greatest application of science ought to be made to teaching? There is, however, complete disagreement between the body of scientists and the body of teachers. One can definitely say that they do not use the same language. No general step has been taken to ensure that advances achieved in science will be immediately passed on to the field of education. There is no broad and sure ladder for descending from theory to practice.

We do not want to belittle those men who by their hard work deserve well of society but are far behind a Descartes, a Pascal, a Newton, or a Leibniz, nor are we trying to depreciate their work, which often presupposes an uncommon degree ability. We are forced to recognize that no great scientific thought dominates or co-ordinates present day scientific concepts. In all this we can discover nothing but a rich collection of individual facts. It is a museum of pretty medallions waiting for a hand to classify them. The lack of order among and within the minds of men has invaded the very sciences, and it must be admitted they offer the sorry spectacle of complete anarchy. In closing, we shall state that the cause of the evil is to be sought in the lack of unity in social outlook; and the remedy will be found in the discovery of this unity.

Industry

Perhaps the marvels of industry have been exalted even more than those of science. Let us attempt to evaluate the efforts undertaken in this direction.

Here, as in the sciences, we shall not try to deny any of the progress that has been made. It is evident that the sciences, which have recently been directed towards applied knowledge, should have thrown light on several branches of technology. It is no less evident, that we, who have profited from the efforts of our predecessors, should have surpassed them. The question is not whether industry has made any advances, which accomplishment no one would welcome more than we; what matters to us is whether the march toward improvement could not have been much more rapid than it has been. We are led, therefore, to observe industry in its three great aspects, namely: (1) its technical component; (2) the organization of work, that is to say the division of labor involved in production with relation to the needs of consumption; (3) the relation of the workers to the owners of the instruments of production.

In the advanced state in which we find science and industry, industry is presented as supposedly constituting in its technological aspects a deduction from science and a direct application of the science's contributions to material production rather than as consisting merely of a collection of routine processes. There has been no organized effort, however, to free industry from the narrow confines within which it is at present restricted so that industrial practices may be raised to the height of scientific theories. In industry, everything is still left to the uncertain performances of individual luminaries. Evidence from experimentation, often lengthy and prejudicial, is almost the only means used by industrialists to evaluate their processes; this is evidence which each one of them must revise, for, thanks to competition, each is interested in surrounding with mystery the discoveries he has attained so that he may keep them as his monopoly. If theory and practice are integrated at all, the process is always incidental, isolated and incomplete.

Undoubtedly, despite these fetters, some improvements have been made. But can one count how much they have cost or how much effort has been wasted, how much capital buried, and how much pain caused by the thought that the founders of the greatest establishments have seldom harvested the fruits? In industry, as in science, we find only isolated efforts; the only feeling that dominates all thoughts is egoism. The industrialist is little concerned with the interests of society. His family, his instruments of production, and the personal fortune he strives to attain, are his mankind, his universe, and his God. He sees nothing but enemies in those who follow the same career; he lies in wait for them; he spies upon them and has made his happiness and glory consist in ruining them. Finally, in what hands have the majority of workshops and industrial instruments been placed? Have they been entrusted to the men who could make the best use of them in the interests of society? Certainly not. In general, they are directed by incompetent managers who until now have shown no evidence of their personal interest having led them to learn what they ought to know.

By no means less serious difficulties have manifested themselves in the *organization of work*.[8] We have said that industry possesses a theory, and one might be led to believe that this theory could show how production and consumption can and ought to be harmonized. But the theory itself is the main source of disorder; the economists apparently have posed the following problem:

"Given leaders more ignorant than those they govern, and supposing, moreover, that far from favoring the rise of industry, these leaders want to fetter it, and that their deputies are the born enemies of the producers, what sort of industrial organization is suitable to society?"

Laissez faire, laissez passer! This has been the necessary solution, and this has been the only general principle they have proclaimed. One knows well enough under what influences this maxim was formulated; it carries its own date with it. The economists thought that with one stroke of the pen they could solve all the questions relating to the production and distribution of wealth. They entrusted personal interest with the realization of that great precept, without wondering whether any individual, no matter how keen his insight, could judge within the limitations of his environment, being, so to speak, in a valley, the totality which can only be seen from the highest mountain peaks. We are the witnesses of the disasters that have already resulted from this principle of circumstance, and if more striking examples were needed, they would appear in throngs to testify to the impotence of such a theory designed to make industry productive. If a few exclusive privileges or monopolies prevail today, the majority of them have their existence only in legislative provisions. Indeed, freedom is extensive, and the maxim of the economists is generally applied in France and England. But what do we see? Every industrialist tries to learn about consumption needs without any guide or compass other than his personal observations, which, no matter however extensive his connections may be, are always incomplete. When there is a rumor that a

[8] "The first use of an expression—we found it neither in Saint-Simon's writings nor in the *Opinions* or in the *Producteur*—which was to become universally popular with the approach of the 1848 Revolution after Louis Blanc . . . had made it the title of a famous pamphlet." B23.

certain branch of production offers good possibilities, all enterprise and capital flow in that direction; everyone hurries there
blindly. No one takes the time to trouble himself about the
proper size and the necessary limits of the enterprise. The
economists cheer at the sight of this overcrowding, for they
recognize from the great number of contestants that the principle
of competition has been widely applied. Alas! What is the
outcome of this death struggle? A few fortunate ones triumph—
but at the price of the complete ruin of innumerable victims.

The necessary consequences of these unco-ordinated efforts
and of this overproduction in some areas is that the balance
between production and consumption is continually threatened.
Hence the numberless catastrophes and the commercial crises
that terrify the speculators and stop the execution of the best
projects. One sees upright and hard-working men ruined, and
morality hurt by such examples, because the crises bring about
the conclusion that in order to succeed, more seems to be needed
than honesty and hard work. A man therefore becomes keen,
clever, and shrewd and even dares to glory in being all these
things. Once this resolution has been taken, he is lost.

Let us add now that the basic principle *laissez faire, laissez
passer* supposes that personal interest is always in harmony with
general interest, a supposition contradicted by innumerable facts.
To choose one example among a thousand: is it not evident that
if society sees its interest in the introduction of steam engines, the
worker who lives by his hands cannot join his voice to that of
society? The answer to this objection is well known. Printing
is taken as an example, and it is established that it employs more
men today than the copyists that ever were before its invention.
Soon the conclusion is drawn that everything ultimately evens
itself out. An admirable conclusion. What shall we do with the
thousands of famished men[9] until this leveling is completed?
Will they feel consoled by our reasoning? Will they take their
misery patiently because statistical calculations prove that in a
certain number of years they will have bread? Certainly technology has basically nothing to offer in this situation; it must

[9] "Sismondi first opposed the optimism of the (classical) school on this
point." B26.

give birth to everything its genius inspires in it. Society, however, ought to see to it that the conquests of industry will not be like those of war. Funeral songs must no longer mingle with songs of joy.

The third connection in which industry is to be considered is in the relationship between the workers and the owners of the instruments of production or of capital. This question, however, refers to the very constitution of property, which we shall carefully examine because it represents one of the general aspects of the social reform that the new doctrine will bring about. We cannot, without anticipating ourselves, have a glimpse of the character of contemporary society in this respect. We shall merely note that land, workshops, capital, and so on, can under one condition alone be employed in production with the greatest advantage possible: they must be entrusted to those hands most skillful in exploiting them, or in other words, to those possessing industrial abilities. Today, however, capacity is only a poor title for credit; to acquire credit, one must first possess something. The accident of birth blindly distributes the instruments of production, whatever they may be; and if the heir, the idle owner, entrusts them to the hands of a skillful worker, it is quite evident that the primary increment accrues to the incapable and lazy owner.* What shall we conclude from this analysis if not that the results at which we marvel may be far surpassed (and without the misfortunes we daily witness) once the exploitation of the whole earth has been subjected to order; once, consequently, a general conception presides over this exploitation. Thus again, unity and coherence is lacking. The leaders of society have shouted: "Save himself who can!" And every member of this great whole has detached himself and said: "Each one for himself; God for none!"

The Fine Arts

After having shown the lack of any common goal in the sciences and in industry, nothing remains for us now except to

* When dealing with the question of property, we shall show how the idle owner exploits the director of work, and how he in turn exploits the worker.

cast a rapid glance at the fine arts, in order that we may encompass all the modes of human activity.

Looking back at the ages of Pericles, Augustus, Leo X, and Louis XIV, and then at the nineteenth century, one cannot help but smile; no one would think of drawing a parallel between the periods. On this point, at least, everyone agrees. It is true that our periodicals console us for this disgrace by assuring us that we are matter-of-fact (*positifs*) to a high degree, but such an explanation is a poor consolation for those of us who know the true meaning of that magic adjective which is so unaccountably abused.

We, too, recognize the state of decline and languor in the fine arts, but we attribute it to basic causes, and it is so much more interesting to go back to these causes that we shall later evaluate the true role of the fine arts and the meaning encompassed by this term.*

The fine arts are the expression of feeling, one of the three modes of being of man, who without the fine arts would lack language. Without them there would be a gap in both individual and social life. Through the fine arts man is induced to social acts and brought to see his private interest in the general interest. They are the source of devotion and of strong and tender affection. The assertion of their inferiority which is rather complacently put forth today is a testimonial to the sterility of general and even of individual sentiments. To what role have the fine arts been reduced when their expressions are considered powerless and their debased functions mere recreation?

There are two aspects of the fine arts, namely poetry or vitality, and form or technique. The former, undoubtedly, determines the latter. We have, however, seen poesy disappear and technical perfection survive. Today, form is the almost exclusive concern; the nature of the emotions of which the form is to be the interpreter is hardly taken into account. We appraise a work of art quite independently of its effect on our sympathies; in other words, we consider only one of its aspects.

* See the brochure entitled: *Aux Artistes. Du passé et de l'avenir des beaux arts.* (Doctrine de Saint-Simon) Paris, 1830, at the office of the Globe, rue Monsigny, No. 6.

Hence the indifference in which art finds us and leaves us. Let us mention, in passing, that the true artists today, men who have been keenly inspired, reflect only antisocial feelings, for the only poetic forms in which vitality has been rediscovered have been satire and the elegy. It is true that today these are the language of delicate souls and of elite groups; but both forms alike attack social feelings, be it by the passionate expression of despair or by a contemptuous infernal laughter attempting to sully everything pure and sacred. But without dwelling any longer on this subject which might easily lead to a critique of the present, we shall turn to an inquiry into general and individual social relations. There we shall find the cause for decadence in the fine arts and at the same time corroborate the disorder presented by the picture of scientific and industrial activity depicted above.

We have explained how the terms organic epochs and critical epochs must be interpreted and have said that paganism up to the time of Socrates and Christianity up to the age of Luther constituted 'two organic states. We shall briefly sketch some of the characteristics of these two eras.

The fundamental basis of the societies of antiquity was slavery. For these people, war was the only way of furnishing themselves with slaves and, consequently, with the material needs of life. The strongest among them were the richest, and their industry was limited to plunder. Woe to the weakling who could not stand up under the weight of armor! The dominant thought of these people and their everyday aim was war. All of their passions and feelings responded to the war cry, and their strongest emotion sprang out of love for the fatherland and hatred for the foreigner. Even the mother offered thanks to the gods when the shield of her son was brought to her. Go through Greece and go through Italy, and you will hear nothing but the noise of arms; Rome ceased to be Rome when the temple of Janus was closed.

Need we be surprised at the strength of the fine arts in that epoch? A common passion animated all hearts, a common idea directed them, a common thought impelled them to devotion; and devotion and poetic inspiration are inseparable.

Later Christianity, its way paved by the Socratic school, destroyed slavery, and at the price of untold heartbreak the

precepts of the Gospel, applied to politics under the name of
Catholicism, gave society a new organization in harmony with its
need. Faith became a spiritual fatherland, common to all children of Christ. And despite the hate and selfishness of nations,
the new fatherland saw a new love reborn. Then, too, there was
a reappearance of great devotion and great inspiration. Eight
crusades in the short interval of two centuries did not weaken
the fervor of the nations. And the centuries of Leo X and Louis
XIV crowned the great work of Catholicism and feudalism,
which organizations had only a short time to live—and in agony
—for after fifteen centuries the organization of the Middle Ages
was threatened on all sides.

The clergy, unable to persevere in the divine mission it had
begun, had abandoned the weak it should have protected and
had subordinated itself to the successors of Caesar. Elsewhere the
nobility, which, in the name of chivalry, had also consecrated
itself to the defense of the weak, had ended by sending the
decrepit among them to the brilliant antechambers of the great
king. And the laymen, who were gradually taking possession of
science and wealth, armed themselves with these powerful
weapons and overthrew the ungodly coalition which had believed
in the eternity of exploitation of man by man.

This is not the place to describe the long struggle that, by
the abolition of serfdom, paved the way for the complete liberation of man. All of us know what was the outcome of the
struggle, under way since the end of the fifteenth century. We
dwell in the midst of the rubble, the living rubble of medieval
society which continues to bemoan its fate. In recalling these
events, we have had no other aim than to establish the distinctive
character of our epoch and to affirm that we live in one of those
periods that we have labeled critical.

The mark of critical epochs, like that of periods of great
confusion, is egoism. All beliefs are overthrown, all common
feelings extinguished, and the vestal virgins no longer preside
over the sacred fires. The poet is no longer the divine singer,
placed at the head of society as man's interpreter to give him
laws, to repress his retrograde inclinations, to reveal to him the
joys of the future, to sustain him and to incite his onward march.

No, the poet can sing only sinister songs. Now he arms himself
with the whip of satire; his verve breathes forth bitter words; he
rages against the entire race; he incites man to distrust, and to
the hatred of his fellow-men. Then, again in a weakened voice,
he sings elegiac verses on the charms of solitude; he abandons
himself to dreams; he paints happiness in isolation (*isolement*).[10]
If, however, a man were seduced by these sad sounds and fled
his fellow-men, he would, once separated from them, find only
despair. But this language no longer has the power to carry us
away. Toward the end of a critical period, one no longer stirs a
man by speaking to his heart, but one must show him that his
fortune is endangered. Look, therefore, at the present leaders of
the critical epoch. When they wanted to make their system
popular, did they call upon our poets, our painters, and our
musicians? What could they do? They could only touch those
strings responding to individual desires. They have, thus, con-
jured up the spectre of feudalism. They have shown it to us
fully armed, coming to win back the tithe with one hand and
with the other snatching back the properties from the purchasers
of national wealth.* When a formidable attack was recently
directed at freedom of the press, the "safeguard of our liberties,"
as political orators would call it, was an attempt made to defend
it on general and moral considerations? Hardly. Who does not

[10] "This is the title of the first poem in Lamartine's *Méditations* (1st
ed., 1820). The Saint-Simonians use this term which characterizes romantic
'individualism' beautifully. This romanticism, at once proud and desperate,
is according to them the perfect sentimental expression of a critical epoch.
It is antisocial, suffers from being so, and finally boasts of its suffering. (See
references to Goethe and Byron in index.) Here is one point where the
Saint-Simonians are 'prophets,' or rather 'initiators.' After the revolutionary
shake-up of 1830, the inspiration of French romanticism changed in conformity with the opinion of the Saint-Simonian preachers and becomes 'social' rather than, as it was formerly, 'lonely.' The poet becomes the 'divine
singer' of progress. See Victor Hugo, *Les Rayons et les Oeuvres*, 1840, the
part called 'The Function of the Poet,' and already the restless 'Prélude' of
Les Chants du Crépuscule." B30.

* Far from pretending that the retrograde attempts of the present leaders of public opinion were mere products of their fearful imagination and
that it was useless to set up such an obstacle against the blind partisans of
the past, we want merely to state this fact: in the critical epochs one can
stir the masses only by fear, never by hope; by hate, never by love; by self-
interest, never by a sense of duty; in short, by egoism never by devotion.

know how limited is the number of those men who are disposed
to do their part for what is called the general interest? Defenders
of the press prudently appealed to something more positive: a
petition was drawn up in the name of bookstore owners, printers,
stationers, book stitchers, book binders, and so on. Indeed, we
are forced to come out and say it; the fine arts no longer have
any voice when there is no longer any love in society. Poetry is
not the interpreter of egoism. To reveal himself, a true artist
needs a chorus which will repeat his songs and be receptive to
his overflowing feelings.

But if social affections do not exist, may not individual affections be very highly developed? Even though the present generation may proudly take refuge in this sphere when accused of
egoism it is very hard to defend our generation against the
reproach of egoism. How are those gentle ties formed today, by
which one sex joins another to share both the joys and the
sorrows of life? We have all learned what is meant by a good
marriage in contrast to what is called a foolish marriage. Poor
girls! You are placed on the auction block like slaves. On holi-
days you are dressed up to enhance your value, and often your
fathers shamelessly place your charms on the scales so that they
may give a little less money to the unworthy husband bargaining
for you. We are only too glad that there are undoubtedly some
men who repudiate this odious traffic, but their number is small,
and everyone ridicules them.

One would believe that paternal and filial affection, born,
so to speak, on the day we receive life, are not of such a nature
as to undergo such great changes; and yet, all emotions are
linked. Any cause that weakens one reacts equally on the others.
To realize its full development, feeling needs to be fully applied.
Have we not heard philosophy coldly question the reciprocal
duties of parents and children? And have inheritances never
soothed sorrow or dried up tears? Without bitterness but with
sorrow we note all these evils and all these miseries. We are
saying that they corrode society and would annihilate it if they
were inherent in it. By naming egoism, we have put our fingers
on the deepest wound of modern societies. Egoism rules as master among nations as it does among individuals. In the Middle

Ages, thanks to religious ties, the peoples of Europe arose more than once and, despite national hatred, marched hand in hand toward a common goal. The sovereigns of our day have tried to re-establish an association among themselves, but their efforts have resulted merely in a sort of parody of the past ornamented by the title, "Holy Alliance." [11] This European pact, based on narrow interests, conceived solely in fear of the revolutionary movement and deprived of that breath of life which animated the old confederation, was destined to have merely an ephemeral existence. It did nothing more than had already been vainly attempted at various periods; namely, it tried to assure peace by the European balance of power, an insoluble problem as long as the peoples of Europe do not feel united by a common goal. Until that time, the members of this great European family, full of mutual distrust, are abandoned to particularism, and are hostile to any power that does not associate itself with their destiny, a destiny they do not yet know but are forever seeking. Such peoples will not feel bound by any common duty or common moral law as in the times of the spiritual brotherhood of the Christians.

We have lamented the recent misfortunes of Italy and Spain. We have seen how these peoples tried to free themselves and to adopt a form of government which we claim to love. What have we done for them? Nothing but make impotent promises. The Greeks who have been massacred by the thousands have implored our pity. Did we take up the cross?*

---

[11] Saint-Simon had advocated a confederation of nations in 1814. In *Du Système industriel,* Saint-Simon criticizes the Holy Alliance as "being exclusively composed of the temporal leaders of the principal nations" and subordinating the spiritual power. (*Oeuvres de Saint-Simon et d'Enfantin,* XXII, 100.) For the Saint-Simonians, the Holy Alliance had to be criticized on two counts: It represented an attempt to restore the past and to squelch revolutionary movements. Here the critique of the Saint-Simonians corresponded to that of liberalism. Yet like Lamennais and ultramontane Catholicism (see Lamennais' "De la sainte-alliance," *Nouveaux mélanges,* 1826, pp. 581 ff.), Saint-Simonianism saw in the Holy Alliance a temporal league, non-religious and non-hierarchical, which in trying to assure the European balance and to protect vested interests expressed the spirit of the critical age. Cf. B32.

* What could we have answered the barbarians of the Middle Ages if they had asked us to account for our lukewarmness in this situation? What

Will it be said that the governments have restrained the spirit of the European nations, and that freed of fetters they have imposed upon us, we would have sped to the help of our brethren and avenged their defeat? But what did America do, that model country, which certainly cannot offer the pretext that she is under governmental constraint? It must be said to her shame that she made an agreement with the Turks to send them provisions. Some parts of South America wanted to shake off the Spanish yoke which still oppresses them. Did the United States, still filled with the bitter memories of colonial rule, with the noise of recently broken chains still in everyone's ears, in any manner whatever facilitate the emancipation of her compatriots? No. Finally, did she offer financial aid to help the Republic of Haiti pay its ransom? No, and again no. This free people, which we are told has shaken off all the prejudices of Old Europe, this people which leads all others in the ways of civilization, protested against the existence of an emancipated people, because it was a nation of Negroes.*

The picture we have just drawn of the present epoch would undoubtedly be heart-rending if it were the picture of the final state of mankind. Fortunately, a better future is reserved for man, and the present, despite its vices, is heavy with the future toward which all our hopes, thoughts, and efforts are directed.

To destroy a social order that was no longer possible, liberty was proclaimed. In the opinion of the people, no idea could have been more powerful against the hierarchies that had fallen and *rightly so.*** But when it was desired to apply this idea to the construction of a new social order, whether in Europe or in America, the situation depicted above was brought about. It was believed that the solution of the problem consisted in put-

---

would we have answered if they had asked us to account for our sworn obligation? No, festivals and concerts had to be given in order to extract donations from us.

* One-seventh of the population of the United States tills the soil of freedom in slavery.

** We have underlined these words in order to answer indirectly those people who, because we know how to do justice to the past, seem to believe that we want to bring it back.

ting a minus sign before all the terms of the formula of the Middle Ages, but this strange solution could only engender anarchy. The publicists of our epoch have remained echoes of the eighteenth-century philosophers without realizing that they had the inverse mission to fulfill. They have continued the attack with the same fervor, as if the enemy were still confronting them, and have exhausted themselves in fighting a phantom.

Has the time come for the formulation of a new social doctrine? Everything foretells it: the deep-rootedness of the evils, the fruitless efforts of some philanthropists, and the distress calls of eminent minds. For several years Guizot,[12] and above all Cousin,[13] have been announcing something different from the eighteenth century, proclaimed for a long time now as the last stage in the progress of the human mind. Saint-Simon had an opportunity to direct his thanks to the former in a postscript which we shall reproduce here.*

As for Cousin, it has been seen how he, a few years ago, brought about as a definitive conclusion of philosophy the concept of representative government; that is, the political state

[12] "The Saint-Simonians were seduced by certain aspects of Guizot's doctrine, by his philosophic conception of history and also, as the text informs us, by a spirit of social conservatism and a feeling for the need for an order based on common beliefs which is lacking among the other liberal publicists." B35.

[13] Victor Cousin (1792-1867), main representative of the early nineteenth-century French philosophic school or eclecticism, conceived of the eighteenth century "as one of the greatest centuries" which had the purely destructive mission of ending the Middle Ages. The nineteenth century must rebuild philosophically and politically. Cf. B36, 38.

* "There are, gentlemen," Saint-Simon said, "men who have rendered great services to inventors as well as the public, namely the *popularizers*. Inventors as well as the public cannot encourage them enough. Voltaire made the critical ideas of Bayle known. M. Guizot has just popularized the observations I published in the *Organisateur* relative to the division of our nation into two peoples, to the alliance between royalty and the Gauls, and to the mistake committed by Louis XIV when he abandoned the Gauls to ally himself anew with the Franks.

"I pray M. Guizot to receive my sincere thanks. I ask him to read this letter with great care. It is highly desirable, both for the public and for me, that he appropriate its content as fully as he did my first ideas on the course of royalty in France." (Henri Saint-Simon, *Système Industriel*, 1821, p. 153.)

which the first quarter of the nineteenth century has made real.
We, who accept neither the Middle Ages nor constitutionalism,
leap beyond the limits of the present; and the present regime,
even when modified and perfected, seems to us as only provisional, for in its very foundation are the evils by which it is
undermined. We are certainly not ungrateful, however, to the
defenders of this system. We know that they set up a healthy
obstacle against the retrogressive attempts of former general interests. They also serve as counterweights to a fraction of society
that could introduce disorder among the European population,
whose first need is peace. We do not, however, expect anything
from their efforts at organizing the peoples; like war, criticism
in all respects has only the power to destroy, and criticism has
fulfilled its mission. The time is approaching when the nations
will abandon the banners of a disorderly and thoughtless liberalism to enter lovingly into a state of peace and happiness, abandoning mistrust and recognizing that legitimate power can exist
on earth.

In carefully scrutinizing social relations, we have recognized
that all the ties that bound men in the past have been broken,
and we have expressed no regrets. We have not even wept at
seeing the exclusive love for the fatherland extinguished, because
in our eyes it was merely the egoism of nations. This pure feeling which has inspired so much noble devotion and so many
generous sacrifices must disappear to give way to a feeling even
purer, greater, and more fertile; namely, the love for the universal family of man. Do we still have to free the word "power"
of its association with "yoke" and "despotism," which it ordinarily awakens in restless minds? Yes, gentlemen, bless with us
the yoke which is imposed by conviction and which satisfies all
the feelings lodged in the hearts of men. Bless a power whose
only thought is to impel the peoples on the way of progress and
to make productive all the sources of public property. The doctrine that we are proclaiming is to take possession of the entire
man, and to give the three great human faculties a common goal
and a harmonious direction. By its means, the sciences will make
unified progress towards the most speedy development; industry,
regulated in the interests of all, will no longer present the fright-

ening spectacle of an arena; and the fine arts, once more animated by ardent sympathy, will reveal to us the feelings of enthusiasm in a common life, whose gentle influence will make itself felt in the most secret joys of private life.

The Law of the Development of Mankind: Verification of This Law by History

We have drawn a painful picture, gentlemen. We were compelled to speak nothing but the truth. It has been unpleasant for us to bring you face to face with society as *criticism*[1] has made it and to uncover its sores in order to make you feel the necessity of and the opportunity for a new general doctrine. We have spared you all the sorrows that one experiences in penetrating the intimacy of families without faith and belief, who, thrown back upon themselves, no longer have any link with society save that of taxation. We have said nothing about that bloody epoch when the crew, in revolt, broke the rudder before building a better one. We could have shown you the altar profaned by the scandalous competition of creeds or overthrown by atheism, and the shattered pieces of the scepter dispersed among a thousand hands, as by soldiers dividing the spoils of the vanquished after victory.[2] But we thought that your minds, once disenchanted of the marvel of liberty, in whose name everything is permitted, would be able to appraise, as we do, everything that emerges from this sinister metaphysics. Now, after announcing a doctrine giving the solution to the great social problem, we shall hasten to expound it in order to turn your thoughts to consoling ideas and relieve you of the uneasiness and anxiety affecting every well-

[1] "This expression has passed over into philosophic language; but it is no longer used in the sense in which the Saint-Simonians used it. Rather it designates the philosophic tendency which places the theory of knowledge, and particularly Kant's theory, at the basis of all speculation. The Saint-Simonians understand the expression in its pejorative sense, as meaning the totality of these forces of disorganization, lack of discipline, and anarchy which predominate during 'critical' epochs; 'criticism' is opposed to 'dogmatism.' " B39.
[2] Allusions to the freedom of worship established by the Revolution, the Cult of Reason, and the confiscation of Church property.

disposed person at this time when society is about to assume a new life and take on new forms.

We have maintained from the beginning that Saint-Simon's concept was verifiable by history. Do not expect from us a discussion of isolated facts, nor enlightenment on details recorded in obscure chronicles. We turn your attention only to the general laws governing the organization of man. The more the chaos and confusion of events have masked these laws for you to this day, the more you will be filled with admiration for the man who unveiled them to us on his death bed.[3]

Saint-Simon's mission was to discover these laws, and he bequeathed them to the world as a sublime heritage. As his disciples, our mission is to continue his revelation, to develop his lofty conceptions, and to disseminate them.

Gentlemen, the head of our school did not escape the persecutions which seem to be the sad privilege of innovators. Picture to yourselves what must have been the frightful martyrdom of this ardent and sublime genius who understood the law of mankind, proclaimed it, and aroused only laughter. He showed the scientists a new road, but they overwhelmed him with their scorn. It may be said that he gave mankind the entire universe for a second time, but he died abandoned and destitute. Pursued by the hooting of the academic crowd and showered with malice, he was lashed by the whips of the nineteenth century, misery and sarcasm. Imagine the indignation of this unrecognized genius, struggling under the burden of abuse with which he was overwhelmed, exhausting himself by fruitless attempts to impress the minds, directing his message to every intellect, and always being sent back to the blind court of public opinion, repulsed by those whom he had nourished, renounced by those whom he had adopted, and looking at last toward the future to find a smile and receive a blessing.

[3] "The Saint-Simonians, who modified the teachings of their master on so many points, still insist on invoking Saint-Simon's authority for their entire doctrine. How did they execute this 'pious fraud'? By presenting themselves as the trustees of Saint-Simon's last thoughts, entrusted to them in the narrow circle of his most intimate friends, 'on his death bed,' subsequently to the publication of his works which were completed, by the way, at a time when his doctrine tended to take on a more sentimental and more religious character. See *Globe*, December 30, 1831." B44.

Gentlemen, this in short was the life of Saint-Simon. This was the lot of one who deserved the honors which grateful humanity bestows on its benefactors, but who received only the painful crown of the martyr. It was during the course of a life filled with humiliations and sacrifices that this man, passionately devoted to humanity, soared above the age that repudiated him and opened new roads through its icy hearts and the narrow intellects that surround him. He was ultimately to prophesy the future and to verify his prophecies by entirely new views concerning the past.

Humanity, he said, is a collective entity. This entity has grown from generation to generation as a man grows in the course of years, according to its own physical law, which has been one of progressive development.

The most general fact in the growth of societies, the one which implicitly includes all the others, is the progress of the moral conception by which man becomes conscious of a social destiny. The political institution is the realization, that is, the putting into practice of this conception, its application to the establishment, preservation and progressive development of social relationships.

A preliminary classification of past facts thus becomes necessary. This is the one already indicated in the preceding session by the terms *organic* and *critical* epochs. Organic epochs present the picture of union among the members of ever widening associations which determine the combination of their efforts toward a common goal. Critical epochs, on the other hand, are filled with disorder; they destroy former social relations, and everywhere tend towards egoism. Let us add that the latter have always been useful, necessary, and indispensable; for in destroying antiquated forms which had contributed for a long time to the development of mankind but had finally become harmful, they have facilitated the conception and realization of better forms.

Next come the three great secondary series,[4] which corre-

---

[4] "This classification into three is shared by Saint-Simon, Auguste Comte and Enfantin. But Saint-Simon puts feeling and science on the same plane and subordinates both to industry and to action. Auguste Comte subordinates

spond to the three modes of human activity; namely feeling, intellect, and material activity. The first comprises all the events in the development of human sympathies, as represented by men who were deeply inspired by them and knew how to communicate them to the masses. The second is composed of the stages in the constant progress of the sciences and is indicative of the development of the human mind. The third, which we are denoting by the words material activity, has been represented in the past by the actions of both war and industry but in the future will be represented by industry alone, for the exploitation of man by man will have been replaced by the harmonious action of man on nature.[5]

---

feeling to science. Enfantin (whose ideas are translated here by Bazard, who is actually less mystical) subordinates science (as well as action) to feeling. Actually, when the Saint-Simonian doctrine was transformed into a religious dogma, its adherents began to see a trinity manifesting the divine life, namely Love, Wisdom and Power. See Eugène Rodrigues, *Lettres sur la Religion et la Politique*, 1832 ed., pp. 121, 159." B47.

[5] "This theory, according to which a regime of the exploitation of man by man is followed by a regime of the exploitation of nature by man in association, had already been expressed by Saint-Simon when he said that a military or governmental regime is followed by an industrial or administrative regime. (*Catéchisme politique des Industriels; Oeuvres de Saint-Simon et d'Enfantin*, XXXVII, 8; cf. *ibid.*, XX, 150.) But one should note that Auguste Comte soon refused to consider a society possible from which all government was excluded (*Système de Politique positive*, 1824, p. 11; 1912 ed., p. 52): 'The government which under any normal circumstances is the head of society, the leader and performer of common action . . .' and 'Considerations about the Spiritual Power' (*Producteur*, II, 316; 1912 ed., p. 52): 'Although it may be useful and even in certain cases necessary to consider the idea of a society as an abstraction from the idea of government, it is universally recognized that these two ideas are actually inseparable.' He did, to be sure, indicate in the same *Système de Politique positive* (1824, p. 117; 1912 ed., p. 102) that in 'scientific' politics, which radically excludes anything 'arbitrary' . . . 'the government of things replaces that of man.' The *Doctrine* seems to avoid intentionally the use of the word *government*, perhaps in order to exclude it from the future organization of society, as being too 'military,' or perhaps in order to adopt it as corresponding to one of the school's preoccupations with organization. But soon the Saint-Simonians become brave and finally arrive at a complete inversion of the original formula. See especially *Globe*, April 4, 1831: 'A worker needs helpers, assistants, laborers. . . . It is up to him not only to administer things, but to rule over men—a difficult, immense, and holy task. The lazy man needs good-natured people, servants, lackeys; he wants them to be docile, at his beck and command, in other words, slaves. . . . The lazy man is a master, the servant is a serf. The master does not *govern*, he *commands*.' It is certainly true that

Saint-Simon, going back to the origin of hatred, shows how it developed to its highest degree from family to family, from city to city, from nation to nation. All antipathy and violence, to be sure, is especially effective outside the circle of association, however small it may be; but within the fatherland, city, caste, or family, all brutal habits which have sprung from hatred of the foreigner are reproduced. Within the family, the man has the right of life and death over all who surround him. In the temple he wins the gods to his side by a bloody sacrifice. He never leaves his dwelling unarmed, for he cannot take a step without meeting an enemy. Gradually, however, less savage feelings appear. Man no longer kills his prisoners, but makes his prisoners work for him and reduces them to slavery. This harsh law was later made milder by imperceptible degrees, and immense progress was achieved the day serfdom was established on the ruins of antiquity under the powerful shield of a religion preaching human brotherhood. Gentlemen, today we consult history to find out what a lord is and to measure the distance between the manorial lord and the serf bound to the sod. Man has a horror of blood, which for a long time was his delight. The apparatus of barbaric punishment has disappeared, even for chastising the guilty. National hatreds are being wiped out from day to day, and peoples who are ready to form a complete and definitive alliance presents us with the beautiful spectacle of mankind gravitating toward universal association.

Moreover, force of war, first deified, has been dethroned by peaceful work. Saint-Simon has shown us how the Greeks and the Romans left the industrial arts to the vile hands of the slave and blushed at what for us is a title of honor. The slave turned over to his master the total increment of his work. But mankind is obeying its own law, which it is fulfilling slowly but inevitably.

---

in the essentially ethical conceptions of final Saint-Simonianism the word *government* suggests the idea of a real but purely spiritual power in contrast to that 'temporal' power whose action was thought of as constituting a government but is now thought of as constituting a 'command.' Whatever it may be, it is strange to see the Saint-Simonians, who are obsessed with organization, arrive at a formula which is almost diametrically opposed to the one which was very successfully popularized by Friedrich Engels, who was inspired by early Saint-Simonianism to designate the future socialist regime: administration of things instead of government of persons." B48.

Soon the slave's tribute diminished. Under the name serf, he turned over only a part of the products of his sweat, and even this part continually decreased until it constituted only a very small fraction, which our fathers knew as *corvées,* feudal rents, and tithes. Look at Europe: the love of peaceful work has succeeded the lust for battle. You no longer see populations devoured by the need for war. A man snatched from the plow can only with difficulty be forced to take up arms. We no longer gird ourselves with swords to satisfy warlike instincts. And Napoleon, that genius whom Rome had forgotten to produce, coming two thousand years later to astonish a Europe which no longer believed in the god of armies, lined up his soldiers for battle while telling them that they were going to win peace and freedom of commerce.*

We shall complete this picture by considering how the intellect, which had first been kept down by brutality, occupied a successively higher place. We are far removed from the age when one went to the slave market to look for a grammarian, and in the Catholic clergy the Middle Ages already offered us an association in which personal merit was the standard for promotion. The sciences, at first limited to observation of the most common phenomena, have extended their realm and have been divided into various fields and in addition have been ordered, systematized, and to some degree unified.

It cannot be our intention here to follow step by step the development of the three manifestations of man. It is up to each of you, gentlemen, to collect your memories and to group around these generalities all the detailed facts you know. It will suffice for us to show you how affectionate feelings succeeded hatred; how peaceful activity continuously expanded at the expense of the military; and how the sciences gradually displaced the darkness of ignorance, to enable you yourselves to trace the development of mankind through its organic epochs. We have just shown you the general stages of the ascending and descending

* Voltaire, who was sensitive to all progress without being able to free himself from his prejudices—one might say from his fanaticism—against the Middle Ages, remarked: "The Princes made war until then (1498) to ravish lands; since then they have waged it to open branch offices." *Essais sur les Moeurs,* III, 344.

series, the simultaneous course of which demonstrates the law
discovered by Saint-Simon. By interpolating corresponding particular facts to these general stages and formulating series subordinated to them, one may descend to the details of human
deeds in history and consider their course of development.

This law is the law of the perfectibility of the human species,* and the method by which it can be verified.

By now it should be apparent what distinguished our master's concept of perfectibility from all others. You see how and
why the word "perfectibility" had for the first time, as he used
it, an exact and positive meaning. It is also comprehensible why
one can foresee the future today by considering the development
of events in each of the series that history presents, by the indications they give. The law of perfectibility is so absolute, it is a
condition so deeply bound up with the existence of our species,
that whenever a people placed at the head of humanity becomes
static, the germs of progress within it are immediately carried
elsewhere to a soil where they can be developed. And it has constantly been observed in such cases how the people which has
rebelled against the law of mankind has been engulfed and annihilated as if it had been crushed under the weight of an
anathema. In this way are to be explained the declines and falls

---

* Thanks to the work of some outstanding men of the eighteenth century, belief in the unlimited perfectibility of men is widespread today. We
are certain that it will hardly be long before Saint-Simon will be treated as
a plagiarist, once the first smiles of disdain have disappeared. That will be
proof that he will not yet have been understood, but very soon will be.

The imperfectly conceived idea of perfectibility remained sterile in the
hands of Vico, Lessing, Turgot, Kant, Herder, and Condorcet because none
of these philosophers knew how to describe the character of progress. None
of them indicated in what it consisted, how it operated, or by what institutions it was brought about and was to be continued; none of them, when
confronted by the great number of historical events, could classify them into
progressive and retrogressive events or co-ordinate them into homogenous
series, the terms of which would be linked together according to a law of
growth and decline. All of them finally overlooked the fact that the only
elements that have appeared repeatedly in the past and would interest the
future were the Fine Arts, the Sciences, and Industry, and that the study of
this triple manifestation of human activity was to constitute social science,
because it served to verify the moral, intellectual, and physical development
of the human race, its ceaseless progress towards the unity of affection, doctrine, and activity.

of empires which have shaken the world and have carried terror into the hearts of the irreligious by making them believe that blind fate was using mankind as a plaything. No, gentlemen, the tradition of progress has never been lost, and perfectibility has never been refuted. Civilization has merely been seen to travel like migrant birds seeking in distant countries a favorite climate and atmosphere which the former home country can no longer offer them. Today everything leads us to assume that in the future, because of the cessation of war and the establishment of a regime that will put an end to violent crises, no retrogression, not even a partial one, will take place. The entire human race will progress rapidly and continuously since peoples will teach and sustain one another.

But perhaps some will ask whether there is any usefulness in explaining progress, provided it exists. This explanation is of the highest importance; for if it were impossible to find a link, or a connection in the succession of past events, the study of history would become valueless. And at this point we should note the immense distance separating the historical view of Saint-Simon from all those formulated before him.

For a long time philosophers have made the human race the object of their investigations. They have studied its history through its various ages and have meditated on the changes it has undergone. But instead of envisaging the race as an organized body which grows progressively according to invariable laws, they have considered it only as the individuals composing it, and they have thought that it reached its full development in every epoch of its existence. Without hesitation, they have acknowledged that in every epoch the same facts could be identically reproduced. From this point of view, history appeared to them as nothing but a vast collection of events and observations; and if they studied the causes of human revolution at all, it was only to find precepts for conduct in similar situations. And this, in all seriousness, is what is meant by the lessons of history! Evidently such lessons can, from the point of view of continuous development, be only illusory,* as the same situation can no

---

* "It has been claimed," Saint-Simon said, "that history is the breviary of kings. By the way in which the kings govern, it can well be seen that the breviary is worthless."

more be reproduced in the different stages of the growth of a
collective being than can the same physiological conditions at
the various ages of an individual, nor can social facts alike in
appearance but occurring at different epochs have either the same
value or the same meaning. Thus history, as it has been presented to this day, rather than serving as a foundation for a
complete and homogenous system, has been nothing but an
arsenal in disorder, from which everyone could get the weapons
of his choice to defend his contradictory opinions. The historians have made of man an abstract and rational being. They
have only seen individual man, manifesting himself at various
places and at various epochs, and they observed him in these
different situations only in order to see him from different points
of view and to extract certain comparisons from them. No one,
however, has studied the life of the human species. Some refer
to the childhood, youth, and manhood of societies, telling us
that we are in a period of old age[6] and persuading old and weary
Europe to look to young America.[7] Others use the words "progress" and "perfectibility," but this terminology represents anything but the idea of continuity and of a chain of events. How
many times have we been told that nations rise to an apogee of
glory only to be plunged back into barbarism. India, Egypt,
Athens, and Rome are cited, and these examples serve as proofs.
There is agreement that some progress has been made and that
beneficial revolutions have taken place; but, according to our historians, the greatest events are due only to contingent causes.

[6] Probably an allusion to Fourier's theory of the four phases of civilization: childhood, adolescence, manhood, and old age. (*Tableau du Nouveau
Monde Industriel,* 1828.) Cf. B54.

[7] The United States, although serving as a model for French liberal
publicists, represented for the Saint-Simonians a society in the critical state,
ruled by a vain bourgeoisie without social ties or social sympathy in any
organic sense. The state was based purely on power and slavery was taken
for granted. (*Globe,* March 6, 1831.) Saint-Simon had already criticized the
Anglo-Saxon, feudal basis of American law and the anti-intellectual character of American society. Cf. B55. Comte in the *Producteur* had described the
United States as the country in which the spiritual disorganization of the
last three hundred years had been most pronounced. (I, 160 f.) Bazard remarked that America lacked a social doctrine as much as Europe did. (*Ibid.,*
III, 556 ff.) Only Blanqui had spoken admiringly of "industrious and free
North America." (*Ibid.,* II, 451.) In brief, America for the Saint-Simonians
was the classical land of liberalism and of the crisis.

Above all, it is chance, namely the unforeseen appearance of a man of genius or the incidental discovery of a scientific fact, that determines them. It is not customary to look upon these facts as consequences of the state of society which made them necessary; nor is it understood that each evolution is the indispensable result of a preceding evolution, each new step, so to speak, a product of stages already passed. There is acknowledgment of the usefulness of the work undertaken by preceding generations, but only insofar as it offers material for future work and multiplies the opportunities favorable to further advances. Let us examine, therefore, the enlightening explanations that emerge from this chaos.

If Christianity ascended the throne with Constantine, it was because the prince wanted to incite the troops which he was leading on Rome to dethrone Maxentius. And then again, for those who are stopped by no obstacles, not even by dates, it was because the pagan priests refused to absolve Constantine of the murder of Crispus and Fausta, and the Christians, being more indulgent, did not fear to cleanse him of his son's and wife's blood. If the communes were freed at the beginning of the twelfth century, it was because Louis the Fat wanted to put an end to the Lords' revolts, incited by his mortal enemy.

The reformation took a possession of fifteen centuries away from the Church. This great event was due only to the jealousy of two monastic orders which were disputing the form of indulgences in a corner of Saxony, and perhaps also to the personal ambitions of the monk Luther or to the whim of some prince.*

The French Revolution was brought about by the extravagance of the court or by the frivolity of Minister Calonne, who threw the finances into disorder. More profound analysts go back to the partition of Poland.

We would actually have to relate all of history to enumerate all the puerile hypotheses of the seventeenth-century[8] critics.

* "Whimsical fate which plays with the world," Voltaire said, "wanted Henry VIII, King of England, to enter into the dispute." *Essais sur les Moeurs,* III, 219, 226.

It is evident how even for the philosophers believing in perfectibility, blind fate brings about the greatest events.

[8] Probably a misprint; the 1830 edition had "eighteenth-century critics."

Speech, writing, the abolition of slavery, and the preaching of
the Gospels are doubtless nothing but matters of chance; for it
would seem, if we understand the historians, that mankind is
gambling in a huge lottery, where it can either ruin itself or grow
rich. Do not accuse us of irony, for this is exactly the way they
reason when they attribute the greatest events in history more
or less to chance. This favorite system has given rise to a popular
proverb: Great effects have little causes.

Far removed from these wretched explanations of human
phenomena is the truly great and imposing sight of mankind
slowly fulfilling the law to which it is subject, offering in the
course of history a long series of corollaries linked with each
other which make possible, by correct appraisal of past events,
the determination of those that will follow.

History, when studied by the method we have just outlined,
becomes something completely different from a collection of experiences or dramatic events suitable for entertaining the imagination. It presents a successive table of the physiological states
of the human species, considered in its collective existence. Indeed, it constitutes a science which takes on the rigorous character of the exact sciences.

Some doubt has been cast, however, upon the logical rigor
of the demonstrations derived by our school from the historical
series. The question has been raised whether this series is long
enough and whether it is not unwise to neglect the whole tradition of the Orient. To this objection we answer that the history
of that series of civilization, of which contemporary European
society forms the last stage, covers approximately three thousand
years, and the development of humanity during this long and
fertile period has not only the advantage of being a long continuation of stages, but also of being better known than any
other historical period, and of constituting in its last stage the
most advanced stage of civilization. The Orientalists are far from
having filled the gaps in the history of Asia, and at each step in
this history there is a dissolution of continuity, so that it is impossible to follow an orderly development. These historical fragments are to be compared with those strips of land about which

the geologist may make more or less ingenious hypotheses, but upon which he will never put the seal of scientific certainty with which he stamps the lands whose layers cover each other successively and uninterruptedly. It can be affirmed in advance, moreover, that if the interpolation of the series of Oriental civilization is completed, it will in its totality offer only one of the stages known to us.* Let us note, moreover, that the Greeks brought home all the progress scattered among the other peoples, and that they represent the summary of all civilizations that had grown up before them. One recalls that Thales, returning from Egypt more than six hundred years before the Christian era, astonished the Greeks by his prediction of a solar eclipse. We know, too, that the philosophers who shone in the Lyceum had broadened their knowledge by long trips into the most enlightened countries of the Orient.

Perhaps, gentlemen, after having heard us lay such stress upon the utility of history for the verification of Saint-Simon's concept of the development of mankind, you will reproach us for not having taken the present sufficiently into account. This reproach is without foundation. If we have placed such value on observations about humanity, it was only to place us upon ground on which the enlightened men of our epoch feel themselves so securely planted, namely that of science. We wanted to show them that if we adopted new views about the social future, that is to say about the predictions of human phenomena which are unknown to them, we are following, in justifying these predictions, the same method that is employed in all the sciences. We wanted to prove to them that our prevision had the same source and the same bases as appear in scientific discoveries in general or, in other words, that the genius of Saint-Simon was of the same nature as that of Kepler or Galileo, and differed only in breadth and in the importance of the laws which he revealed to us.

The present is undoubtedly only a point in space and a

* We do not even hesitate to say that the Europeans alone are able to teach the Indians their own history and to see in their traditions and monuments ideas and facts which could not be discovered by the Indians themselves.

moment in time. It is the link that cannot be grasped between past and future. We know, however, that it encloses the summary of the former and the seed of the latter. We know that it is by and through the environment in which we live, incited by memories and attracted by hopes, and in it and by it that we march unceasingly toward a better future.

Saint-Simon keenly felt the emptiness and chill of the egoistic environment he was forced to enter. He did not despair of mankind, however, because he felt within himself enough life and enough love to reanimate the world. He did not forget the present, for with the conviction of a genius he knew how to read in it that his word, which had been sown on soil that seemed to reject it, would sprout before long. Gentlemen, do we lose sight of the present when we address you, when we come to teach you what it is important to love, to know, and to practice today, namely, the doctrine of our master?

Yes, gentlemen, if we have insisted on the scientific character of the *Doctrine,* and if we have tried to calm the concerns which are quite natural to an epoch with doubt as to its distinctive characteristic, we shall be happy if you will attach to science, reason, demonstrations,* observations of facts and consequently to traditions only the importance they deserve and we ourselves attribute to them. We who are filled with faith in the future which Saint-Simon has proclaimed to us do of course not repudiate the purely rational method whereby we can demonstrate to the staunchest unbelievers that this future is a necessary consequence of the progress accomplished in the past. But these attempts at logic are not those we would like most to see under-

---

* The claim made for the rigor of demonstrations and the horror of fictions may seem strange in an epoch when the majority of political dogmas are fictions. Thus in the highest constitutional theories, a king has the right to name his ministers, but the chambers may send them back by rejecting the budget. If a king acts well, it is he who has acted; when he acts badly, it is not he. He can declare war, but one has the right to refuse him the resources he needs to wage it. All men are equal before the law, but the laws, without having any other basis than fortune, distributed by the chance of birth, sanction certain inequalities (for example, peerages, and qualifications for voting, juries, and the national guard). All these contradictions and mysteries have the approval of a public which considers itself completely positivistic.

taken by the generous souls we long to feel around us, seeking with us to awaken the sympathies of mankind and to mingle all hearts in one same love.

Before concluding, we feel the need for giving an answer to an objection which "feeling" might raise to our ideas. If there is such rigor in the interlinking of events that the future will be a necessary consequence of the past, will the human race not be subject to a fatalistic law? Yes, if a man could make a complete abstraction of his desires and hopes and coldly deduce the future from the past by rational means alone, then this man ought to think of himself as subject to fatalism. But such a man does not exist in nature. Everyone is moved more or less by "sympathy" for society; all look interestedly toward the future, and there begins for them the providential point of view.

In the realm of a brutal fatalism such as that conceived by antiquity, man, a passive being in respect to events, was dragged along without foreseeing or understanding anything. Pushed onward by a blind and inscrutable force towards a destiny which awakened only fear and repulsion in his soul, he asked without hoping and sowed with an insecure hand, without daring to expect anything from his efforts. Does that law which we proclaim, a law full of hope and promises, deserve the same name? Well, gentlemen, you would hardly think so. Man foresees his destiny; and when he has verified the predictions of his sympathies by science, and has assured himself of the legitimacy of his desires, he advances calmly and confidently towards the future which he knows. Of course, his foresight cannot extend to details and dates, but he feels that his efforts can hasten his fortune. Certain of his destiny, he directs toward it his heart and his spontaneity. Before acting, he knows what will be the general outcome of his action, and he applies all the power of his faculties toward it. In this way, he becomes a free and intelligent agent of his destiny, which he can at least hasten by his work, even if he cannot change it and would not want to. Fatalism cannot inspire any virtue other than dull resignation, for man is ignorant and fearful of the inevitable fate awaiting him. On the other hand, through the providential view an activity full of confidence and love manifests itself; for the more conscious man becomes of his destiny, the more he works in concert with God himself to achieve it.[9]

Rid yourselves of all fear, gentlemen, and do not struggle against the torrent which carries you onward to a happy future; put an end to the uncertainty which weakens your hearts and strikes you with impotence. Embrace the altar of reconciliation lovingly, for the times have been fulfilled and the hour is about to strike when, according to the Saint-Simonian transformation of the Christian word, all shall be called and all shall be chosen.

[9] "Since the second session, we have been informed that the doctrine of Saint-Simon was only provisionally presented as a form of 'positivism'; that, as will be established in the last sessions, it is a religion founded on a meta-physics of feeling or of 'sympathy' proving the existence of God." B65.

THIRD SESSION (January 14, 1829)

Conception, Method, and Historical Classification

Gentlemen:

We ought to take into account the general state of mind which claims that it analyzes before believing, that it dissects the elements of its beliefs or, better yet, demonstrates axioms. We must first destroy the weapons with which one might attempt to oppose the introduction of our master's doctrine. To do so we must prove the superiority of this doctrine on the very ground of its adversaries, in order to acquire the right to lead them onto his ground. We must show an age—which considers itself rational[1] above all—that our beliefs about the future of mankind, revealed by intense feeling and by an ardent desire to contribute to man's happiness, are justified by the most rigorous observation of facts. We even must prove that the title, "age of reason," which our century gives itself expresses a claim rather than a reality. The world today contains three classes of thinkers: the more or less specialized scientists, the publicists, and the philosophers. It is useless to occupy ourselves at this point with the first group, the specialized scientists. Their incompetence in the subjects with which we deal is evident. We are hastening all the more to refute these men since we hope to have judged in its true light that absurd charge so often brought against our master, namely, that he assigned the leadership of society to chemists,

[1] "In order to understand the import of this beginning and of all the following development, it is necessary to be aware of the date of this session. It was six days after Auguste Comte resumed before a select audience his 'Course in Positive Philosophy.' Bazard thought of him primarily in his denunciation of 'reasoners.' This session is essentially a rough draft of the long polemic with Auguste Comte, which will be resumed in the fifteenth session." B67.

41

physicists and astronomers,[2] or, as he was reproached at other times, that he wanted to entrust social destiny into the hands of the painters and musicians, and even into those of the mechanics, masons, and laborers. And what do the publicists[3] do? They exhaust themselves by fighting day after day, without any foresight, against an ephemeral power whose claim to public support is based on the struggle among various parties within the political institution. The philosophers are busily justifying this state of struggle by showing with the help of a few historical events or some old metaphysical notions that it is a necessary and final consequence of the progress of civilization and of the free development of man's faculties. All these thinkers remain without any influence on the direction of society. The practical life of their contemporaries escapes them completely and remains outside the intellectual movement of which they have made themselves the leaders. Despite the names with which the publicists are honored, no one is ready to acknowledge that there exists in their contradictory theories a social science, namely politics, or in the abstractions of our philosophers a science of man, morality.

Moreover, while attributing to reason all the importance that it deserves, where can one find among the minds that are in popular favor men who can be compared in breadth or force of logic to a Leibniz, a Descartes, a Malebranche, or, and we are not afraid to say so in spite of the scorn of the eighteenth century, to a Saint Augustine or a Saint Thomas?

But if our epoch appears inferior to some that preceded it

[2] "In the *Lettres d'un Habitant de Génève à ses contemporains*, 1803 (*Oeuvres de Saint-Simon et d'Enfantin*, XV, 13), Saint-Simon proposed that a subscription be organized in front of Newton's grave, and that each subscriber should name three mathematicians, three physicists, three chemists, three physiologists, three writers, three painters, and three musicians who are destined to become 'masters.' But this does not mean by any means that Saint-Simon wanted to return authority to 'specialists.' In his *Lettres au Bureau des Longitudes* (1808), he asks the scholars to elevate themselves to the conceptions of the totality in order to exercise the decisive influence which society needs." B68.

[3] "While this word is often used today as a synonym for journalist, it had then a more exact meaning; it was originally applied to writers dealing with public law, then in a general way to political writers. In Saint-Simon's language it is almost synonymous with author or intellectual." B69.

in terms of the greatness of its conceptions and their influence on practical life, it differs at least in its pretense to have faith only in facts. It admits no other means for the solution of problems but factual observation. The procedure that is used to unite the various parts of any discovery, invention, or new idea is the so-called positive[4] method. Positive—a marvelous adjective before which the masses bow respectfully without quite understanding it, and which those who never stop repeating it do not understand much better either. Let us add that this method has nowhere been put to use, either in its full rigor or in awareness of its true nature.

We are told that the positive method consists in the observer's making an inventory of the facts he has observed while completely uninfluenced by any feeling of desire or apprehension. If the inventory is exact, it should present to the observer the law of the succession of all the facts, that the description of the relationship existing between them and binding them.

Some preliminaries are necessary before we examine the false and incomplete elements of this definition of positive method.

The exercise of the human intellect may be divided into two distinct modes: conception and verification, or invention and method. The intellect discovers, conjectures, and creates with the former; it justifies its foresights, its inspirations, and its revelations with the latter. We shall not break down, analyze, and define the process of conception or invention in a more detailed way, for that would be to attempt to define genius. But for us genius is indefinable. By nature, genius is a unique phenomenon which we cannot grasp. It is the principle underlying all human knowledge. It is in the realm of the mind what movement is in the material order and what life is for every creature in love.

To appraise the nature of these two processes of the human

[4] "The term *positive* has two meanings in Saint-Simonian terminology, which, although inseparable, are yet distinct and correspond to the dual, experimental and organic character of the doctrine. In its first meaning, *positive* is the opposite of *conjectural*. Saint-Simon used it in this sense from his first works on. . . . In its second meaning, *positive* applied to the social sciences is opposed to *negative*. This use is very frequent in the *Doctrine*." B71.

intellect, conception and verification, it will be necessary to take into account the situation in which man is found when he uses the one or the other.

In reality, man is never isolated in the environment surrounding him. However, by his abstraction, sometimes the world and at other times his own individuality absorb him almost exclusively. On the one hand, when he follows these abstractions as far as he can, the world seems to him as a pure creation of his mind. And then, on the other hand, he is annihilated in the face of the immense phenomenon that surrounds him. In other words, at times his creative powers, his activity, and his spontaneity are exalted, and he impresses the forms of his being on the facts he views. And then again, in contrast, he, a mere passive and unproductive observer, reflects within himself things created outside of him. In the former case, he wishes, he commands, he speaks; in the latter, he lets himself be dragged along, he listens and obeys. In the one state he invents, in the other he verifies. Alternately he is a poet and a man of reason and so becomes a scientist.*

In passing from the active view to the passive, from the role of the creator to that of the observer, from imagination to reason, man attains the fullness of his scientific power.

As the validation of original thought, method impresses on the creation of genius the stamp that clearly distinguishes the work of the scientist from that of the poet.

What is method? The same philosophic principles that we have just applied to the examination of the processes of man's faculty of knowing will now give us an account of method—that is, of the means employed by man to justify his foresights and

* Let us also recall that the philosophical or, better yet, metaphysical analysis in which we are engaged here and by which we divide the unity of man's intellectual existence into two distinct parts has no value other than that which abstractions can have. Using Newtonian language, we might have said: Things happen *as if* man was alternately active and passive, actor and spectator, inventor and verifier, but in reality, at every moment of his existence, of whatever duration this moment may be, he is at once active *and* passive. The division we have made expresses therefore only predominant traits which are constant in certain individuals when compared with others, but which vary in every man.

discoveries. For we repeat that this is always his aim. However, before applying this formula, we again want to take up the definition of the positive method mentioned above. It has been said that it consists in making an inventory of facts without letting oneself be influenced by any feeling of desire or apprehension. But in what order are these facts to be classified? Which will be the first and which the last? And above all, why want, why desire to put them in order? The scientist believes that a certain order exists among facts. He believes this firmly, for he tries hard to discover it. But that is not all. It is not enough to believe that an order exists; one must discover what this order is. Which one of the infinite number of hypotheses that appear will he choose to verify, that is to say, to see whether all the facts which he thinks the hypothesis should embrace are effectively included by it?* Before stopping at one of these hypotheses, must he have observed all the facts? How many facts must he have observed before caring to formulate a hypothesis? And even to observe the facts, must he not discover a relationship between an already observed fact and the one he is observing? But to affirm that a relation of such and such a nature exists between two facts, one must necessarily suppose that all the conditions under which the facts are brought about are well known, something which surpasses human capability. For if one of these conditions should change, the relationship would be different. Thus human science would in no way be certain, nor even probable, because the number of conditions of existence known to man is always infinitely small in relation to those he does not know.

We shall, no doubt, be accused of injustice. The magnificent work of the scholars of our day on the calculus of probabilities will be held up to us. But this kind of research proves the full truth of what we have just said. Under what conditions does the word "probability" mean anything? And which hypotheses must

---

* We are using the word "infinite" intentionally. A man would be confronted by an infinite number of choices if his own nature did not make him prefer some hypothesis to another, if before observing fact, before acting, he had not felt the desire to observe certain facts, to produce certain acts, or in other words, if he had no will, principle, cause, or motive for all his physical and intellectual activity.

be admitted, and what beliefs held previously, if the work of M. de Laplace[5] is not to be an empty collection of words? There we reason as if all the balls contained within an urn were perfectly alike, and as if the urn were made in such a way that all the balls had an equal chance to fall out. But in reality any calculation would be impossible, for no ball would fall out. We foresee the recurrence of the sunrise as if all the conditions that permitted the sun to rise over a long span of time (and what is this long span of time in the face of eternity—a point?) were to continue obviously unchanged. Finally, everywhere the belief prevails, without which, it is true, no human science is possible or useful, namely that there is constancy, regularity, and order in the succession of phenomena. As we have just said, the number of hypotheses which can be conceived about an expected phenomenon, for example, the rising of the sun, is infinite. Mankind adopts the one that has been justified by observations of the past and says that that hypothesis is the most probable because mankind believes in order. But if this belief is examined it will be seen that the finite number of observations that have been made are valueless in the presence of the infinite number of possible phenomena.

Let us return to method. All philosophic schools have recognized two distinct modes of human reasoning by which an observer may go through a given series of facts. He may ascend from particular facts to general, or descend from general to particular facts. One recalls the image through which Bacon expresses this idea, namely the double ladder. Saint-Simon has reproduced it in a large number of forms. What needs to be ascertained here is that these two modes of the mind, which properly speaking constitute logic, have a like importance. To discuss the superiority of analysis over synthesis is, as Saint-Simon said, to study whether it is better to lower or to raise the piston of a pump in order to make it work.

[5] "Reference either to the *Théorie analytique des probabilités* (1812) or the *Essai philosophiques sur les probabilités* (1814) by Pierre-Simon Laplace, the Marquis de Laplace (1749-1827). This treatise, which originated in a lecture given in 1795 to the normal schools, has remained the great classical work which has inspired to this day later authors who dealt with this subject." B73.

Once a new conception seems to be able to link the facts, there are two means of verifying the conception. One can go through the series of facts by descending from the fact that has been designated by the conception itself as the most general to the most particular facts and observing whether all intermediary facts can be arranged in this series in order of increasing particularization, or one can ascend from the fact that has been designated by the conception as the most particular one to the most general fact by classifying the intermediate ones according to degree of generalization.

The two aspects from which we have just viewed method each have a distinct underlying principle and a distinct result. The first is the operation by which the scientist can proclaim that a certain phenomenon will take place once the law of the appearance of the phenomena is known. On the other hand, Saint-Simon affirms by means of the second that a certain phenomenon which has taken place was derived from the conceived law. The former is thus especially applicable to prediction, the latter to recounting. But both are the validations in the future and in the past, that is, by what will be and by what has been, of the inspiration brought about within man by what is, which is to say, by the way a being feels the universal life manifested within himself and outside himself.*

Here you have all of method and all of logic. But logic and method presuppose conceptions, instead of creating them, as poetics presupposes poems but does not inspire them. What we have said is not intended to offer new indications about the processes of the human mind, but merely to point out the confusion of invention and method which has been so frequent until

* We repeat at this point what we have said about concerning the division made between conception and reasoning, poetry and science. Synthesis and analysis are never completely isolated from each other, but the one or the other manifests itself more in particular to us, depending on whether the science with which we are dealing takes on a speculative or a descriptive character. Doubtless one can, given a law, prophesy according to it events that must have taken place as well as events that will take place. But the very word "to prophesy," which we use here, when referring to the past has evidently been taken from an extension of its true meaning. This is to say that when man looks at the past he considers it known in particular while from the point of view of unity it is as unknown as the future.

now, and the inconvenience which results from the preference given by all metaphysicians to one or the other mode of reasoning as the one leading to discovery. Some prefer synthesis, others analysis; the synthesists, as Saint-Simon says, contemplate general principles, general facts, general interests; the analysts observe minutely secondary principle, particular facts, and private interests.

To sum up the above: man conceives and verifies. Thus he becomes a scientist, a knower; for he knows when after having imagined he validates his creation and hypothesis. He knows when he links his predictions to his memories by an uninterrupted chain of causes and effects. And finally he knows and wants to know, because, being a lover of order, he finds in the past, in which he believes, a token of the future he desires.

The common opinion is that the human mind, when observing a large number of facts, passes successively from one to another and proceeds thus uninterruptedly from particular facts to the general fact, to the law which links them. That would be to say that the conception, the discovery of this law, would be the consequence, the logical result of the last observed fact. There has been no example of such a course in the history of human discoveries. Certainly the facts surrounding us constitute the circumstances exterior to man which inspire an idea of co-ordination. But between this idea and the occasional fact that has taken place, there is no immediate contact. Rather there exists a gap that cannot be overcome by any method, and which genius alone can span. There is no doubt that all successive conceptions are linked with each other, and that the last one can only manifest itself after all preceding ones. But it is not yet a deduction from them. Its author has not told himself beforehand: Since such general views have been produced, it is time now to conceive a new one of the same sort. It was indisputably necessary that mankind make all the progress that preceded the age of Socrates before it could attain the conception of unity of cause, which was to contribute to changing the face of the sciences and that of the entire earth. It was also necessary that the road opened by Socrates's conception had been traveled completely for Saint-Simon to appear in his turn. But when their time had arrived, these two extraordinary men arrived at their creative thought by the inspiration of genius, and not by means of any method.

However, we must not be considered unjust for having assigned method the role to which it may lay just claim. Doubtless science was confused too long with poetry, and imagination has too often failed to recognize the support it might find in reason. Should, therefore, science today reject, disregard, and vilify the breast from which it springs and which nourishes it? Forgive us if we see in our scientists mere collectors of facts who use dead instruments of observation and ingenious mental acrobatics to bring together, distrustfully and enviously, the materials for a structure whose plan was drawn by a creative master. No, we do not fail to recognize the importance of reasoning, nor of the method that directs it and perfects its process. Have we not said ourselves that the study of mankind will truly form a science worthy of the name only when history, that vast field of observations, illumined by the light which the genius of Saint-Simon shed on it, presents itself to the eyes of the strictest logician as an uninterrupted sequence of progress from the narrowest and most savage association to the most loving, most learned, and richest society that man may be able to conceive and desire?

But one should not be deceived: the favor which the positive method enjoys today, its popularity, does not stem from or depend on the services it has rendered science. Its repute comes from higher up; something else has been seen in it than a weapon of the academy. It is loved and extolled above all as a war machine, as a handspike of destruction against a religious law and against a social order that has weighed as a burden on Europe for two centuries.

And, indeed, what more powerful weapon could have been used against a doctrine which represented the world as permeated with spontaneity, with life and with love, and which ceaselessly called man's mind into a new world, to be conceived by mind alone? In brief, what weapon could have been more powerful against Christian beliefs than a method which clothed the universe and man himself in a shroud and showed men to each other as incidental collections of molecules subject to a purely mechanical order, as corpses deprived of the sacred fire which until then

had united them with each other and had made them march
shoulder to shoulder toward a common destiny? These are the
true reasons for the favor and acknowledgment which this
method enjoys today. For the happiness of mankind requires
that the work of destruction, to which this method has been
applied with such effect, be completed.

We have already said that no one today is more aware than
we of the usefulness of a division between poetry and science,[6]
between imagination and reasoning. No one knows better than
we how their primitive confusion was a condition for progress,
that at the beginning of societies the leaders of mankind had to
be at the same time poets of knowledge, and even warriors,
prophets, legislators, and kings.* But it is precisely because we
know all this that we can apply and realize this division more
rigorously than the scientists, who seem to claim exclusive ownership of this division, but who have not completely submitted
to it.

Gentlemen, we long to apply broadly to the history of mankind the principles we have just established.

Must we not ask ourselves, when regarding the past and observing in detail the facts that tradition has transmitted to us,
which thread will lead us into that immense labyrinth? All these
facts, up to our time, have already been observed, classified, and
named. The monuments of various civilizations have been described or are still standing. The books they have produced are
available, translated with commentaries and explained. And

---

[6] "Here the Saint-Simonians admit the necessity of some kind of division
of labor between poetry and science, a temporary necessity, to be sure, which
they themselves hope to overcome. The Saint-Simonian systematization of
ideas must go hand in hand with a systematization of feelings." B79.

* We shall see later how the division of the powers in the Middle Ages
into spiritual and temporal ones facilitated the progressive development of
mankind. Let us merely note in regard to the topic under discussion here
that this confusion still existed in the spiritual power, and how there the
same men dealt with poetry and science. In any case, the division of the
clergy into secular and regular (the latter particularly concerned with preaching and with the service of God in the presence of the faithful; the former
shut up in cloisters and working, outside the ever impassioned movement of
the masses, at the elaboration of the dogma and the constitution of the
science of God), gave witness to the tendency of mankind not to estrange
religion and science, poetry and reason, but to give each its proper role and
to entrust its development to different hands.

finally the great men that moved these masses, the laws which
these masses obeyed, the beliefs that filled their souls are there;
all are living for him who loves mankind and who knows its destinies and applies himself to their realization.

Of what use are these facts to us if we do not know how to
read from them clearly a wish, a desire, a sought for goal, never
attained but which mankind is approaching ceaselessly, and toward which we ourselves shall help to guide her? Of what use
are they if we do not know how to link them by a general conception which, embracing all, indicates to us the place each one
of them should occupy in the sequence of the development of
the human species? And what mighty genius will reveal this
conception to us?

A man passionately concerned about mankind, who loved
order but lived in the midst of a society in disorder, who burned
with the desire to see his fellow-men united and brethren at the
very moment when everyone around him was struggling, warring,
destroying each other; an eminently sympathetic man, a poet before being a scientist, came to give human science a new basis
and new axioms. Saint-Simon said: "Order, peace, and love are
for the future. The past has always loved, studied, and practiced
war, hatred and antagonism. However, the human species
marched ceaselessly towards its peaceful destiny, passing by successive steps from an imperfect order to a better order and from a
weak and narrow association to a stronger and wider one. Each
step mankind made was at first a crisis, for it had to deny its past
and break violently the bonds which had been healthy in its
childhood but which had become obstacles to its development." [7]
With these words of our master, history takes on an altogether
new character. The observer, the scientist, verifies that sublime
inspiration of the genius by a new examination of the past. He
studies how the savage's hut was replaced by the city, the city
by the fatherland, the fatherland by mankind. In the long succession of centuries that preceded us, he observes which are the
epochs in which men, belonging first to a family, then to a city,

[7] "Saint-Simon has never said this. This is the terminology of the
Saint-Simonians of 1829, not of the master. But the Saint-Simonians give
their doctrine a religious character by allusions to a mysterious oral teaching
by their master." B80.

and later even to a fatherland, appeared bound by love to the destiny of their race, their fellow citizens, and their compatriots; and, on the other hand, those epochs in which the bonds of affections have been broken, and an order, formerly loved, has become oppressive and incompatible with the new desires that move hearts. In the first epochs all efforts seemed to converge towards one goal; in the latter epochs everyone was isolated. In the former all the elements of the social body come together, combine, and organize; in the latter, dissolution and death seem nearer every day, until a seed of love comes to call the members of this body, weary from a terrible crisis, back to life and to unite them more strongly than ever.

Thus we are given the first extensive classification of the past. We can divide it into organic epochs in each of which a social order is developed, incomplete since it is not universal, provisional since it is not yet peaceful; and into critical epochs in which the former order is criticized, attacked, and destroyed; epochs which extend up to the moment when a new principle of order is revealed to the world.

Let us look at the epochs of civilization to which we are tied directly, and which are best known to us. To us, educated in Greek and Roman letters, sons of Christians, witnesses of the decline of Catholicism and even of the luke-warm reformation, two clearly pronounced critical epochs appear during the period of twenty-three centuries: the first separates polytheism from Christianity and extends from the appearance of the first Greek philosophers to the preaching of the Gospels; the second separates the Catholic doctrine from that of the future and includes the three centuries from Luther to our day. The corresponding organic periods are the one when Greek and Roman polytheism was in full vigor, which ends in the centuries of Pericles and Augustus; and the period when Catholicism and feudalism were at their greatest might and splendor, which came to an end as far as its religious side was concerned with Leo X and from the political point of view with Louis XIV.

What is man's destiny in relation to his fellow-man and in relation to the universe? These are the general terms of the dual problem which mankind has always posed. All organic epochs have been at least temporary solutions of these problems. But soon the progress achieved with the help of these solutions, and sheltered by social institutions based on these solutions, makes even them insufficient and new solutions are called for. The critical epochs, the moments of contest, of protest,[8] of expectation, and transition, follow—to fill the interval with doubt, with indifference concerning these great problems, with egoism, a necessary consequence of this doubt and indifference. Wherever these great social problems have been solved, there has been an organic epoch; when they have remained unsolved, there has been a critical period.

During organic periods, the goal of activity is clearly defined. We have said that all efforts are dedicated to achieving this goal, toward which man is continuously directed by education and legislation during his entire life.* If general relations are fixed, individual relations are modeled on them and are also fixed. The goal that society intends to attain is revealed to all hearts and all intellects. It becomes easy to recognize the men of capacity most suited to further this trend, and the truly superior are, of course, in possession of power. Legitimacy, sovereignty, and authority exist in the real meaning of these words. Harmony rules in social relationships.

Man then sees the totality of phenomena administered by a providence and by a benevolent will. The very principle of human societies, the law which they obey, appears to him as an expression of this will. And this common belief is manifested by a cult which binds the strong to the weak, and the weak to the strong. It may be said that in this sense the character of the organic epoch is essentially religious.

The unity existing in the sphere of social relations is reflected in an order of facts which we should mention here, in particular, because of the importance attached to it today. We

---

[8] "No doubt the word is underlined in order to indicate that the Saint-Simonians mean Protestantism, whose critical tendency they cannot forgive." B83.

* We refer to the lectures in which these two subjects, education and legislation, are treated from the point of view of the doctrine of Saint-Simon. But we shall say here already that these two words signify to us something different than our codes or the instruction in our colleges.

wish to speak of the sciences. The different special fields of
which they are composed appear in the organic epoch only in a
series of subdivisions of the general conception of the fundamental dogma. There really exists then an encyclopedia of the
sciences, if we keep the true meaning of the word "encyclopedia," [9] which is the connectedness of human knowledge.*

The critical epochs offer a diametrically opposed picture.
True, at their beginning one can observe co-operation determined by the generally felt need for destruction. But soon differences appear and become insurmountable. Everywhere anarchy
manifests itself, and soon everyone is busy appropriating ruins of
the structure which crumbles and is scattered until it is reduced
to dust. The goal of social activity is completely ignored. The
uncertainty in general relationships passes over into private ones.
The true men of ability no longer are or can be appreciated.
The legitimacy of the power of those who exercise it is contested.
Governors and governed are at war; a similar war begins among
particular interests, which daily acquire a more and more marked
predominance over general interest. Egoism finally succeeds devotion as atheism replaces godliness.

Man has ceased to understand his relation to his fellow-men
as well as the relation which unites his destiny with universal
destiny. He passes from faith to doubt, from doubt to unbelief,
or rather to the negation of the former faith, for that negation
itself is a new faith. He believes in fatalism, as he believed in

[9] "The Saint-Simonians have often defined their undertaking by declaring
that they considered it their task to compose a 'new encyclopedia.' One of
Saint-Simon's earliest works carried the title: *Sketch of a New Encyclopedia
or Introduction to the Philosophy of the 19th Century. A Work Dedicated
to Thinkers.* Here this definition of the word *encyclopedia* is to be found:
'*Encyclopedia,* a word of Greek origin, means the connectedness of knowledge.' (*Oeuvres de Saint-Simon et d'Enfantin,* XV, 91.) In one of his last
works, Saint-Simon writes: 'The philosophers of the eighteenth century composed an encyclopedia in order to overthrow the theological and feudal system. The philosophers of the nineteenth century must also compose an
encyclopedia to establish the industrial and scientific system.' (*Ibid.,* XXXIX,
104.) Four years later, Bazard develops this theme, which he takes up here
again in a discussion of the definition proposed by Guizot . . . (*Producteur,*
IV, 112)." B84.

* We shall see later, however, how certain sciences have not been included directly in the Catholic Encyclopedia, which is to say, the Christian
dogma; for example, the physical sciences.

Providence. He loves and sings of disorder as he adored and extolled harmony.

In these epochs one sees a large number of systems appear that more or less win the sympathy of some factions of society and which divide society more and more while, almost unnoticed, the former doctrine and the old institutions continue to serve society as a link, or at least a barrier against excessive disorder.

The different systems of human knowledge no longer form a unity. Man's knowledge no longer constitutes dogma: the collection of the sciences no longer deserves the name encyclopedia, for the tomes containing them, however voluminous, are merely an aggregation lacking connection.

At such epochs, when all social ties have been broken, the masses experience only imperfectly the immense gap in moral activity. For them this gap is overcome by a surplus in spiritual or material activity without any sympathetic goal—without any inspiration of love. But the men of superior mind view the abyss with terror. The more the moral nothingness places bitter and bloody satire in their mouths, the more they are inspired by songs of sadness and despair. In such epochs a Juvenal appears, or a Persius, a Goethe, or a Byron.[10]

In summary, the distinct characteristics of the organic epoch are unity and harmony in all spheres of human activity, while the critical epoch is distinguished by anarchy, confusion, and disorder in all directions. In the former, the totality of general ideas has until now been given the name "religion"; in the latter, they are formulated under the name "philosophy," a term which in this sense had only a destructive meaning in regard to the former beliefs. However, it may be observed that ideas destined to serve in later reorganization, too, adopt the name "philosophy" at their birth. In the organic epochs the highest manifesta-

[10] "This association of the names of Goethe and Byron is disconcerting at first. However, for Bazard, Goethe always remains the author of *Werther*, the inspirer of romantic pessimism, even when he disavows his origin and attempts in the second part of his *Faust* to integrate his romantic philosophy with a superior philosophy." B86.

Goethe's classical period was viewed as an expression of the indifference of the critical age. (Cf. *Globe*, May 29, 1831.)

tions of feelings bear the name "cult" in the most exact sense of this word; in the critical periods they take on the name "fine arts," an expression that comprehends the same critical thought in respect to cult that the term "philosophy" has in regard to religion. We have now determined the general characteristics of the organic and critical epochs. In all epochs of the same nature, whether organic or critical, whatever the time and place, men are always occupied in building during the former, and destroying during the latter. The differences that can be noticed between two organic epochs or two critical epochs depend solely on the nature of the object that is to be constructed or to be destroyed. The intensity of belief, and the extent of association give each epoch its distinctive expression. But an appraisal of the details distinguishing one epoch from another of the same nature is of little importance and can easily be made, once the characteristics common to every critical epoch and those pertaining to all organic epochs have been grasped.

Throughout this exposition, we shall repeat the division we have just made and shall justify it by a new evaluation of the facts with which human tradition furnishes us. This great conception will be a real compass in our return to the past, just as it will serve in a different form to guide us toward the future.

We say "in a different form" because today mankind is traveling toward a final state which will be exempted from the long and painful alternatives and under which progress will take place without interruption, without crises, in a continuous, regular, and constant fashion. We are marching toward a world where religion and philosophy, cult and the fine arts, dogma and science will no longer be divided; where duty and interest, theory and practice, far from being at war, will lead to the same goal, to the moral elevation of man; and where science and industry will daily have us know and cultivate the world.

Then reason and power, united as two sisters, shall offer to the spring from which they draw their life, to love, a thanksgiving, a hymn of acknowledgement, and shall there receive the inspiration, the creative breath without which they would remain in nothingness.

Gentlemen, the critical era which began three centuries ago

has fully accomplished its task. The destruction of the former order of things has been as radical as possible in the absence of the revelation of the new order to be established. The doctrines born in the sixteenth century and those they came to fight are almost balanced today. What remained of the latter suffices to maintain order[11] in the heart of society. What has been established of the former suffices to set up an invincible barrier against retrogression. The men who want the happiness of mankind, those who feel powerfully incited by the desire to prepare its definitive[12] organization, to realize its peaceful destiny, can, in the presence of two aged societies, abandon two interests belonging to the past. And leaving an arena in which efforts are squandered in vain struggle, they can consecrate all they possess of love, intelligence, and power to the realization of the future which Saint-Simon has revealed to us.

[11] "Here the Saint-Simonians have in mind the spirit of the Reformation, which they contrast with that of the Catholic Middle Ages. They have always seen in Catholicism what Enfantin called means of order and of union. (*Producteur*, IV, 389; V, 39.)" B89. Refer to Catholicism in index.

[12] "The Saint-Simonians try to reconcile the idea of a *definitive* organization with that of an indefinitely *progressive* solution. In their opinion there will always be progress, but without antagonism. 'The organization of the future will be definitive because society will only then be directly oriented toward progress.' It is interesting to see how Karl Marx inherited this Saint-Simonian idea. See the final sentence of his *Misère de la Philosophie* (cf. *The Poverty of Philosophy*, trans. by H. Quelch, Chicago, 1910): 'Must one be astonished that a society which is based on the opposition of classes shall finally arrive at a brutal conflict, at hand-to-hand struggle as its final solution? . . . Only in an order where there will no longer be classes and class antagonism will social evolutions no longer be political revolutions.'" B90.

Antagonism and Universal Association

The Decline of the One and the Stages
in the Progress of the Other

Gentlemen:

At our last meeting we showed you what the general characteristics of the organic and the critical epochs of the past were. You must have understood that this alternation of epochs of order and of disorder was the condition underlying social progress. It remains for us to make you understand how this continuous succession of seeming grandeur and apparent decline, commonly called the vicissitudes of mankind, is nothing but the regular series of efforts made by mankind to attain a final goal.

This goal is *universal association*,[1] which is to say, the association of all men on the entire surface of the globe in all spheres of their relationships. But perhaps it will be said that association is only a means; that it is more important to determine the goal towards which mankind must travel. For anyone who would reflect on the strict meaning of the terms, it should be evident that the end and the means are expressed at the same time, at least in a general fashion, as we employ the terms here, and that *universal association* can be understood only through the combination of human forces into a peaceful direction.

Nevertheless, since the word "association" is being applied in our time only to narrow combinations that embrace but one type of interest, it seems necessary to distinguish among historical

[1] This term, which occupies a focal place in Saint-Simonian terminology, does not occur in Saint-Simon. For a history of the term's use in Saint-Simonian and socialist literature, see B91.

phenomena those that place mankind outside of association and those which by their development have brought mankind closer to association. In this way, one may understand the full scope of the terms "association" and "universal" as used by us.

From a viewpoint high enough to embrace at once the past and the future of mankind—terms inseparable from each other, since both are parts of one process and one cannot be judged without the other—one recognizes that society in its entire duration contains two distinct general states: a provisional one belonging to the past and a final one reserved for the future, the state of antagonism and the state of association. In the former, the different partial, coexisting aggregations consider themselves as reciprocal obstacles and feel for each other nothing but distrust and hatred. Each aspires only to destroy its rivals and subject them to its domination. On the other hand, in the state of association, the division of the human family into classes is presented as a division of labor, as a systematization of efforts to attain a common goal. Each particular aggregation sees its prosperity and growth bound up with the prosperity and growth of all other aggregations.

We certainly do not maintain that the march of mankind is subject to the action of two general laws, antagonism[2] and association. The successive development of the human species recognizes only one single law, the uninterrupted progress of association. But precisely because there has been progress in regard to association, it is evident that while this progress was taking place facts must have emerged which to a greater or lesser degree were outside of association. We call this state of things antagonism, a

---

[2] "This word does not occur a single time in Saint-Simon's writings. Nor is it found in the works of his first collaborators before the master's death. It first appears in the *Producteur*, III, 367 f . . . (in) an article by Auguste Comte" and then in one by Enfantin (*ibid.*, IV, 380). "It was probably borrowed from Kant, who had used it in a work ('Idee zu einer allgemeinen Geschichte in weltbürgerlicher Absicht,' cf. 'Idea of a Universal History from a Cosmopolitan Point of View,' in *Kant's Principles of Politics*, ed. and trans. by W. Hastie, Edinburgh, 1891) in which he tried to establish that war itself had contributed in the past to paving the way for universal peace. Auguste Comte was the first among the Saint-Simonians to draw attention to this work." B93.

state which, strictly speaking, expresses only a negation. It should, nevertheless, be studied apart if one wants clearly to appraise the differences between the first and the last stage of social development.

The further we go back into the past, the narrower and the more incomplete we find the sphere of association. The most confined circle, one which is thought of as necessarily having developed first, is the family. History has shown us societies which had no other bond. Today tribes on the globe* exist among whom association seems not to have spread beyond this limit. Finally, even among us in Europe certain peoples (for example, the clans of Scotland and the inhabitants of Corsica), which through particular circumstances have been isolated to a certain extent from the movement of civilization, still reveal in their social relationships traces of this primitive state.

The first progress that takes place in the development of association is the union of several families into a city. The second is that of several cities into a national body. The third is that of several nations, linked by a common belief, into a federation. We have already stated that mankind has remained at this last stage, which was realized by the Catholic association. And however immense this progress may be if one compares the social state that it created with those that preceded it, it must yet be recognized that the degree of association attained at this stage is still, from the dual standpoint of depth and extent, far from the one which it is to attain. Indeed, Christianity, whose principle and expansive force have long since been exhausted, embraced in its love and sanctified by its law only one of the modes of human existence, and did not succeed in establishing its rule —now failing—over more than a portion of mankind.

If we look at history, the different phases of the progress of association can easily be identified. It is true that we have not witnessed the union of several families into one city, but we have later seen cities unite in national bodies. The phenomenon of such a fusion occurred in Greece, Italy, Spain, Gaul, and Germany. Much closer to us and much more distinctly, we have seen nations associate to a certain degree under the authority of the

* Australia.

same belief and form the great Catholic alliance that was dissolved by the critical works of the three last centuries.[3]

The series of social states that we have just indicated (namely
the family, the city, the nation, and the church) offer the observer
a picture of perpetual struggle. This struggle successively rules
in all its intensity first from family to family, then from city to
city, from nation to nation, and from belief to belief. But it is
not only between the various associations of which we just spoke
that struggle is witnessed: it is also found in the very bosom of
each of them considered separately. We have seen the wars which
the people composing the Catholic association waged among
themselves, even though these people had so often demonstrated
the power of the link uniting them; notably when they combined
their efforts to curb the rise of Islam and stop its conquests. History shows us rivalry of the same nature between cities or provinces which formed part of the same nation, and even within the
city between the different classes of men composing it.* Finally,
struggle is to be found even in the bosom of the family, between
the sexes and between the ages, between brothers and sisters, and
between older and younger children. The seeds of division
within every association are perpetuated after their fusion into
a larger association, but with an intensity decreasing in direct
proportion to the extension of the circle.

The political structure of the Middle Ages presents us with

[3] "This desire to re-establish the integrity of the theory of continual
progress, which Condorcet jeopardized by his anti-Catholic prejudices, brings
Saint-Simon and his disciples closer to the theocrats Joseph de Maistre and
de Bonald. The problem is well expressed by Saint-Simon after 1811: *Correspondence avec M. de Redern (Oeuvres de Saint-Simon et d'Enfantin)*, XV,
115 f.: '(Condorcet's) second mistake: to have presented the religions as having
been an obstacle to the happiness of mankind, which is essentially a wrong
idea . . . Condorcet, struck by the faults of the Catholic religion in its decline, lost sight of the fact that it was that same religion to which the Europeans owed the restoration of Roman morals, the civilization of the barbarians who lived in the North, as well as the purification of the countries
which they inhabit.'" B96.

* Undoubtedly, in these last cases, struggle does not appear in the same
way for all the parties engaged in it. Between the slave and the patrician,
struggle is progressive in character, because its object is the performance of
peaceful work. With the patrician and the master, on the other hand, it is
stationary or retrogressive in tendency, since its object is the maintenance of
the interests of conquests and the prolongation of the reign of violence.

a striking example of the phenomenon of antagonism in the relations of the two great powers that divided society between them, the temporal and the spiritual power; antagonism between two forces that balanced each other, considered each other as enemies, and sought unceasingly to invade each other's realm.*

Finally, in order to exhaust all aspects of antagonism, we can follow it into the very heart of the Catholic priesthood, that is to say into the midst of the most imposing, the most homogenous society, and if mankind's final goal is taken into consideration, the most legitimate that ever existed. National clergies and the central clergy are often in opposition. Quarrels arise between the regular and the secular clergy and are reproduced among the various monastic congregations. These conflicts in the very heart of a peaceful society doubtless depended on the heterogeneous elements with which the clergy was in contact. We shall have to examine that later; at present it is sufficient to mention these struggles as facts.

Having explained what antagonism is at the different stages of human association, we must hasten to add that antagonism has never been powerful enough at the beginning of any social organization to prevent it from preserving itself and from spreading within the limits necessary for mankind to pass on to a more advanced organization. But neither has political organization ever had enough strength to prevent the elements of antagonism which it harbored from developing and acquiring sufficient power to overthrow and destroy it the day when, new needs having made themselves felt by men, these needs called upon men to enjoy a better organization. However, it may be said that antagonism, by preparing the way for a wider association and hastening the day of universal association, is destroying itself[4] bit by bit and tends completely to disappear.

* At this point it is expedient to repeat the observation which we just made. Struggle does not have the same character for both sides. In temporal power, struggle is in general godless, which is to say retrogressive, for it tends to assure the triumph of the sword. In spiritual power it may be considered holy, which is to say progressive, for its aim is generally to subordinate military to peaceful power and the rights of conquest and of birth to those of ability.

[4] "The expression reminds one of Hegelian dialectics which was going to inspire the Marxist philosophy of history. The antagonism which destroys itself is the negation which negates itself: but on this point, as on so many

Let us conclude all that preceded by saying that, properly speaking, true associations in the past have existed only in opposition to rival associations in such a way that the past may be viewed in relation to the future as a vast state of systematized war.

When we speak thus we are far from wanting to arraign the preceding generations. The states through which they passed were necessary in the progressive evolution of mankind. We should take into consideration the general facts characterizing them as the means man had to use to reach his destination.

It is evident, moreover, that the principle of association has always been more powerful than that of antagonism; that association has in the course of time prevailed more and more; and that the impetus of the latter principle has only helped to assure the former's complete triumph. Thus the strongest manifestation of antagonism, war, in determining aggregations of previously isolated tribes later made their association possible.

We have seen that in the march of mankind the circle of association has been steadily widening and that at the same time the inner principle of order, harmony, and union has taken deep root. That is to say that the elements of struggle contained in the heart of every association weaken as several societies unite into one.

A number of developments will suffice to give evidence of this important fact. We shall consider the state of antagonism first of all in respect to its principle and its general results.

Physical force and the exploitation of man by man are two coexisting, corresponding facts. The latter is the consequence of the former. The realm of physical force and the exploitation of man by man[5] are the cause and effect of the state of antagonism.

others, de Maistre's formulations foreshadow the Saint-Simonian formulations. See in *Principe générateur des Constitutions*, 1814: 'The remedy for abuse is born out of abuse . . . when evil arrives at a certain point, it kills itself, and this has to be so; for evil . . . is only a negation.' (*Oeuvres complètes*, I, 282.)" B101.

[5] "The formula, the 'exploitation of the earth,' appears from the first numbers of the *Producteur* on (I, 73, 95, 100). But the expression 'the exploitation of man by man' does not appear prior to the *Doctrine*. One can, however, follow the progressive elaboration of this phrase in the *Producteur*, particularly in Enfantin's articles. See particularly, I, 555 . . . III, 67." B104.

Antagonism, having physical force as its cause and the exploitation of man by man as its result, has been the most outstanding fact in all the past. Antagonism, too, arouses most strongly the sympathy that we feel for the development of mankind, since, from this point of view, this development may be expressed as the constant growth of the rule of love, harmony, and peace.

This proposition, that the rule of force manifests itself more absolutely as we go into the past, may evoke an objection drawn from the existence of priestly castes in antiquity, which up to this day have been considered as having achieved the domination of intelligence. We reply that this objection will disappear if the very nature of the social organization over which these castes presided is taken into consideration, as well as the order of relationships which it was their mission to maintain and to consecrate by the authority of intelligence, and the type of force which this intelligence used as support and principal means of action. Indeed, it will then be seen that among ancient peoples under the government of priests, just as under the government of patricians, the realm of force was always consecrated, and that in India and Egypt as well as in Greece and Rome the distinctions that were established between classes or castes were at the same time the political expressions of the different degrees of man's exploitation by man.

These various states of society are doubtless separated by important particular differences; but the most general fact they present is the same.

The following questions may now be raised: Why is it that in the same general state of mankind social power is either in the hands of the priestly or the warrior castes? To what fact may the establishment of the rule of force be traced directly? Did it take place after a conquest, or did it develop spontaneously with every society as the immediate consequence of human nature and organization?

These questions, however pressing they may be, do not enter into the framework of our exposition at this moment.

It is sufficient to have stated that the exploitation of man by his fellows, whatever its origin may be, is the most characteristic phenomenon of the past. Let us now see what this exploitation was at its beginning and how its progressive decline took place.

It is useless for us to dwell on the times of savagery, when the realm of force manifested itself only in destruction, and when the savage killed his enemy and often even ate him. Let us first turn to the epoch when the vanquished became the property of the victor and when the latter made of him an instrument of work or pleasure. In short, let us look back at the institution of slavery. When we reckon from this epoch, facts interlink in an orderly fashion without interruption; and one may say that only then, properly speaking, the exploitation of man by man began.

The passing from the state of anthropophagy and extermination to the first stage of civilization, marked by the establishment of slavery, is an immense progress, perhaps the most difficult, but it is impossible for us to grasp the intermediary steps. We shall therefore take as the point of departure the moment when this progress had been achieved and when the interlinking of events no longer escapes us.

In the beginning, exploitation embraces the entirety of the material, intellectual, and moral life of the man who is subjected to it. The slave is placed outside mankind; he belongs to his master like the land, the cattle, and the stock. The slave is property the same as they; he has no recognized right, not even that of living. The master can dispose of his days, can mutilate him at will, and can use him for whatever function he decides. The slave is not only condemned to misery and physical suffering, but also to intellectual and moral brutalization. He has no name, no family, no property, and no religious existence. In short, he can never lay claim to the acquisition of any of the benefits that have been denied him, or even come nearer to them.

Such was slavery in the beginning. In the course of time the condition of the slave became less rigorous. The legislator intervened in the slave's relationship to his master, and little by little he ceased to be a purely passive object. He was granted a small part of the profit of his own work and was given some guarantees for his existence. Not very much later he claimed through his emancipation, a still rare and exceptional event, to be making a step toward civil and religious society and to be introducing his race into mankind, without, however, his race being freed from proscription and exploitation as long as its origin could be recognized.

In the republics of antiquity a class of men is to be found holding a middle place between the masters and the slaves, namely the plebeians.

The origin of plebeianism is unknown. But whether through the slow evolution of the slaves it represents the first conquest of any status in society, or whether it is the result of a primitive transaction between victors and vanquished, the plebeian was always exploited by the patrician, as the slave was by the master—not with the same rigor, or in a brutal way, but still to a high degree and in the same respects. The plebeian's religious, political, and even civil existence was not recognized, for he could not have property or family. These rights were reserved for the patrician. It is true that the plebeian could acquire them, but only by delegation, a sanction from a patrician, and by the invocation of, the latter's name. This is the basic reason for ancient patronage. At all times the original inferiority of the dependent did not permit him to attain, even through adoption by the patron, the fullness of religious and social existence. He was barred from the priesthood and the mysteries set apart for this office. Only a patrician was judged worthy of interpreting the divine will.

The plebeian, who from the beginning had been placed in a more favorable position than the slave, attained his liberation sooner than the latter. His emancipation, hastened by the devotion of the Gracchi, was completed under the Empire as far as it could be within Roman society. This society had to be transformed as the emancipation became complete. It occurred when Christianity, in proclaiming simultaneously the unity of God and the brotherhood of man, completely changed religious and political relationships, and the relation of man to God and of men among themselves.

It was in the Occident that the political realization of this new religious conception began. At the beginning of its domination two classes of men still existed; one of them was subject to the other, but the condition of this class had improved noticeably. The serf was no longer the direct property of the master as the slave had been. He was bound only to the sod, and could not be separated from it. He received a part of the fruits of his labor; he had a family; his existence was protected by civil law and, even better, by religious law. The moral life of the slave had nothing in common with that of his master. [*Sic!*] Lord and serf had the same God, the same belief, and received the same religious instruction. The same spiritual assistance was given them by the ministers of the altars. The soul of the serf was no less precious in the eyes of the Church than that of the baron. It was even more so, for according to the Gospels the poor were the chosen of God. And finally, the serf's family was hallowed like the lord's.

This situation, incomparably superior to slavery, was, however, still only provisional. The serf was later detached from the soil and received what might be called the right of movement. He might then choose his own master. Doubtless, after what, strictly speaking, may be considered his emancipation, the former serf remained in many respects marked by the impress of servitude. For a long time still he was subject to personal services, to corvées, and to feudal rents, which were the price of his labor and liberty. But these burdens were lightened from day to day.

At last the whole class of workers in the material order, a class that is merely the prolongation of those of slavery and serfdom, made a decisive advance by acquiring political capacity through the establishment of the communes.

The decline of the exploitation of man by man gives rise to a number of observations. In the institution of the priestly castes, intelligence always leans for support on military force, the principal means of its power. In the Christian institution, not only does intelligence separate its cause from that of force, but it also pronounces an anathema against it and requires that in its actions force takes on a completely new character. Thus the nations that until that time had openly waged wars of destruction, then of pillage and conquest, appeared to blush in the presence of the peaceful society constituted within the Church. They felt obliged to look for pretexts to make war. When war was undertaken, it was supposedly fought for the defense of one's

territory or to avenge an outrage. No longer does one dare
recognize war as the goal of social activity, but only as a means
for peace. A revolution in general sentiments thus took place.
The narrower the associations had been, the greater was the sway
of hatred. This was the inevitable outcome of the repeated
injuries these associations had inflicted on each other as well as
of the struggle within each one of their component classes of
men. On the other hand, to the extent that associations grew,
hatred ceased to be the exclusive form of social feeling. At last,
Christianity, by proclaiming universal brotherhood, virtually
substituted love for hatred and hope for fear, a transformation
to which we owe the progress achieved since that epoch and
which even affects the time when this transformation will become
final and definitive.

Under the influence of Christianity, man's material activity
gradually turned away from the exploitation of his fellow-men
and was directed more and more towards the exploitation of the
globe, without, however, being directly inspired by Christian
doctrine. In considering progress from this point of view one
sees how the decline of man's exploitation by man reveals a no
less general fact, namely, the development of all human faculties
in a peaceful direction.

The Catholic clergy offers the first outline of a society based
upon the combination of peaceful forces, from whose midst the
principle of the exploitation of man by man, from whatever
point of view it may be conceived, is completely excluded. This
association could only be very incomplete, considering the external circumstances that surrounded it. But in an age ac-
customed to barbarism, the Catholic clergy strongly voiced its
horror of blood and reiterated the maxims: Render therefore
unto Caesar the things that are Caesar's! My kingdom is not of
this world! This is to say: Leave the world; it is still subjected
to the sword. In the midst of a society originally divided into
classes by the sword, where an aristocracy based on birth ruled,
this totally peaceful association trampled on the privileges of the
nobility and of birth, proclaimed equality before God, the
distribution of heavenly punishments and rewards according to
works, and realized in its earthly hierarchy a new way to dis-

tribute functions and ranks, not according to birth but according to ability and personal merit. The history of the popes offers striking testimony. At the time of the zenith of the Catholic Church, nearly all of them were chosen from average men of lowly origin who had been distinguished solely by their ability. Although the so-called temporal society refused to imitate spiritual society, it was dominated, nevertheless, by its moral influence and by its teachings to such an extent that in the midst of all their efforts to restrain its power, the heads of nations were seen bowing their heads before the clergy, and glorying in the name of sons of the Church.

To sum up: to the degree that the circle of association became wider, exploitation of man by man diminished, antagonism became less violent, and all human faculties were developed more and more in a peaceful direction.

This continuous tendency suffices to indicate the general character of the final state towards which mankind is traveling. In any case, a clear idea can be obtained of the universal association which is gradually becoming established only after, in a general way, the nature and relations of the different components of the social institution in that epoch are understood. This picture should appear from the course of our exposition.

But before continuing, we think it necessary to anticipate an objection that might be suggested by the word "final," with which we describe the state of universal association toward which the human species is advancing.

We do not want to say that mankind, once it has reached this state, will no longer have any progress to make. On the contrary, it will march faster than ever towards perfection. But this epoch will be final for mankind in the sense that it will have realized the political combination most favorable to progress. Man will always have to love and to know more and more and to assimilate the outside world more completely to himself. The fields of science and industry will gather daily more abundant harvests and will furnish man with new ways to express his love even more nobly. He will broaden the sphere of his intelligence, that of his physical power, and that of his sympathies, for the course of his progress is unlimited. But the social combination that will be most favorable to his moral, intellectual, and physical development, and in which every individual, whatever his birth, will be loved, honored, and rewarded according to his works, which is to say according to his efforts to improve the moral, intellectual, and physical existence of the masses, and consequently his own, and in which all will be ceaselessly moved to rise in this threefold direction, is not susceptible of perfection. In other words, the organization of the future will be final because only then will society be formed directly for progress.

A Digression on the General Development
of the Human Species

Gentlemen:

The entire world is progressing toward unity of doctrine and action. This is our most general profession of faith. This is the direction which a philosophical examination of the past permits us to trace. Until the day when this great concept, born of the genius of our master, together with its general developments, can become the direct object of the endeavors of the human spirit, all previous social progress must be considered as preparatory, all attempts at organization as partial and successive initiations to the cult of unity and to the reign of order over the entire globe, the territorial possession of the great human family. However, when these preparatory labors, this provisional organization of families of castes, of races, and of past nations are studied in the light of a new day, they will show evidence of the goal at which we are aiming and of the means by which to attain it.

Indeed, gentlemen, the need for unity and the love of order are so deeply inherent in man that before they can be experienced and satisfied to their limit in the universal association, we see them established on a provisional basis at least: first in the family through marriage, then in small associations, finally in entire nations, over ever wider areas. In this way the various elements of general progress have been able to germinate and grow strong among peoples who somehow were successively chosen to represent at every epoch the new stage attained by the human species.

We shall observe here, however, that these attempts of the human mind and these political organizations, which are provisional merely because they do not embrace the sphere of the total development of mankind, must contain a cause for dissolution.

This seed of death, cultivated constantly by the work done out-side the ruling doctrines and institutions, brings its destruction little by little. This is the reason for our first classification of the past into organic and critical epochs.

In the organic epochs it may be observed from every point on the social circumference how all minds and deeds are directed sympathetically toward a center of affection. In the critical epochs the old beliefs crumble everywhere, because their defects have been pointed out by feelings which the old social bond could not comprehend and have been attacked by a present no longer bound to traditions or attached to a future. These epochs deserve yet another name. In the true sense of the words they are religious in the first case and irreligious in the latter.

We have just presented our broadest conception of the past of the human species, considered from the point of view of the general character of the doctrines under the influence of which mankind has successively accomplished its mission and prepared its destiny.

Before passing on to the presentation of the most important historical events, whose connection will demonstrate the truth of the above philosophic perceptions, we shall call your attention to the most general form of human activity until now.

The exploitation of man by man describes the state of human relations in the past. The future offers the picture of exploitation of nature by man associated with man. Doubtless the exploitation of external nature goes back to remotest antiq-uity; industry is not a discovery reserved for the future. More-over, without any doubt, the exploitation of man by man has been weakened today. It is no longer a matter of breaking the slave's chains. But the progress of the spirit of association and the relative decadence of antagonism do not represent the most complete expression of man's development. In other words, war and peace are the distinguishing characteristics of the past and future, respectively, when considered from the point of view given us by Saint-Simon.

War, properly speaking, is the object of antagonism; slavery is its means and result. But it is antagonism which first civilized the world. Kant has already noted this before us. Yes, gentlemen, the institution of slavery, following upon the fiercest brutality and the most savage appetites, was favorable to the development of human society in its beginning. The conquerors sought to save the life of the conquered when newly born industry claimed slavery as the foremost instrument of material production. The traditional history of the human race has not transmitted to us the details of this primitive barbarism; some savage American tribes have, however, given us a living image of it. Gentlemen, what do we see in the first state of the human race but physical force exploiting weakness? The immediate appetites alone incite man's activity; women, children, old people, and all those who are weak groan under the yoke of brutality. Hunting and war are the noble customs of heroes, and their passions are those acquired by barbarous work.

Men may then be divided into two classes, the exploiters and the exploited. One may even say, as Aristotle and Saint-Simon have done (each in a different sense, however) that the past shows us two distinct species, that of masters and that of slaves. The second species is regarded by the first as something strange. It constitutes a part of the stock or mobile property. It is put by law and by fact in the same category with the animals. History tells us how this *most numerous*[1] class constantly improved its relative position in society through the *peaceful* work to which it was dedicated. It also tells us how this improvement, subject to the general principles of social relations of the past, took place only through the successive admission of the most advanced men of the exploited class to the ranks of the privileged, which formed the class of the masters. Finally mankind will break all the chains with which antagonism has burdened it. One day man, liberated and completely separated from the animals, will organize for peace, after having undergone and consequently rejected the education of war.

[1] "The New Christianity (*Nouveau Christianisme, Oeuvres de Saint-Simon et d'Enfantin*, XXIII, 152): 'The general aim which you must present to all men in their work is the improvement of the moral and physical existence of the most numerous class. . . . To improve most rapidly the existence of the poorest class . . .' The motto of the Saint-Simonian *Globe* was: 'All social institutions must have as their aim the improvement of the moral, physical, and intellectual lot of the most numerous and poorest class.' " **B**119.

This, gentlemen, is the second point of view from which we envisage the march of human society. Let us now consider the great events of history.

Europe is the center of the world. Since Christianity, the East has ceased to shed its light upon the West, and Christianity, in linking the development of the European peoples to the progress realized before by the people of Moses, permits our mind to grasp the summary of the Oriental doctrines.

Indeed, the traditions of history show the Mosaic organization contemporaneous with the Egyptian colonizations of Greece. All other histories are subsequent to these events, prior to which no precise tradition or document has been found. A mass of circumstances, not known to us today, permitted the Hebrew people, who had left Egypt at the time when the first colonies were established in Greece, to receive from Moses a much stronger and much more unitary organization than that of their companions in emigration or exile.

The unity of God, the real link of the unity of activity and doctrine, does not appear among the Greeks before Socrates. Even then, as will be demonstrated presently, it plays only a critical role which, to be sure, is very important in the series of human progress. It is therefore mainly to Moses that the organic or religious chain of the European people must go back.

What was the character of that first social unity? What was the will of the God of Moses? Being confined within the limits of a small area and unknown to the rest of the world, Hebraic unity was not the peaceful and definitive unity of the human race. Arriving at the fullness of their political constitution by the extermination of the peoples that opposed them, and undergoing themselves a most severe discipline, the Hebrew people, nevertheless, were not primarily warriors in so far as they lived under the powerful sway of Mosaic law. Their mission was not to civilize the world by conquest but to elaborate and bequeath to their successors the philosophic conception of unity. Thus slavery was made relatively less harsh under the influence of the religious and political unity founded by Moses.

However, the political unity of the Hebrew people was broken. First the establishment of a military kingdom led to the dissolution of the tribes of Jacob. The people were reduced to captivity a second time. Everything proclaimed a great change in the interpretation of the divine will. The Law became at last subject to the criticism of the reformers.

Elsewhere, Greek polytheism was decaying. The mysteries preserved polytheism's ruins when Socrates recapitulated, by his proclamation of unity, the critique of all the old dogmas, and in dying returned the fatal stroke with which they had struck him.

Thus the unity of activity and doctrine reappears, based on a foundation which Roman power and the labor of the Platonists were to spread far. In maintaining the unity of God against Greek polytheism, the student of Socrates freed his conception from any idea of place or time, an admirable preparation for the approaching realization through Christ of the mission of the Gentiles. In another part of the world, Rome, still representing the aged genius of war, linked all the peoples to its fortune. Being the mistress of their temporal destinies, Rome opened an immense field to the doctrine which was to unite their beliefs. At last the Hebrews went beyond the boundaries of Judea, and the people of God began to feel that they had brothers outside the Holy Land.

At this time Alexandria opened its schools; Greek philosophy and Oriental dogmas faced each other. The spiritual destiny of humanity, heatedly debated far away from the power of the sword and completely separated from the laws of Caesar, was determined while the laws of Caesar, so powerful until then, were not even discussed. In short, Christianity no longer sanctified war. It still represented war but promised peace to the world.

We have just dwelt on the most important political fact which Christianity brought forth, namely the division of power into temporal and spiritual, the separation of Church and State, and of peaceful and warlike society. But before demonstrating the beneficial influence which this division exerted on the future of mankind, some historical considerations will still be necessary to confirm what preceded and to make you understand the state of the old world which Christianity regenerated.

The colonies founded by Cecrops, Inachus, and many others

had doubtless brought the public doctrine of the Egyptian priests to Greece at the time when Moses took their secret doctrine to perfect it. Moses, as we have already indicated, could not bring about a truly peaceful association. The slave still played a very important role in that extremely compact and religious society. War was still honored in Jerusalem; and the bloody practices, the remains of ancient barbarism, could merely be modified, but not abolished.

The organization of the Greek colonies was priestly and military. In Rome this double organization was repeated by two founders, one military, the other priestly.* The unity of God, the basis for the harmony of dogma and cult, remained unknown to these people, who were, nevertheless, destined to facilitate the establishment of Christianity through conquest.

To the extent that the invasion of Asia Minor and of the adjacent islands was accomplished by the Greeks and after Alexander annihilated the political influence which Asia exercised on Europe by carrying the war into Persia, and as far as India, and by subjecting the entire known world to his laws; and to the extent that the material bases of civilized society in Europe spread, two noteworthy events occurred: the religious tie of the Greek and Roman peoples was broken at the same time that they found themselves sated with military glory. The first of these two facts has been clearly developed by the classical historians who inform us of the long critique of Greek and Italic doctrines. Despite the seductive powers of the fine arts in Greece and Rome, despite Homer, Hesiod and Virgil, skepticism and the doctrines of Epicurus proclaimed from the tribune and repeated at the theaters soon dethroned the pagan divinities.

It would seem that this sight of destruction might make one despair of human destiny. But recall the second fact which we just mentioned: Rome was sick of glory.

Gentlemen, look at slavery, which had first been established in Greece and Rome with all the rigor with which victory could endow it. Think of the military discipline which transformed authority in nearly all its relations into despotism when sustained

---

* See the preceding session on the identity of the power of the priests and that of the patricians.

by religion itself or incited by the spirit of conquest. Recall finally the terrible right over life and death which the father still had over his children, like the master over his slaves.

Indeed, gentlemen, another critique was at work quietly, but nevertheless filled with hope. The weak, the poor, the slave— and does that not also mean woman?—were waiting for a savior.

But let us return to that great separation, established by Christianity under the name of Catholicism, between spiritual and temporal power. We shall not deal at length here with the betterment which resulted from it for the human species. We shall merely stress the general character of this separation.

The doctrines of the Church, completely foreign to military power, had been elaborated, as we have said, without the rights of Caesar being taken into account. Persecuted, but nevertheless peaceful, the Church respected the hierarchies of antagonism, but within its midst based dignity upon personal merit, not upon birth. She did not intervene between master and slave to recognize the realm of conquest by sanctifying it as the religions of the past had done. On the contrary, she taught the masters that God is no respecter of persons, that in his eyes the temporal hierarch is nothing, since he prefers the poor to the rich and the weak to the mighty of the earth.

Thus the essentially peaceful Church, or Christian association, founded its power on the brotherhood of mankind. The temporal power, on the other hand, was the military power of Caesar, to whom the Church by necessity left most of the worldly discipline and administration of a society which had been ruled entirely by the sword in the era when Christianity appeared.

This separation between two powers which were made rivals by their goal and origin inevitably had to lead to a struggle profitable to all mankind, which is to say fatal to the sword. But this struggle, which occupied the Church ceaselessly, contributed not a little to preventing the Church from developing the sublime doctrine it had received. Its dogma and cult, even its morality, were to be affected and consequently to remain almost stationary despite the constant progress of human societies.

The works of Aristotle on the physical sciences had been forgotten, while Plato's work was fused with Jewish doctrines into the elaboration of Christianity. Aristotle's writings, which tended directly to reverse the former theories, appeared in the eleventh century, brought to Europe chiefly by the translations and commentaries of the Arabs. The Church, then in the fullness of her influence on the kings who gloried in being exalted by the Church, took possession of a part of these works. While foreshadowing a struggle which was soon to be under way, the Church identified herself above all with the discoveries of Aristotle about the mechanics of reasoning, and scholasticism came into being. But the other parts of the works of Aristotle, although equally accepted by the clergy, doubtless arrived too late to be directly fashioned religiously, and thus too late to help in the perfecting of the dogma which had been accepted and triumphant for several centuries.

Here began a series of advances outside the Church, which the kings themselves soon did not mind using in order to oppose what they called the encroachments by the spiritual power.

On the other hand, the organization of the clergy, perfect in principle since it was peaceful, could not fail to be soon polluted by its perpetual contact with a society held together in its material aspects by sword and slavery. The abuses of worldly society were introduced into the Church. From that time on the fall of the Church became certain.

The beginning of the Reformation and the support it found in attacking the very core of the Church among the philosophers who had been strengthened by the progress of Arabic science hardly awakened the clergy from its lethargy. Moreover, Catholicism, which had forgotten its peaceful mission, became in turn a bloody persecutor. The giant of the Middle Ages, about to abandon her moral hold on the world, and already having lost the powerful message by which it had once won mankind, was to astonish and enlighten Europe once more in a final effort. In the sixteenth century she attempted to rekindle the sympathies of man through master works of art, and the vigorous Jesuit institution threw one brilliant ray on the last days of her agony. Yet all these admirable efforts were wasted, and the outburst of the French Revolution, as it overthrew the ancient throne of Caesar, at the same time gave the final blow to the throne of Saint Peter.

The authors of destruction attempted in vain to reconstruct the social order with the instruments of its ruin. The structures erected by them crumbled as soon as they were raised. At last a final attempt at reorganization was made by the modern Caesar. But he still rested upon the sword eighteen hundred years after the word of peace, and the sword dug his grave at the remote border of the civilized world.

Society is awaiting the peaceful organization which it has been promised. Saint-Simon, gentlemen, has laid its foundations. He has shown us the definitive goal towards which all human capacities must converge: the complete abolition of antagonism and the attainment of *universal association by and for the constantly progressive amelioration of the moral, physical, and intellectual condition of the human race.*

The Successive Transformation of Man's Exploitation by Man and of the Rights of Property

Master and Slave; Patrician and Plebeian; Lord and Serf; Idle and Worker

Gentlemen:

After having shown antagonism to be the most striking characteristic of all past social organizations, we have traced in the most general terms the decline of man's exploitation by man, to this day the strongest expression of antagonism. In showing you the constant decline of the driving power of the associations of the past, which were always military to some extent, since they were not universal, we wanted to give you a first idea of the goal toward which the human species is traveling, as represented chiefly by the most enlightened nations of the globe. We have arrived at the conclusion that the future toward which we are advancing is a state in which all forces will be united in the direction of peace.

However, this short account, which has shown you how mankind comes ever nearer to universal association, could not explain clearly the exact economic organization, once society will have reached this stage, and more than the possibility of its realization. To arrive at a precise understanding of these two things, one must follow the successive transformations of the most important social institutions and define the modifications they must experience in order to take on their new form and their final character. We have said that, from this moment on, mankind was to work directly toward the realization of universal association. Indeed, this social combination is the first and only organic state which offers itself to mankind as a fulfillment of all the steps it has made in its forward march. But we do not claim here that to achieve such a result there is nothing more to be done today but to unite and combine the scattered elements of the social order. When the present state of these elements is compared with that of previous epochs, the present seems undeniably much closer to the demands of the future toward which we are moving. It may even be noted that most of these elements are instinctively moving more or less in the direction of the future. Nevertheless, it would be very wrong to suppose that they need undergo no further changes; and when we say that mankind must work from this day on to achieve universal association, we understand above all that it must occupy itself with transforming education, legislation, and the organization of property and all other social relations in such a way as to actualize its future condition as soon as possible.

Antagonism, the realm of physical force, and man's exploitation by man are doubtless greatly weakened today. They manifest themselves only in forms tempered and transformed to such an extent that at first it seems difficult fully to recognize them. Nevertheless, they continue to exist very intensely in these forms. We do not mean to speak here of the phenomena of the critical struggle which began in the sixteenth century, but only of the main events which arose in the last organic epoch and which have been prolonged up to our day. We shall try to point out the principal ones.

For a long time no wars of destruction or conquest have taken place at all similar to those of antiquity and the first centuries of the Middle Ages. The form and purpose of wars have changed. Wars have lost their barbarous character. Pillage and even territorial possessions are no longer coveted by the belligerent parties. In most cases, nowadays, commercial privileges are in dispute. But although the purpose of war has changed, antagonism exists nonetheless among peoples, and the sword is still the highest arbiter of their blind disputes.

At the basis of modern societies, force is still clearly manifest in government, legislation, and above all in the relations between the sexes, in which woman remains burdened with the anathema the warrior formerly placed upon her and is supposed to be subjected to an eternal guardianship.[1]

At last the exploitation of man by man, which we have shown in its most direct and uncouth form in the past, namely slavery, continues to a very large extent in the relations between owners and workers, masters and wage earners. Of course, the respective conditions of the classes today are far from those of masters and slaves, patricians and plebeians, or lords and serfs in the past. At first sight it seems as if no comparison could be made. However, it must be realized that the more recent situation is only a prolongation of the earlier. The relation of master and wage earner is the last transformation which slavery has undergone. If the exploitation of man by man no longer has the brutal character of antiquity and assumes more gentle forms today, it is, nevertheless, no less real. The worker is not like the slave, the direct property of his master. His condition, which is never permanent, is fixed by a transaction with a master. But is this transaction free on the part of the worker? It is not, since he is obliged to accept it under penalty of death, for he is reduced to expecting his nourishment each day only from his work of the previous day.

The moral dogma which declared that no man should be disqualified because of his birth has been impressing itself upon men's minds for a long time, and the political constitutions of our day have expressly sanctioned it. It seems then that among the various classes of society a continuous change in the families and individuals composing them should take place today, and that, as a consequence of this change, the exploitation of man by man, if it should continue, would be in a state of flux, at least in respect to the races which are its victims. But in reality this change has not taken place; and except for a few cases, the advantages and disadvantages proper to every social position are

[1] The only important mention of the question of woman in Saint-Simon occurs in *Lettres d'un habitant de Génève* in which he grants women the right to subscribe to and be nominated for the "Council of Newton." (*Oeuvres de Saint-Simon et d'Enfantin*, XV, 11.) The role of woman was not yet mentioned in the *Producteur*. See the Introduction to this translation; also cf. B128.

transmitted through inheritance. The economists have taken care to establish one aspect of this fact, namely *hereditary misery,* when they recognized within society the existence of a class of proletarians. Today the entire mass of workers is exploited by the men whose property they utilize. The managers of industry themselves undergo such exploitation in their relation with the owners, but to an incomparably smaller extent. And in turn they participate in the privileges of exploitation which bears down with all its weight upon the laboring classes, which is to say, on the majority of the workers. In such a state of affairs, the worker appears as the direct descendent of the slave and the serf. His person is free; he is no longer bound to the soil; but that is all he has gained. And in this state of legal emancipation he can exist only under the conditions imposed upon him by a class small in numbers, namely the class of those men who have been invested through legislation, the daughter of conquest, with the monopoly of riches, which is to say, with the capacity to dispose at their will, even in idleness, of the instruments of work.

A glance at what is happening around us will be sufficient to make us recognize that the worker is exploited materially, intellectually, and morally in the same way as the slave was, only less intensely so. It is indeed evident that he can hardly provide for his own wants by his work, and whether or not he wishes to work is not up to him. He worsens his position if he is imprudent enough to believe that he is destined to enjoy the things that constitute the happiness of the rich, and if he takes a companion and establishes a family. Can the worker, who is restricted by the misery to which he has been reduced, have the time to develop his intellectual faculties and his moral desires? Can he even desire to do so? And if he should experience this desire, who will furnish him the means of satisfying it? Who will place science within his reach? Who will receive the effusions of his heart? No one cares for him. Physical misery reduces him to brutishness, and brutishness to a depravity which is the source of new misery. Thus a vicious circle develops which inspires in us only disgust and horror with each step when we should be filled with pity.

This is the situation of most workers, who compose the immense majority of the population[2] in every society. And nevertheless, this fact, which should arouse all feelings, is passed unnoticed by our political speculators. The privileged of our age enumerate complacently the great advances made by liberty and philanthropy. They boast of the rule of equality which, they say, our constitutions have hallowed by declaring that every citizen is eligible for public employment; and they ascribe all these advances to the love and admiration of the masses as the highest and last stage of our civilization. It would indeed be cruel irony if one could suppose that those who speak in this manner had seriously examined the surrounding society.

All other lasting and legitimate revolutions that deserve to be preserved in the memory of mankind must improve the fate of the most numerous class. All those revolutions which up to this day have been of this character have successively weakened the exploitation of man by man. Only one revolution can take place today, capable of exalting the hearts and of filling them with an everlasting feeling of gratitude. That revolution will put a complete end in all its forms to this exploitation which has become godless in its very foundation. But this revolution is inevitable, and until it is achieved, these so frequently repeated expressions about the last stage of civilization and the enlightenment of the age will remain mere phrases for the use of a few privileged egoists.

In listing the social forces which the last organic period has bequeathed to ours, we spoke of the antagonism perpetuated among the peoples in the new form of commercial rivalry. We

[2] "Since Saint-Simon assigns to positive philosophy the task of ameliorating the lot of the most numerous and poorest class, and declares in his last work that because the 'class of proletarians is as advanced in fundamental civilization as that of proprietors, the law ought to classify them as partners' (*Opinions littéraires, philosophiques et industrielles,* p. 108), one is at first inclined to attribute to him the honor of having first criticized salaried work. Actually, his thoughts remain extremely confused in this respect. . . . After the death of Saint-Simon the editors of the *Producteur* drew the logical conclusions from his thought and declared that there are within industrial society itself relationships which are still relationships of governmental oppression." B132.

shall return to this subject when dealing with universal association from the point of view of industry, a state in which the
various nations, scattered over the face of the earth, shall appear
only as members of one vast workshop,[3] working under a common law for the accomplishment of one and the same destiny.
We have shown brute force manifesting itself in governmental
forms and in legislation. We shall return to this subject, too,
when dealing with education and its beneficent and progressive
power and with the gradual substitution of its sanction (which
will correct evil inclinations and direct them toward the good)
for those purely material sanctions of a coercive legislation which,
while letting evil grow freely, can only accuse, condemn, and
punish. We have indicated the relations association establishes
between the sexes as one of its most important aspects. This
point will be the topic of a special discussion in which we shall
show how woman, who at first was a slave, or at least in a condition bordering on slavery, was associated little by little with man,
and acquired each day a greater influence in the social order, and
how the causes which to this day have determined her subordination have been successively weakened and shall at last disappear
and carry away with them that domination, tutelage, and perpetual minority which even now are imposed on women, and which
would be incompatible with the social state of the future which
we foresee.

The subject matter of our examination at this point will be
the exploitation of man by his fellow, which is continued and
exemplified today by the relations of the owner with the worker,
and the master with the wage earner. We shall observe this
exploitation in the light of that which dominates it and is its

[3] "The Saint-Simonians borrowed this metaphor from their master, who
had said in his first work (*Lettres d'un Habitant de Génève; Oeuvres de
Saint-Simon et d'Enfantin,* XV, 55): 'All men will work; they will consider
themselves workers connected with a shop, which in its work aims to bring
human intelligence and my divine foresight closer together.' This is characteristic of Saint-Simon's industrialism and differentiates him from the
industrialism of the liberal economists. For them, the distribution of tasks
works by way of exchange among independent producers. For Saint-Simon
it tends to operate in mankind as a whole in the same way as in a factory
or a workshop in a unitary direction." B133.

most immediate cause, namely the constitution of property and the transmission of riches by inheritance within families.[4]

According to general prejudice, whatever revolutions may suddenly occur in society, none can take place within property, which is an unchangeable institution. Men of the most diverse political and religious opinions are completely in agreement on this point; and at the least symptom of innovation in this respect, all call immediately upon universal conscience which, they say, proclaims property as the very foundation of the political order.

We, too, while confining ourselves to these general terms, repeat, if you wish, that property is the foundation of the political order. But property is a social institution, subject, as are all other social institutions, to the law of progress. Property may thus at various epochs be understood, defined, and regulated in different ways.

If it is admitted that the exploitation of man by man has gradually decreased; if sympathy proclaims that it must disappear completely; if it is true that mankind is moving toward a state of things in which all men, without distinction of birth, will receive from society the education which can give their faculties their fullest realization, if they shall be classed by society according to their merits and be renumerated according to their work; then it is evident that the constitution of property must be changed, since, by virtue of this constitution, some men are born with the privilege of living without doing anything, namely at the expense of others, which practice is nothing else than the continuation of the exploitation of man by man. From one of these facts the other can be deduced logically: the exploitation of man by man must disappear. The constitution of property which is hereby perpetuated must, therefore, also disappear.

But it will be said that the owner and the capitalist do not

---

[4] Unlike the *Doctrine*, Saint-Simon did not question the right of inheritance, except possibly in one place and there only by implication. He declared that "wealth is generally a proof of ability among industrialists even in cases where they have inherited individual fortunes." (*Système industriel; Oeuvres de Saint-Simon et d'Enfantin*, XXXI, 49.) He did, however, point out that "the industrial system is based on the principle of perfect equality . . ." and that "it is opposed to the establishment of all birth rights and of all privileges." (*Catéchisme politique des Industriels; Oeuvres de Saint-Simon et d'Enfantin*, VIII, 61.) Cf. B135.

at all live at the expense of others. That which the worker pays him is only the fee for the productive services of the instruments of work lent to the worker. While admitting that these productive services are real, an opinion which we shall not test at this moment, we must still know, in regard to the question before us, who ought to dispose of these inanimate servants, whose property they should be, and to whom they should be transmitted.

In order to justify the privileges that property bestows today, it is absolutely necessary to go back to one of the great principles which until now has been recurrently invoked for this purpose, namely divine right, natural right, or utility. But whichever of these principles one may espouse, one must yet acknowledge, if one admits man to be progressive, that divine right and natural right are equally progressive and that utility varies with the stages of progress. The question is therefore one of knowing what divine right, natural right, and utility would prescribe today in respect to property.

We have observed that property has generally been considered an unchangeable institution. However, it will be noted in studying history that legislation has never ceased to intervene in determining the nature of objects that could be appropriated and in regulating their use and transfer.

In the beginning the right of property embraced both things and men, who even formed the most important and most valuable part: the slave belonged to the master on the same basis as cattle and material objects. No restriction existed yet regarding the exercise of property right over a person. Later the legislator defined the limits of the privilege of use and abuse which man *qua* owner had over the slave, which is to say, over man *qua* property. These limits became progressively narrower. The master each day lost some moral, intellectual, or material share of his slave, until finally moralist and legislator agreed to the principle that man could no longer be the property of his fellow. This intervention into the rights of property by moralist and legislator corresponds to the most complete transformation which human association has undergone.

In the same manner the legislator has intervened to regulate the transfer of property. And thus, for example, one may observe in the epoch of civilization to which we directly belong, in the space of approximately fifteen centuries, three states of property in respect to transfer, each of which is sanctioned by legislation and custom. At first the owner had the right of disposing, in whatever way he wanted, of the goods in his possession. He could disinherit his family or distribute his belongings arbitrarily among the members of his family. He was told: The law henceforth shall determine your heir. Your wealth can be transferred only to male children and among them only to the oldest. Later the legislator again changed the rules governing inheritance in dividing their father's fortune equally among all children.

These revolutionary changes which legislation brought about in property rights could not have been effectively carried through if they had lacked moral sanction. This was never the case. Conscience always found itself in harmony with the wishes of the legislator, at least for long periods of time. Conscience has constantly seen in every epoch the wishes of God or, to use the critical terminology, those of nature, in the expression of its own desires.

When, as is customarily done, the law of property is considered abstractly and by itself, it has reached its last transformation as the consequence of the revolutions which we have just recalled and which generally resulted in the ever widening distribution of riches. And even in this state, it may be observed how it daily loses some of its remaining importance, an importance which is based on the privilege of levying a tribute on another person's work. But this tribute—represented today by interest and rent—is steadily decreasing. The conditions which regulate the relations of owner and capitalist with the workers are becoming increasingly advantageous for the latter. In other words, the privilege of living in idleness has become more and more difficult to acquire and to preserve.

This short account suffices to prove that the law of property, generally considered to be protected from all moral or legal revolutions, has actually been constantly subject to intervention both from the moralist and from the legislator concerning the nature of possessions as well as their use and their transfer. We see that the last stage of modifications in the transfer of property has been the assignment of a greater part of the property to a greater number of the workers, the result of which has been that the social importance of the idle owner was weakened because of the importance which the workers acquire daily. Now a last change has become necessary. The moralist must prepare the way; the legislator must then prescribe it. The law of progress that we have observed seems to establish an order of things in which the state, and no longer the family, will inherit the accumulated riches insofar as these form what the economists call production resources.

We must anticipate that some people will confuse this system with what they know as community of goods. These systems are, however, not related. As we have said, in the organization of the future each one will be classified according to his ability and remunerated according to his work. This indicates sufficiently the inequality of distribution. In the system of the community of goods, on the other hand, all shares are equal; and against such a mode of distribution, there necessarily are many objections. The principle of emulation is destroyed when the idle man receives the same share as the industrious man, and the latter consequently sees all the burden of the community fall upon himself. What we have just said suffices also to show that such distribution is evidently contrary to the principle of equality which has been invoked for its establishment. Moreover, in such a system, the equilibrium would constantly be broken. There would be a constant tendency toward the return of inequalities, and inequality would re-emerge again and again, necessitating constant redistribution.

These objections are well founded and cannot be answered when they attack the system of the community of goods. But they have no value when they oppose the principle of classification and remuneration according to ability and work, a principle which we believe is destined to rule the future. You will easily be convinced by what follows.

The Constitution of Property and the Organization of the Banks

Gentlemen:

Examination of the various questions relating to the regulation of society ordinarily give rise to two types of considerations: right and utility. After we carefully observe the importance given to this distinction in the most serious controversies, the moral order seems in a state of perpetual antagonism, and societies seem constant prey to the contradictory solicitations of two principles: one good, right; the other bad, utility. Man, who is never supposed to be able to conciliate the two, has no other choice but to choose between them. What is remarkable in this state of uncertainty is that the men who are reputed to be the wisest and who enjoy perhaps the highest esteem are precisely those who have decided in favor of utility, that is to say, in favor of what in moral speculations is identified with the bad principle. If this dichotomy were real, man would constantly find himself confronted by the alternatives of duty or interest, of devotion or egoism, of perpetual sacrifice or perpetual immorality. Fortunately mankind's fate is not so rigid. The incompatibility of duty and interest, like that which one sees between theory and practice, systems and facts, general welfare and particular welfare, is real only in critical epochs; that is to say, in those epochs of mistrust, hate, and disorder, when one loses sight of that moral bond which unites the intellectual and the material, the interest of all with that of each, general facts with particular ones. In the organic epochs—and mankind is no longer to know any others—these distinctions tend ceaselessly to disappear, not only for each separately organized association, but for all of mankind which shall be united in one association.* Then unity is established among all the proclivities of man. The moral order presides equally over the intellectual and material orders, over thoughts and actions. At last egoism and devotion, interest and duty, right and utility converge toward a common goal or, better yet, become identical: they are but two different aspects, two distinct manifestations under which each social fact is presented, just as industry and science are the two aspects of individual and collective life.

If we take this distinction into account in dealing with the question of property, if we consider this question separately from each of these two points of view, we are merely bowing to established ideas and conforming to the present habits of speech and reasoning.**

Divine right, natural right, and utility are each invoked in their turn to consecrate the inviolability, one may almost say the sanctity, of the present organization of property. In the name of these principles, reforms are considered impossible and outside the intervention of moralists and legislators. The more these opinions are generally spread and the deeper roots they have taken, the more we must take care to combat them. We have already shown that these three principles, by which property is defended as an absolute and invariable right, have successively sanctioned the various revolutions which this essentially changeable right has undergone. In order to justify the new change which we announce will take place in the constitution of property, we have shown that the modifications imposed by the legislator in respect to its nature, its uses, and its transfer have

* Let us recall that all the epochs of the past which we have called organic were only incompletely so and were all only provisional.

** In all the preceding, the great question is indicated, or rather posed, which has occupied man in many forms: the two principles, good and evil, original sin and redemption, free will and grace, and so forth. The Saint-Simonian solution will be given in the following volume. (See Nos. 33, 35, and 37 of the *Organisateur*, first year.) But we now call this to the reader's attention. For there is the whole Saint-Simonian doctrine, since it will put an end to the antagonism that has ruled among men until now, the cause of which has been the steadfast belief in a primitive, eternal dualism contradictory *per se*.

never lacked the sanction of the moralist. We have shown that the human conscience has always found itself in harmony with the different states of property. We have also seen that the part of the total product attributed to the workers has been gradually augmented, whereas the right of the owner lost in importance in the hands of the idle; and that in the series of civilization to which we directly belong, one can observe several successive states of property viewed from its three principal aspects (its nature, its use, and its transfer), each of which has been sanctified by human conscience, manners, and habits. As an example of the mode of transfer, we cite the right of the father arbitrarily to dispose of his wealth after his death; after that the exclusive right of inheritance granted to the oldest son; and at last the equal division among all the children.

As we have said, a new order is now being established. It consists in the transference of the right of inheritance, today still confined to the domestic family, to the state, which has become the association of the workers. The privileges of birth, which have already received blows in many respects, will disappear completely. The only right to wealth, that is to the disposal of the instruments of work, will be the ability to put them to work.

If past progress forecasts new progress, if it leads toward better relations among the members of society, human conscience will harmonize with this change, as it always has; and this change will itself be justified by a new divine right, a new natural right, and a new principle of utility, developed from divine right, natural right, and the principle of utility of the past.

Until now the only right to property has been directly or indirectly derived from force. In the future this right will be based on peaceful work. Perhaps it will be said that right through force has been eradicated long ago, and that there is no longer any property which is not at least indirectly the result of work. But by virtue of what authority does the present owner enjoy his wealth and transfer it to his successors? By virtue of legislation, the principle of which goes back to conquest, and which, no matter how far removed it may be from its source, still reflects its origin from the exploitation of man by man, of poor by rich, of the industrious producer by the idle consumer.

The advantages which property confers, whether they come from inheritance or whether they are acquired through work, are only functions of the right of the strongest, transferred by the accident of birth or ceded to the worker under various conditions.

We say that in the future the only right to property will be the ability to do peaceful work; the only title to consideration, work. To express ourselves more precisely, we shall add here that this title must be given to each owner specifically, which implicitly comprehends another idea, namely that the only right transferred by the owner's title is the direction, use, and exploitation of property.

If, as we have proclaimed, mankind moves toward a state in which all individuals will be classed according to their ability and rewarded according to their work, it is evident that property, as it exists now, must be abolished; for in giving a certain class of men the right to live in complete idleness from the work of others, property supports the exploitation of one part of the population, namely the most useful one which works and produces, for the profit of those who know only to destroy.* Thus we may consider the change we have announced justified from the standpoint of divine and natural right, since for the religious all men are of the same family and ought consequently not to exploit but to love and help each other. For the partisan of

* When new ideas are explained, all objections must be anticipated, even those which would be rejected upon the least reflection. We will be asked: If you want everyone to work, what will you do with the old people and the children? We shall answer: We do not desire that all men work, but that they all be raised successively for and by work, and that all can count on rest after having worked. The old and the children die miserably in critical epochs, because a considerable mass of strong, young, and intelligent men steadily consume much but produce nothing. To these latter we promise in the future the noble exercise of their feelings, their intelligence, and their vigor. As for the others, they will no longer be a prey to corruption, brutalization, and exhaustion from the most tender years on, or to the sufferings of a miserable old age. Then it will be true that France will no longer count a million of its men armed or manufacturing arms and munitions, inspecting and controlling all that pertains to war; but peace will have gained a million more workers. Then the glamorous company of our young idlers will no longer flutter around on our promenades or linger in our salons, but those who today live from the sweat of the old and the tears of the orphans will be making bread for the children and the old.

natural right, the nature of things calls men to freedom and not to the most cruel slavery to which misery condemns, or to the most unjust despotism, namely that founded merely on the accident of birth, without consideration of work, intelligence, or morality.

We must now justify this change from the standpoint of utility. But we repeat that we have adopted this division between right and utility only because of the prejudices of the day. We are assuming the approach of our adversaries in order to convince them of what they will call the practical value of our system; for without this value they would have been able to object that this system is based on right but has not been confirmed by utility; that feeling accepted it but reason rejected it; in short that it was a theory, a system, but not a realizable fact.

Let us therefore examine the value of the present organization of property from the viewpoint of utility, that is to say examine in what way it benefits material or industrial production.

Property, in the most customary sense of the word, is composed of wealth not intended for immediate consumption which today entitles the owner to an income. In this sense it includes land funds and capital: in the language of the economists, production funds.[1] For us land resources and capital, whatever they may be, are instruments of work. Owners and capitalists, two classes that cannot be distinguished in this sense, are the trustees of these instruments. Their function is to distribute them to the workers.* [2]

To what extent do the owners or capitalists fulfill this function, the only one they fulfill intelligently, cheaply, and to the advantage of increased industrial production? Seeing the relative abundance in which these men, whose number is considerable,

[1] Capital goods. Cf. B146.

* This distribution is undertaken by operations giving rise to interest, ground and property rent, and farm rent.

[2] "This is the first appearance of the word "function" in connection with the idea of property in the *Doctrine*. One could not imagine oneself assigning a part of the production funds without being socially responsible for their management. One is a functionary of industry, i.e. of production. Hence property is a function." (B147)

live, and weighing the large share granted them from the annual production, one must agree that they do not perform their services without a considerable charge. On the other hand, if the violent crises and the somber catastrophes that so often desolate industry are taken into consideration, it becomes evident that the distributors of the instruments of work show little intelligence in the exercise of their function. But it would be unjust to reproach them for this lack. For if one realizes that this distribution, if it is to be well performed, demands a deep understanding of the relations existing between production and consumption and a long acquaintance with the mechanism that turns the wheels of industry, it will be recognized how impossible it is for these conditions ever to be met by men who are given their function by the accident of birth, and who remain strangers to the work for which they furnish the instruments.

The following conditions are necessary if industry is to attain the maximum possible perfection: first, the instruments must be distributed according to the needs of each locality and each branch of industry; second, they must be distributed according to individual capacities so that they are put to work by the most capable men; and finally, production must be so organized that short supply or glut need not be feared in any of its branches.

In the present state of affairs, where the distribution is made by capitalists and owners, none of the conditions is either being or can be realized except after a large number of trial-and-error attempts, frequent blunders, and sad experiences. And even then the result that is obtained is always imperfect and momentary. Each individual is left to his own limited knowledge and no common view presides over production, which takes place without discrimination and foresight. At one point it is lacking, at another excessive. Industrial crises, about whose origin so many errors have been and still are being circulated daily, must be attributed to this lack of a general view of the needs of consumption and the resources of production. If so many disturbances and disorders are observed in this important branch of social activity, it is because the distribution of the instruments of

work is made by isolated individuals ignorant of the needs of
industry and of men, as well as of the means able to satisfy these
needs. The cause of the evil lies nowhere else.[3]

Indeed, how are things carried on today? A man thinks of
an industrial speculation. He makes every effort to call together
all the men of intelligence and all the documents in his reach
in order to assure himself that his undertaking is practical and
that he has a chance of success. But isolated as he is, he cannot

[3] "The year 1824 saw the first industrial crisis in France, similar to those
which England had experienced in 1816 and 1819. Sismondi published in
1826 the second edition of his *Nouveaux Principes d'Economie politique ou
de la Richesse dans ses rapports avec la Population,* preceded by a triumphant
preface. The facts verified his theory of 1819, founded on the English experience and on Robert Owen's theory. Big industry dumped on the market
products of common use, produced in great quantities, which consequently
only the working class could absorb. But the big industrialist's profit consists
in the difference between the net cost and the sale price of his products, and
since the net cost consists largely of the worker's pay, the big industrialist
can only sell at a profit if he pays his workers wages with which they cannot
buy all the products of their labor. There is therefore in modern society
chronic overproduction because of the very fact that it rests on paid workers.
Big industry can only solve the problem by something as major as the conquest of foreign markets where the rule of the wage workers and of big
industry are not yet established. The Saint-Simonians could have and
should have departed from this theory; they have read Sismondi and speak
of him with esteem. However, they ignore his theory of depressions and
explain them ultimately like James Mill and J. B. Say, by the bad distribution of products under the rule of competition. The difference lies in the
fact that they do not, like the latter, count on freedom to repair the evils of
which freedom is the cause; they want centralization in order systematically
to regulate production for the needs of consumption on the entire world
market. Cf. *Producteur,* I, 330, IV, 319 ff. . . . In other words, the Saint-
Simonians have two objections to the critical epochs: (1) Not having any
other historical function than to destroy the organic epochs immediately
preceding them in so far as they are bad, they present all the vices of
anarchic liberty themselves; (2) They retain a vice fundamental to all organic
epochs through which mankind has passed until now and are still based on
the 'military' principle of 'the exploitation of man by man.' But the Saint-
Simonians with their theory of crises seem to be attached to the first of these
two aspects exclusively. If they had made use of Sismondi they could have
taken the second into account. Is it necessary to conjecture that, being
fanatical about centralization, they defied a theory which had for a long time
been an indictment against industrial concentration?" B148.

"It was not possible for him (Enfantin) to become enthusiastic about a
theory which assigned no other purpose to the 'social power' than to slow
down the progress of wealth. . . . In the final analysis, the influence which
Sismondi exercised over the Saint-Simonians must be considered to have been
slight." B166.

have access to all the experts and documents needed. However favorable his individual position may be considered, it is impossible for him to evaluate rightly the expediency of his undertaking and to know, for example, whether at that moment others are not already busy answering the need which his undertaking is intended to satisfy. Let us now suppose that this speculation is really useful, and that the man who conceived it is the most competent person to direct it. What shall he do if the material means of performing the undertaking, without which his idea would remain sterile, are not at his disposal? How can he procure them? He should turn to the proprietors and capitalists, the owners of the instruments which he needs, and submit himself to their decision. But are these people, who are thus called to judge upon his project, competent judges? Can they derive from their relation with the workers sufficient insight to appraise the ability of the borrower and the advisability of the use of the capital he requires? Doubtless not. They are strangers to industry, and to the men who conceive, direct, and execute industrial work. They cannot therefore estimate the guarantees of morality and intelligence which the entrepreneur offers and the enterprise demands. They are reduced to stipulating certain material guarantees, the only ones they can evaluate.

Thus the choice of directors and heads of industry and the determination of industrial enterprises are left to chance.* The small number of men who can offer or promise material guarantees alone obtain capital, and these men find themselves immediately subject to supervision, to control by creditors and their blind, impotent, and troublesome policies; troublesome because they do not love work; blind because they do not know how to work; and impotent because they do not work.

But now let us look at a new world where there are no

---

* If we put the words "war" and "warlike" in place of "industry" and "industrialist," and if we said, for example, that there were no armies where the choice of the leaders and the determination of the enterprise were left to chance, no one would challenge us. But when we are dealing with industry it is a different story. Why? Because society has already its military but not yet its industrial organization. The question is then whether the social organization of the future will be peaceful. If this is answered affirmatively, then with a little logic anyone will reach the same conclusions as we.

longer owners, isolated capitalists, by their very habits strangers
to industrial work, who yet determine the selection of projects
and the destiny of the workers. A social institution is then
entrusted with these functions that are performed so poorly today. The institution is the trustee of all the instruments of production. It presides over all material exploitation, and therefore
is in a position to have a total view which permits it to see all
parts of the industrial workshop at once. Through its branches it
is in contact with every locality, with every kind of industry, and
with all the workers. It can therefore take into account general
and individual needs, and direct manpower and industry where
most needed. To be brief, it can regulate production, bring it
into harmony with consumption, and entrust the instruments of
production to the worthiest industrialists, for it can ceaselessly
make every effort to recognize their abilities and is in the best
position to develop them.

In this hypothetical new world everything appears differently. Moral and intellectual guarantees exist as well as material
ones. Work is done as well as the state of human society and of
the earth that man inhabits will permit. All men can hope to
become leaders and princes of industry. The possibilities of good
selections are multiplied and there are better ways of making
them. The disorders resulting from the lack of general agreement and from the blind distribution of the agents and instruments of production disappear, and with them also the misfortunes and the bankruptcies from which no peaceful worker
can feel safe today. In short, industry is organized, everything is
interlinked, and all is planned. The division of work is improved, and the combination of efforts becomes more powerful
every day.

We shall return to the mechanism of this institution presently. At this time it is important that we anticipate and refute
an objection which is bound to occur to you. No, only a few
people consider it possible today to subject industrial work and
the men that dedicate themselves to it to a complete and uniform
system, and those who believe it possible and useful can offer us
only antiquated and rightly condemned institutions for attaining
this goal. Those who consider such a thing impossible do so

because they imagine that there has been no attempt of this kind in the past; those who propose antiquated institutions do so because they have not understood the purpose of the various previous attempts. It is quite true that no attempt has been made to co-ordinate the efforts of men's material activity and the use of his powers? Does history not rather show that societies have ceaselessly tried to subject the works of this order to a common direction?

If one recalls that material activity was formerly exercised in war above all, and that peoples sought riches through conquest, and that the power with which man is endowed was deployed worthily and nobly only in combat, one will note that institutions in all past organic epochs had as their goal the organization of distribution of the instruments of work and of functions, which then consisted in arms, military posts, and ranks. These institutions direct the total efforts of these hierarchically classified barbaric workers towards the achievement of a common goal. Production through pillage and conquest, distribution of these products, consumption of the pillaged and conquered objects are regulated, to the extent which the ignorance and ferocity of the time allow, by a competent authority, for the leaders of the warrior people are skilled warriors. The government of ancient cities, the Germanic tribes, and the temporal power of the Middle Ages are in reality only unitary and more or less complete organizations of material activity.

In this respect the last organic period offers a valuable subject for observation in the works of those barbaric times before feudalism was firmly established. At that time there existed a spirit of individualism and of egoism similar to that dominating our industrialists today. The principle of competition, of liberty, reigned then not only among the warriors of different countries, but within the same country among the warriors of different provinces, cantons, towns, and castles. In our time, too, the principle of competition, of liberty, and of war exists among the merchants and manufacturers of the same country. It exists between province and province, between town and town, between factory and factory, and, we may add, between shop and shop. Feudalism put an end to military anarchy by binding dukes, counts, barons, and all independent proprietors and men of arms through reciprocal services and protection, an immense advantage that was never fully appreciated by any of the historians of the last century. It was indeed an immense advantage for all warriors to pass from the anarchy of the ninth century to the feudal association of the tenth, and this advantage can be explained only by the sudden conversion of freeholds into fiefs, an explanation from which even the genius of Montesquieu shied away. The owners of the freeholds were proprietors free from any public burden, dependent only on themselves, and consequently in a state of independence and antisocial isolation. These free owners, who were not bound to any service, due, or homage, nevertheless consented to becoming vassals of a lord, that is, to giving him their freehold and to receiving from him only the title to the fief or benefice. They consented because they found in protection and help by this suzerain lord a fair price for the services, the homage, in short, for all the new obligations which vassalage imposed upon them.*

The true reason for the general conversion of freeholds into fiefs was that men always prefer the state of society to the state of isolation, even if the former is called a state of independence, and that in the Middle Ages feudal government offered the best combination of material efforts and the best authority for directing military works, which were still the most important and the only ones considered noble.

Just as warlike work in the ninth century led to the formation of a society which had its hierarchy and leaders and which systematized completely all interests and duties, so today peaceful work is creating one society, having leaders, a hierarchy, an organization, and a common destiny.

Industry has already made a step towards this definitive or-

* Guizot, who has thoroughly understood that freehold property was antisocial, since it did not imply any bond between isolated leaders of society, and who was moved by the love for so-called freedom, has not understood the significance of this great event, the transformation of freeholds into fiefs. According to him, the great owners forced the small through violence to convert their freeholds into fiefs. Doubtless some stragglers in this extremely rapid movement were induced only by violence common in that epoch. But these examples are only exceptional cases rather than the common rule.

ganization since the time when peaceful work and peaceful workers began to assume real importance in society. Before the great political revolution of the last century, legislative provisions had as a goal the establishment of order within industry. An institution then existed which particularly impressed the minds of the men of those times, and which answered the need for union and association to the extent that the state of society then permitted it. We want to speak about the corporations. In this system the admission of every new entrepreneur presupposed that conditions had previously been filled, namely, that his ability had been recognized by competent judges, and that equally competent judges had ascertained the need for the employment of new hands and capital in the branch of industry to which he was intended to dedicate himself.

Certainly this organization was faulty in many ways. Limited to small localities, it was necessarily insufficient for regulating the totality of industrial work. In several aspects it was even vicious, since it had not been conceived altogether with regard to industry, but mainly as a defensive system against the military institutions, confronted by which and under whose yoke industry was rising. It bore the stamp of its origin and thus aided the struggle unleashed by selfish inclinations and antisocial attitudes. Each corporation was to other corporations what one baron had been to the other barons. There was war among them and within them as it had been formerly between count and count, castle and castle. These corporations developed antisocial tendencies, since all of them tended to exploit each branch of industry as a monopoly and to treat the consumer as the men of arms had treated the peasant. But all of these selfish inclinations came to the foreground with increasing force as the social doctrine in its religious or political, spiritual or temporal aspects failed to take peaceful industry into account and permitted most of the industrial system to escape from the judgments and influence of moral authority.*

* The clergy in obeying its dogma had to preach the mortification of the flesh and hence had to neglect or scorn industry. The nobility from its standpoint was lowering itself when allying itself with industry. Devotion and honor did not therefore bring their usual fruits of love and order to industry.

In spite of the defects of this institution, one cannot deny that it has rendered great services for several centuries, since the first organization of the communes. But in the course of time it took on a different character. Once the military class had stopped threatening the workers and their property directly, the institution of the corporation, as an institution, lost all defensive value. From that moment on, antisocial tendencies developed within it with ever growing intensity. Soon it offered more disadvantages than benefits. And at last it disappeared without one voice being raised to defend it.

We no doubt rightly congratulate ourselves on no longer seeing corporations, wardenships, and masterships governing industry. However, this achievement is hardly a positive one in the strict sense of the word.

A bad organization has been abolished but nothing has been constructed in its place. All the endeavors of the publicists and economists seem to have only one purpose, namely to bear down with a few last strokes upon an enemy who has already been knocked down and deprived of life.

We shall recall what we have just said concerning the anarchy which preceded the military organization of the Middle Ages. We noted that those principles of freedom and of unlimited competition, principles which always shape the dogmas of the epochs of transition and the belief of the critical moments of the life of society, have only a negative value; and as long as these principles prevail, no common view presides over material activity; no equilibrium, proportion, or harmony can exist between the various types of work; and finally, these works are as badly conceived and as badly executed as can be expected from an association in which the selection of the leaders is left to chance.

Let us look at the society surrounding us. Numerous crises and deplorable catastrophes afflict industry daily. A few minds are beginning to be impressed by this, but they can neither account for the cause of such great disorder nor realize that it is the result of the application of the principle of unlimited competition.

What indeed has competition achieved if not a murderous

war which in a new form is being perpetuated from individual to individual and from nation to nation? All the theories which this dogma tends to develop are necessarily based on sentiments of hostility. However, men are called upon not to war eternally but to live in peace, not to hurt but to help each other. Competition, in keeping all individual efforts in a state of isolation and struggle in respect to others, perverts individual as well as social morality.

From the moment when each believes that he can increase his chances for success only by diminishing those of his competitors, fraud will appear as the most efficient means of sustaining the struggle, and the conscientious men that shy away from using this means are usually the first to become its victims.

However, in the midst of the disorder we have just described, instinctive endeavors appear whose manifest purpose is to restore order by leading toward an organization of material work. Here we have in mind an industry which may be considered new if we take into account the particular character and the considerable development of the banking industry in recent times. The creation of this industry is evidently a first step toward order. Indeed what role are the bankers to play today? They serve as intermediaries between the workers, who are in need of the instruments of work, and the owners of these instruments who either cannot or do not want to use them. To a certain extent, they fulfill the function of distributors which we have seen so badly exercised by capitalists and owners. In the transactions of this nature that take place through the mediation of the bankers, the inconveniences we have pointed out are found to be greatly diminished, or at least to be easily diminishable. For the bankers, because of their knowledge and connections, are much more in a position to appraise the needs of industry and the ability of the industrialists than are idle and isolated individuals. The capital that passes through their hands is therefore at the same time put to greater and more equitable use.*

* It should be easily understood that despite the organic germs enclosed within the institution of the bank, which we shall uncover here, the advantage that might result from the intermediary position of the bankers between the idle and the workers is often counterbalanced and even destroyed by the facilities which our disorganized society offers to egoism to express

Still another advantage derives from their mediation. By the very fact that they can judge better the value of an enterprise and the merits of the entrepreneur, they can considerably reduce that part of the rent of the instruments of work which some economists call the insurance premium and which protects the capitalists against the accidents to which they expose themselves in lending their funds. Just as they have let themselves be paid for their own intervention, they can also procure instruments for the industrialists at much lower cost, that is to say at a lower interest than the owners and capitalists can who are more exposed to deception in their selection of borrowers. The bankers therefore contribute a great deal to facilitating industrial work and consequently to increasing wealth. Because of their intervention, the instruments of work circulate more easily, are less exposed to remaining idle, are offered more—to use the expression of the economists—a practice that results in a competition for workers on the part of the capitalists which, while not ideal, at least benefits the workers.

However, credit, bankers, and banks all constitute only the most unrefined rudiments of the industrial institution, the basis of which we are going to outline. The present organization of the banks reflects in part the vices of the system in which the owners of the instruments of work are at the same time the distributors of these instruments, that is, of a system in which the distributor is constantly induced to levy the heaviest tax possible on the products of work.* Moreover, if the position of the bankers permits them to evaluate the needs of some industrialists, and perhaps of an entire branch of industry more exactly, still no one

---

itself in various forms of fraud and charlatanism. The bankers often place themselves between the workers and the idle to exploit both to the detriment of society as a whole. We know this, and by showing what is antisocial in their acts and consequently retrogressive, as well as what is progressive, we indicate what must be destroyed but also what must rapidly develop.

* The debates which have been taking place for several years now at the Bank of France concerning the reduction of the discount rate, which has always been rejected, are a striking proof of what we have said. The very opposition which this institution, whose mission is to procure funds easily for the workers, has put up against any project for reducing the rate of annuities paid by the state is another no less indicative proof. The bankers then acted like the idle and not like the workers.

among them (not even a bank, since it is not the center where all industrial operations converge) can grasp the totality, evaluate the needs of each of the parts of the social workshop, activate its movement where it lags, and stop it or slow it down where it is no longer or not to the same extent necessary. We shall add that the greatest part of material activity escapes from their influence. This is true of agricultural works, which doubtless form the most important part of industry today, because of special legislation which still regulates landed property, and which bears the stamp of the dogma of immobility of ancient societies which was still the seal of civil society in the Middle Ages.[4]

It may also be observed that most of the properly called industrial transactions take place without the participation of the bankers. Finally, in granting credits the banks are primarily guided by material guarantees and to a large extent neglect considerations involving the ability of those to whom they extend credit, although these considerations are most important.

We do not claim to say that the general political circumstances under which we live must first be completely changed in order that the banks can be improved. For us politics is not that narrow sphere within which a few ephemeral petty personalities act. Politics without industry is a word void of meaning. But the best side of industry today is presented by the bankers and the banks. If political circumstances are to be changed, it becomes necessary to modify bankers and banks. On the other hand, improvements in the banks and in the social-industrial functions of the bankers are improvements of a political nature.

[4] "Saint-Simon (*L'Industrie*, Part II, *Oeuvres de Saint-Simon et d'Enfantin*, XX, 111) and O. Rodrigues (*Opinions littéraires, philosophiques et industrielles*, p. 196) had already presented this last objection to the system of banks as it functions under our eyes. But the first objection is new and marks the progress accomplished by the Saint-Simonians on the road to 'socialism' since the death of the master. It seemed then that by its spontaneous development, the institution of banks ought to be sufficient for the realization of the future 'industrial regime.' Now it seems that the banks have all the faults characteristic of our critical epoch: the banker himself is a capitalist who exploits the workers. He is subject to the anarchical law of competition which prevents the unification of the banking system. If these faults are to be eradicated, instinct has to be enlightened and directed by science and the Saint-Simonian doctrine has to make the 'general staff' of bankers aware of its 'function,' its 'social destiny.' " B156.

Consequently, improvements in this last realm could result from changes which the publicists of our day consider purely industrial and which for us would be a thousand times more important than most of the discussions occupying our best political minds today.

Hence the centralization of the most general banks and the most skillful bankers into a unitary and directing bank dominating them all, which can bring the needs for credit in all areas of industry into exact balance. On the other hand, there will be progressively increasing specialization by particular banks in such a way that each will be charged with the supervision, protection, and guidance of one type of industry. According to us, these are political facts of the greatest importance. Every act that results in centralizing the general banks, in making particular banks more specialized and in binding them together in a hierarchy will necessarily result in better harmony between the means of production and the needs of consumption. At the same time, this presupposes a more exact classification of workers and a more enlightened distribution of the instruments of industry, a more exact evaluation of the workers and a more equitable remuneration of work.*

The series of improvements which the banks can undergo directly through the unique influence of the bankers is nevertheless limited by the present state of things. The present-day system of banks can come very much closer to the social institution of which we are foreseeing the foundation. But this institution will be realized in its fullness only when the association of the workers will have been prepared by education and sanctioned by legislation. It will be realized completely only when the constitution of property will have undergone the changes we have announced.

We have pointed out the conditions necessary for the

---

* In an industrial society, conceived as such, one will always see a leader and inferiors, bosses and dependents, masters and apprentices. Everywhere *legitimate* authority exists because the leader is more capable; everywhere there is free obedience because the leader is loved; there is order everywhere. No worker lacks guidance and support in this vast workshop. All have instruments they know how to use, work they love to do. All work—no longer to exploit men, not even to exploit the globe—but to embellish the globe by their endeavors, and to adorn themselves with all the riches the globe can give them.

achievement of the highest degree of order and prosperity and the direction which the first progress of the banking system must take. It should be easy now to form a first idea of the social institution of the future which will govern all industries in the interest of all society, but especially in the interest of the peaceful and industrial workers. We shall label this institution for the time being as the "general system of banks," although we have reservations with regard to the narrow interpretation which this expression may be given today.

This system would comprise a central bank representing the government in the material order. This bank would be the depository of all the riches, of the total fund of production, and of all the instruments of work; in brief, of that which today composes the entire mass of individual properties.

On this central bank would depend banks of the second order which would be merely extensions of the first, by means of which the central bank would keep in touch with the principal localities to know their needs and productive power. The second order would command within the territorial area of their jurisdiction increasingly specialized banks which embrace a less extensive field, the weaker branches of the tree of industry.

All needs would converge in the superior banks; from them all endeavors would emanate. The general bank would grant credit to the localities, which is to say, transfer instruments of work to them only after having balanced and combined the various operations. And these credits would then be divided among the workers by the special banks, representing the different branches of industry.*

* If one reflects for a moment on the picture of the industrial government of a peaceful society which we have just drawn, it will be easy to see that from the industrial point of view, at least, the solution to the great question which occupies the publicists of today so intensely, namely communal and departmental organization, is given here. Today they all want to organize cities and provinces, but since none of them knows the purpose of cities, provinces, or nations, the reasons why men unite or what they should do, all their conceptions are powerless. Or, rather, they suppose an aim, namely resistance to power; a motive for union, namely resistance against power; at last a duty, namely, again, resistance against power; and thus by establishing everywhere revolt and nothing but revolt, they disorganize instead of organizing, instead of binding commune to prefecture and prefecture to administration, France to Europe and Europe to the earth, and

A question arises at this point which is quite secondary for us but of great importance today, since only on this plane do our statesmen concern themselves with industry and seem to perceive that there are men who produce the wealth which they themselves consume. We want to speak of taxes, or more generally speaking of what is called the budget, since the latter contains taxes among its receipts and uses them for its expenses. In the system of industrial organization which we have just presented, the assets of the budget are the totality of the annual products of industry. The liabilities consist of the distribution of all these products to the secondary banks, each one of which establishes its own budget in the same manner. That which under this system might properly be called taxation of the classes producing the wealth, that is to say on industry, would consist of that part of production dedicated to the support of the other two great social classes: that is, to providing for the physical needs of the men whose mission it is to develop the intelligence and sentiments of all. But for the moment we must concern ourselves with the particular budget of industry. Since each person is rewarded according to his function, what is now called income will no longer be anything but a salary or a retirement pension. An industrialist will no more possess a workshop, workers, and instruments than a colonel today possesses a barracks, soldiers, and weapons. But nevertheless all work ardently, for who produces can love glory and have honor as well as he who destroys.

Let us spend a moment retracing our steps. The industrial organization which we have just briefly described unites, on a broad scale, all the advantages of the corporations, of the wardenships and the masterships, and of all the legislative provisions by which the governments have tried to regulate industry up to this day. It presents none of their disadvantages. On the one hand, capital is brought where its necessity is recognized, for there can be no monopoly. On the other hand, it is at the disposal of the men most able to use it profitably. And the injustices, the acts of

---

even the earth to the Universe, they break, divide into fractions, divide the world and the earth down to the village, because they see only little sovereign individualities, satellites without planets, rising up against the universal law of attraction.

violence, and the egoistical inclinations with which the former privileged bodies, of which we just spoke, were reproached are no longer to be feared. Indeed, every industrial body is only a part, a member, so to speak, of the great social body which includes all men without exception. At the head of the social body are the general administrators whose function it is to assign each man to the place where he is most needed for his sake and for the sake of others. If one branch of industry is refused credit, it is because it has been found that the capital can be put to better use in the interest of all. If a man should not obtain the instruments of work for which he has asked, it is because the competent chiefs have recognized him as more qualified to fulfill another function. Doubtless error is inherent in human imperfection, but it must always be admitted that men of superior ability, in a position to have a general point of view free of the shackles of specialization, should be exposed to the least possible chance of error in the decisions with which they are entrusted. Their feelings, and even their personal desires, cause them to be directly interested in bringing maximum prosperity to industry and in providing each branch with as many instruments of work as the state of wealth and human activity allows.*

By pursuing the examination of banking, by concerning ourselves more particularly with the mechanism of the institution of industry, we would lose sight of the question of property, properly so called, and would be dealing with that of industry. Although these two questions may be nearly identical, we believe that the word "industry" refers to a large number of considerations of an altogether special character. With Saint-Simon the

* The general great objection to injustice, partiality, and arbitrariness on the part of the governing is always raised, no matter which part of the social order one examines. The answer may be reduced to these simple terms: (a) either all men are equal in morality, intelligence and activity; or (b) there are different degrees of morality, intelligence and activity. In the first case, there is evidently no place for hierarchy, power, or guidance; there are no inferiors or superiors, neither governed nor governors. In the second case, on the other hand, there is necessarily authority and obedience. But it is enough to open one's eyes to reject the first hypothesis. The whole question then consists in ascertaining who is to have authority, who will classify men according to their abilities, and who will appraise and reward their works. And our answer is that whatever circle of association one has in mind, it should be that person who has the destiny of society most at heart.

goal of the material activity of the human species has changed completely. In the future industry will assume a political importance more powerful than that which war ever held in the most bellicose ancient societies. We must, therefore, consider industry from this point of view. This will be our opportunity to present the general institution of the banks, which we have proclaimed as the future organization of the army of peaceful workers,[5] from a new angle.

But in order that our ideas on property be clearly understood, they must not be separated from those set forth previously concerning the development of mankind, the law of its development, and the promised future which we anticipate. This part of the social system cannot be judged outside the totality of ideas and facts by which it is justified.

Gentlemen, we are discussing a serious question. We must expect not only intellectual prejudice but strong, even if merely instinctive, resistance on the part of material interests, the only ones whose activity has remained vigorous to any extent. When we restricted ourselves to the sphere of abstract ideas, we exposed ourselves merely to the risk of being scorned. But on the ground on which we now stand, as we embrace at the same time the speculative idea and its application, theory, and practice in our exposition, we must fear that we provoke more than scorn. Doubtless we shall even be accused of aiming to overthrow society and of provoking disorder. However unfounded such a reproach would be, we cannot dispense with anticipating and answering it in general terms now.

The doctrine of Saint-Simon, like all new general doctrines, assuredly does not propose to preserve the existing order or to modify it superficially. Its object is to change profoundly and radically the system of feelings, ideas, and interests. But nevertheless, it has not come to overthrow society. The word "overthrow" always carries with it the idea of blind and brutal force which aims at and results in destruction. But these characteristics are far from Saint-Simon's doctrine. This doctrine neither advocates nor recognizes for the guidance of men any force other than persuasion and conviction. Its aim is to construct, not to

[5] Cf. the Introduction to this translation.

destroy. It always takes its stand with orders, harmony, and positive construction in mind, whether it produces a purely speculative idea or calls for the material realization of this idea. We want to repeat that the doctrine of Saint-Simon does not want to bring about an upheaval or a revolution. It comes to predict and to achieve a transformation, an evolution.[6] It brings the world a new education, a definitive regeneration.

It is true that to this day the great evolutions which have taken place within human society have had a different character. They have been violent because they found mankind unprepared and hence ready to throw itself enthusiastically into new directions without a clear consciousness of its destiny. Consequently, ignoring the endeavors it had to make to attain this destiny, mankind marched instinctively, without calling on reason to verify the visions of its enthusiasm, without reason paving the way for the changes for which these visions called. Thus all the great evolutions of the past, even the most legitimate, that is to say, those which have contributed most to the happiness of mankind, all seemed to have the characteristics of common catastrophe or upheavals at their beginning.

Today the situation is no longer the same: mankind knows that it has experienced progressive evolutions. It is acquainted with their nature and extent. It knows the law of these crises which have ceaselessly modified mankind and brought man ever nearer to the normal conditions of existence. Now man can, through the progress of the past, verify the future which his feelings show him. Above all, man can pave the way for the realization of this future through slow and successive transformation of the present. Mankind should therefore foresee and avoid disorders and violence which have been the conditions for all past progress.

It would be quite wrong for anyone to suppose that we intend to offer a sort of excuse for the boldness of our predictions. The view that today mankind, in its definitive evolution, should

⁶ Bouglé and Halévy believe that Bazard borrowed the term "evolution," as used here, from Ballanche's *Essais de palingénésie sociale* which had just appeared and which the Saint-Simonians were reading in 1829. Cf. B161; see index for references to Ballanche.

avoid the violence and disorders which have characterized the evolutions, and consequently the revolutions, of the past, was not suddenly invented by us in order to defend the doctrine of Saint-Simon against attack. It is one of the most elevated dogmas of the doctrine and one of the first rules of conduct our belief imposes on us. Consequently, it is a part of what we are trying to teach. Not to understand it means not to understand the thought of our master.

So when we announce a coming change in social organization, for example that the present constitution of property must yield to an altogether new constitution, we mean to say and to demonstrate that the passing from the one to the other cannot be brusque and violent but must be peaceful and gradual, because it can be conceived and prepared only by the simultaneous action of imagination and demonstration, of enthusiasm and reason. For it can be realized only by those men who are most animated by sentiments of peace, who love force when it produces and when it gives life, and leave to the past the force which destroys and spreads death.

Modern Theories of Property

Foreword

Gentlemen:

During the last three centuries, which saw the destruction of the social order of the Middle Ages, the most resolute defenders of papal government clearly realized that once religious unity and the political or military hierarchy were breached, the past they cherished was doomed. But their efforts were in vain; the nobility is dead and freedom of worship has been proclaimed. De Maistre, de Lamennais, and de Montlosier[1] have nobly expressed their regrets and their indignation. They have shown their contempt for this new society, devoid of authority and faith, delivered to indifference and anarchy, and living in memories of bygone days. But their dirges, drowned out by the shouts of the victors, have not touched the masses, or if they were heard, they have aroused anger and hate. Some individuals have responded warmly and have repeated their cries with conviction. But very few have been able to appreciate all that which was great and at the same time weak in the last sighs of the expiring Middle Ages.

The former feudal or military hierarchy no longer exists. Catholic unity has dissolved into individual beliefs, all equally respectable before the law, and this result of the persistent labors of our fathers finds large numbers of admirers today. So we no

---

[1] François Dominique Reynaud, Comte de Montlosier (1755-1838), a defender of the traditional aristocratic institutions, was during the Restoration period an ardent opponent of the Jesuits. Montlosier held the Revolution responsible for the success of ultramontanism through its destruction of the old aristocratic institutions. The Saint-Simonians here throw him together with the ultramontane de Maistre and Lamennais (see Introduction) under the assumption that, as the *Producteur* had already noted (III, 172), they all were "reactionary publicists." Cf. B164.

longer hear the publicists, with the approval of public opinion, propose a community of religious beliefs as the basis of the social order and try to strengthen it by a political cement analogous to that which united sovereign and serf in the Middle Ages. But this is not all. The public listens indulgently to the doctrines that tend to individualize beliefs or interests more and more. In short, egoism, expressed in political or religious terms, finds grace before it in whatever form it may appear. On the other hand, a devoted defender of throne and altar is regarded by the public as an enemy that must be fought, not because the altar is the chair of Saint Peter, and not because the throne is that of Caesar who rules by the sword, but because both must always create fear that one common belief and common actions may be imposed upon the masses by a few privileged men.

The critics of religious and political authority are generally well received today. If, on one hand, they hurt a few persons, as they undoubtedly do, on the other hand those whose curiosity they arouse and whom they amuse are numerous enough so that these critics, even if they are not encouraged excessively, are tolerated complacently and decorated with the honorable name of "opposition."

We shall not further develop these ideas, which are but indirectly connected with the goal we have in mind. The foregoing should suffice to prepare what remains to be said.

The complete abolition of slavery and the destruction of almost all privileges of birth have been carried to their conclusion. Mankind has broken the ties necessary to its childhood but harmful to its manhood. Mankind has shaken off the yoke of the past by force. It has broken it, but fortunately is still weighed down by the yoke—fortunately because mankind is not yet conscious of the new ties that are to unite it. We would see a distressing spectacle of extreme confusion and bloody anarchy if all the past means of order had been destroyed, and if there were not today a few such means of order left upon which the social structure, tottering to be sure, still maintains itself.

We have said that almost all privileges of birth have disappeared. Only one has remained, and the importance of the role it occupies in our disintegrating political situation shows the strength of the social constitution to which it owes its life. Let us congratulate ourselves on the inconsistency of the men who have preserved this anchor of health as a precious thing in the revolutionary storm. We saw that they were inconsistent because nothing in their theory makes legitimate such an exception in favor of the strongest support of the past.

This heritage of our fathers is surrounded by an aura of respect. It is the forbidden ground upon which even the hothead cannot tread without incurring excommunication by the very high priests of liberty. We are not speaking here of the thunder-bolts of the reactionary party which are ready to strike the sacrilegious hand that would dare to attack this last vestige of the Middle Ages. These bolts are spent and are not even forged any longer in the arsenals of the criminal police.

This truly religious susceptibility is doubtless miraculous when found among the enemies of superstition and fanaticism, among the apostles of the emancipation of thought, free inquiry, and doubt, but above all among the partisans of human perfecti-bility. And we congratulate ourselves on it, since it upholds a certain material order in the midst of the intellectual and moral anarchy into which we have been plunged. But when we have reached the moment when this means of order should be attacked by a doctrine destined to replace the one which gave it birth, we become aware of the obstacles which these retrogressive preju-dices, bequeathed to us by a hybrid civilization, present to the innovators who want to overthrow it—prejudices so obstinate that they resisted the fire of criticism and came out of the revolu-tionary crucible just as they had entered it. We are convinced of the imprudence of wanting to destroy the only principle of order that still remains without immediately replacing it by a wider principle, adapted to future needs. But at the same time we are aware of the strong resistance which even the wisest and most carefully considered endeavor, the one most clearly beneficial to the progress of mankind, will encounter, in this respect, as we enter with equally great confidence and devotion on the road Saint-Simon has opened.

We are not addressing ourselves to popular passions. How shall we make ourselves understood today? We call for order and proclaim the strongest and most unitary hierarchy for the future. The people need a different education than the one which they have been receiving from their masters (who march like slaves behind the people) if a powerful feeling of sympathy is to bind them to our ideas. The people have been taught to fear and despise force and ceaselessly to defy power as long as these words will recall their former slavery to them and make them weary and perhaps hostile toward those men who would proclaim a new power worthy of their love and devotion.

Our position will permit us to march ahead safely. Our frankness can be fatal only to us.

Yes, we have a firm conviction. We shall arouse the passions of the most violent adversaries of the past against ourselves by attacking a privilege which they do not hesitate to enjoy, although they have taken it from their vanquished enemy. The fate of Hercules, who was destroyed by the spoils of the Centaur, does not frighten them. They have attached themselves to the skeleton of the Middle Ages, to the corpse of their victim, and they will defend it like the ashes of a beloved until they themselves crumble into dust.

We already hear them say, while they are sharpening the cherished weapon of criticism: Well, what is this dress of the Centaur, what is the skeleton, the object of our tender love? And we shall answer: It is property by right of birth and not by right of ability. It is inheritance.

Opinions of the Economists, Jurists, and Publicists, and in General of all Political Theorists Concerning Property

Property is the foundation of the social order. This is the dogma proclaimed by all the doctors of political science. We, too, think that property is the material basis of the social order. However, our views on political organization are completely opposed to the doctrines professed in our day. The difference between us and our publicists on this subject is the same as that between them and the clerics of the Middle Ages, or between the latter and the Roman consuls. This great word "property" has represented something different at every epoch of history. It has resulted in diverse ideas, although it has been upheld by mores and laws wherever mankind was not troubled by general revolutions during which no time-hallowed right or interest was respected, and when new rights and interests became legitimate.

And thus, for example, the power to use and to abuse a man, his work, even his life—in short, slavery—has rightly been considered the foundation of Greek and Roman societies. Aristotle himself thundered forcefully against the extremists who would attack this sacred right. No one would consider calling this philosopher a barbarian when he advised the young citizens to go to war to hunt slaves. And Cato was not deceived—for he could read the future—when, weeping about the patriciate in the face of the proud freedmen, he mourned in advance for the old Republic. Similarly, the right of property in the Middle Ages, originally based on conquest, represented all the rights of the vassal in relation to the serfs and his duties to the suzerain. It consisted, moreover, in the power of transmitting through inheritance all the privileges or services attached to it. Respect for property was, therefore, in the eyes of the most enlightened men of the twelfth century, respect for feudal property in its purest sense.

No one believes that our publicists refer to slavery or serfdom when they speak of property. They must therefore base their proof of the importance of property on our modern societies and above all on the societies of the future rather than on the political constitution of the Roman Republic, the codes of the empire, or the legislation of our former monarchy. Undoubtedly they will find it in a new political theory, that is to say in a new way of looking at human needs and at the order most capable of satisfying them. Indeed, if the general needs of society were the same as formerly; if, for example, the people in a year of dearth would demand loudly that a barbaric province be handed over to them so that they might live from the spoils; if conquest were still the noblest way of acquiring power, one would necessarily have to draw the logical conclusion and praise slavery and war as did Aristotle, for the student of Plato was as great a logician as are our legislators and publicists.

What then is this new social doctrine from which our political theoretists deduce their ideas on the present constitution of property?

The Economists

It is difficult to find such a social doctrine among the economists. The majority of them, and above all Say (in whom nearly all the others are summed up), consider property as an existing fact, the origin, progress, and utility of which they do not examine.

They all speak of the necessity of maintaining the rights of property. But slavery and serfdom were also rights of property. Must Christianity be cursed because it did not respect them?

Sismondi, who has, to be sure, a very vague inkling of the future, and who because of this alone has placed himself in opposition to the principal organs of economic science on important points, has seen that different interests necessarily motivate the idle owner and the worker who puts the former's property to work.

After having indicated that the classification into owners, directors of works or tenant farmers, and finally journeymen is not indispensable to production, since these three qualities can be united into the same hands, he expresses himself in the following way: "The owners of land often imagine that a system of agriculture is good in direct proportion to their net income (that is to say, to the portion of the products of the land that remains after all the cultivation costs have been paid). However, what matters to the nation and should occupy the economists' attention is the gross product or the sum total of the harvest. The owner understands only the income of the idle rich; the economist understands also the income of 'all those who work.' " * If, instead of dealing only with the system of agriculture, Sismondi had applied these ideas to the entire political system, he would have formulated the most comprehensive and fruitful idea that an economist can advance about the social order. This very fearfulness and reserve always permitted him merely to touch the

---

* *Principes d'économie politique*, Book III, chap. 1, p. 153.

surface and prevented him from thoroughly examining the radical question of the idle and the workers. Thus the second chapter of his third book is entitled: "Of the Laws Intended to Perpetuate Landed Property in Families." It seems that by singling out "landed" property alone, Sismondi does not dare to attack property in its entirety. Yet he fights forcefully against the opinion of the legislators who always wanted to be able to keep in leisure what had been acquired through work.* His critique of substitutions, and of the majorats is remarkably vigorous in its logic, but, nevertheless, he did not understand that the different ways of transmitting property into idle hands are only particular cases of a general principle, namely inheritance. He passes over this immense question and his critique of substitutions really remains valueless because he does not go to the roots, that is to the spirit which has dictated all the laws pertaining to the transmission of property.

The works of the English economists are even further removed from any conception of social order. Malthus and Ricardo, it is true, finally arrive at a very important conclusion in their very thorough investigations of rent, namely that the differences in the quality or exploited lands make it possible for a part of the social products easily to be used for things other than the maintenance of the cultivator. But they conclude from this very simple, even if not yet clearly expressed truth, that the disposable part of the products was and should be used to nourish the noble owners in their idleness. In short, they justify as best they can the political organization in which one part of the population lives at the expense of the other part.

The speed with which these two writers concluded one of the most important principles of the social order from one datum of simple agricultural statistics would seem miraculous had it not been determined by the absense of a general social doctrine.

Rent and interest, that is to say the "rent of workshops and of instruments of work," constitute a part of the products of industry of which the worker can be deprived under duress: for some among them, the most wretched, to be sure, live on lands which yield no rent. When they were deprived of the rent in

* *Principes d'économie politique,* Book III, chap. 2, pp. 252 ff.

order to feed warriors, counts, barons, knights, and squires, nothing could have been better, since they needed warriors to work in peace without having to fear robbery by neighboring barbarians. But therefore to conclude that they ought to be condemned to this privation for the benefit of people who do nothing for them, who live in complete idleness, who distract them from their work by the example of this idleness, or rather by the demoralization which such a curse brings in its train, would be amazingly to abuse man's faculty of connecting ideas.

Besides, it is not our intention to discuss the opinions by means of which the present organization of property is defended. We merely want to establish that the men who have approached this great question have never linked it to a general view of the social order toward which mankind is moving, but have, on the contrary, received it in the form given it by the Middle Ages. Later we shall even show that they have taken away some of the color of property and have stripped it of all that constituted its grandeur and strength in the past.

The economists of the eighteenth century based their political system on the interest of the owners.* From their master's elevated point of view, the economists understood that their system would be of value only as long as the owners played another role than that of the idlers and rendered services which largely recompensed society for the sacrifices imposed upon it for their sake. But here their efforts were in vain. It was useless to preach to the rich idlers, and to try to persuade them to live on their properties and to direct their cultivation wisely, in short to become the first farmers of the state, opening model farms as does the Emperor of China. Their appeal did not go beyond the antechambers of the owners' palaces, did not trouble them at their splendid banquets or startle them out of their sleep.

Admittedly, however, a very vague feeling revealed to some of the enlightened philanthropists of the eighteenth century, as

* Say seems to share the love of Quesnay and his students for the owners when he says in Book I, chap. 4, p. 140, 4th edition: "Who does not know that no one knows better than the owner the profit which he can draw from his possession." If he had expressed himself like this about the tenant no one would have challenged him. But to say this about the owner!

for example to Necker,[2] that the following problem would be interesting to solve: How can the men who share the products of work with the worker not only justify their own share but also make the workers respect and love this division? No doctrine then recognized offered a solution, and the doctrines of the economists did so even to a lesser extent because they were concerned with the interests of the owners and not directly with those of the workers. Thus they had not advanced any idea concerning the successive modifications which the exercise of property right had undergone or concerning the obligations and benefits that should accompany it. They considered the right of property a perfect institution just as it was. In this respect they were less advanced than their successors and did not even strike the first blow against feudal privileges. Or at least, when some of them contributed to the destruction of these privileges, they were not obeying a general principle for the reorganization of property. One economist alone, doubtless the one most worthy of the respect and affection of mankind, namely Turgot, was aware of the faults of Quesnay's nomenclature, which designated owners and tillers by the same name: "productive classes." He created for the owners the name "available class," and justified this designation by saying that this class consisted of individuals who ought to be occupied with supplying the general needs of society.* Turgot thus foresaw the application which one day was to be made of Malthus's and Ricardo's rent theories. In other words he conceived of the best use to which could be put the excess product of the good lands over the bad lands, or the part of the social wealth available after the payment of all the costs of cultivation.

But the time had not yet come. The book of human destiny was closed even to Turgot. He did not know what the general needs of the new society would be and, consequently, what abil-

---

[2] A reference to Necker's work, *Sur la Législation et le Commerce du Grain* (1775), in which he takes issue with the laissez faire approach of the physiocratic school and sees in the power of the property-owning class the source of the suffering of the "most numerous and wretched class in society." Cf. B172.

* *Sur la formation et la distribution des richesses,* chap. XV.

ities the individuals composing this available class in charge of foreseeing and satisfying the needs of society should have.

This should suffice as far as the political economists' views of property are concerned. The jurists could have reversed the decrees of this science, and would only have been right in doing so, for at least the most recent economists, who alone have any authority today, were not afraid to explain that they consider themselves incompetent in political matters. Their modesty in this respect should be enough to make us stop looking in their writings for the principles of the social order according to which property as we see it today is instituted. They actually claim to show how wealth is created, distributed, and consumed.* It does not matter to them whether this wealth, created by work, is always distributed according to birth and consumed to a large extent by the idle. They are even indifferent as to whether the producer is a slave and the distributor a warrior, and which one of the two, master or slave, consumes the greater share of the products.

Either these problems seem to them to belong to an order higher than their science, in which case we must repeat our praise of their modesty; or they consider them of too little importance to merit their attention, and if this is the case, we should feel obliged to complain. In any case we should stop to examine their works in more detail for what they themselves did not feel obliged to put there. We have proved that our ideas on the political organization of property could not be attacked by their science. And that was all we intended when we occupied ourselves with the present state of economic doctrines.

Jurists and Publicists

We would be even more embarrassed if we had to find a single clear principle on this subject in our law codes. The *Code* says that the right of property is the right to enjoy things and to dispose of them in the most absolute manner, provided that no use be made of them that is prohibited by the laws and regulations.

* J. B. Say, *Traité d'économie politique,* "Discours préliminaire."

Two important points in this definition must be examined. First, it should be noted that our legislation recognizes the right to enjoy and to dispose of things but not of persons. That alone differentiates our laws from all past ones. Secondly, it should be observed that the definition of property, as vague and as negative as that accepted for liberty,* does not in any way indicate to what end the laws restricting this absolute right will be instituted. Consequently it offers no idea of the right of property, since these restrictions can be such that the right to enjoy and to dispose can be reduced to almost nothing, or on the other hand extended with practically no limit. And if, for example, no social function were necessarily attached to property, and the benefits, minus any burden, constituted the lot of the owner, should the laws then permit the transfer through inheritance of this magnificent privilege, namely the right to live abundantly in idleness? The definition we have cited above leaves this question open, for it can be applied equally to two societies, one of which would adopt the feudal principles of succession, which is to say inheritance by birth, and the other of which would regulate by laws the transfer of *workshops* and *instruments of industry*** to the hands of the individuals most fitted to use them, whatever their birth.

We shall be told that this principle is useless. Read the *Code* and you will find there all the restrictive laws on the absolute right to dispose of things. You will see there that a father can transfer his fortune to his idiot or immoral children, but that he is not permitted to deprive them of their legitimate hopes based on the event of his death.

It is undoubtedly a noble idea that honors the principle from which it springs. But it is foreign to the subject with which we are dealing at the moment. We are complaining neither about the conciseness nor the silence of the laws and the jurists. We merely seek to speak with men who know a large number of written lines by heart, and who are in doubt concerning the way in which these lines are connected, that is to say, about the

---

* Liberty is the right to do everything not forbidden by the law.
** These words comprehend for us the same idea as the division of goods into movable and landed property.

principle that dictated them. But in order to apply this to the definition of property, we must know on what general principle are based the exceptions which are imposed on the right of property by the legislator, or in other words, what principle guided him when he drew up the rules for the exercise of this right. In short, we must know the "why" of all these isolated laws.

It must be admitted that we are in an unfavorable position to attack the *Code,* since revisions in our laws are demanded daily. We must therefore seek the reason and spirit of the property laws elsewhere. These words indicate sufficiently which book we should open: that of Montesquieu. Here we ask forgiveness of all our romantic jurists, who no longer bow down before the master's name. We know that a great many of them see in the *Spirit of the Laws* a beautiful literary monument and nothing more. We, who were not brought up in social science by the illustrious president,[3] nor by Sieyès,[4] Delorme,[5] or even Bentham, view this work differently. Montesquieu, we believe, has made the profoundest criticism possible in the eighteenth century of all the social organization of the past. But our admiration for this great man, whose work has served as the basis for all the publicists who prepared or directly provoked our revolution, cannot prevent us from recognizing that there exists no passage in the *Spirit of the Laws* in which property is treated as a general principle of social order.

Montesquieu, however, while approaching the system of feudal laws respectfully and digging deep to find, as he himself said, the roots of the ancient oak whose foliage spread so far that its trunk was perceived only with difficulty, sensed that he was contemplating a great event that occurred once in the world, and which had built a new society upon the ruins of antiquity. Everything had to be created there. "These Teutons, who ac-

[3] Montesquieu held the judicial position of *président à mortier* in the Bordeau *parlement.*

[4] Emmanuel Joseph Sieyès, the Abbé Sieyès (1748-1836), revolutionary statesman and author of the famous pamphlet, *Qu'est-ce que c'est le Tiers-Etat?* (What is the Third Estate?) published in 1789.

[5] Jean Louis Delolme had glorified English institutions in his work, *De la constitution de l'Angleterre,* published in 1771.

cording to Caesar* had neither lands nor boundaries of their
own, among whom the princes and magistrates gave to the individuals shares of land which they desired, and obliged them
the following year to go elsewhere" were soon to know freeholds,
and then fiefs. How were these great institutions established?
Why was this new order which these institutions consolidated
preferred to the variable, personal, and nontransferable distribution of property? Finally, for what purpose, in the end, was not
only the inheritance of functions but also that of the privileges
of wealth accepted, in other words, the inheritance of benefits
resulting from services which formed the appanage of these functions?

These roots Montesquieu should have sought to uncover.
But they were too deeply buried in the ground. Unaware and
preoccupied with the state of the society in which he lived, he did
not feel compelled to find the basis for a new organization. It
was left for his successors to sense the need for a complete revolution. To them he left the task of summing up his work, of putting in order the scattered materials he had extracted from the
mines of history, and finally of bringing about a formidable
union of all the weapons which they had forged and which soon
were to destroy the colossus of the Middle Ages.

Rousseau undertook this task.[6] In the *Social Contract* he

* *Esprit des Lois,* Book XXX, chap. 3; Caesar, *De bello Gallico,* Book V.

[6] "This homage to Rousseau, who is presented as superior to Montesquieu,
is new in the history of Saint-Simonian thought. For Saint-Simon and his
immediate disciples, J. J. Rousseau represented that type of Jacobin egalitarianism which was the very expression of metaphysical and critical
philosophy. . . . In the text of tne *Doctrine,* the respective positions of
Montesquieu and Rousseau are almost reversed: Montesquieu is presented as
too little preoccupied with 'reorganizing' economic society through the
suppression of hereditary property, while to J. J. Rousseau is attributed the
honor of having at least perceived the problem. Rousseau is, of course,
reproached with still having remained too 'critical,' and of having restricted
himself to denouncing the 'thieves' without demanding their systematic ex-
propriation. Buonarotti's work about the Conspiracy of Babeuf suggested no
doubt to Bazard and to Enfantin the idea of his rehabilitation of Rousseau.
If they rejected the egalitarian, communistic consequences of Babeuf's and
Buonarotti's philosophy, they could not help being struck by their critique
of hereditary property." B178.

Filippo Buonarotti, who in 1828 published the *Conspiration de Babeuf,*
had collaborated with Babeuf in the unsuccessful communist insurrection
during the Revolution.

intended to take care of an omission of Montesquieu. It was to serve as the prolegomena or as the concluding remarks of the *Spirit of the Laws,* and was to lay down the general principles of the constitution of all peoples according to the climates which they inhabited or the state of demoralization to which the progress of civilization had led them. When we recall in these terms the philosophic views by which he was guided and which he himself expressed so eloquently,* it would seem to us that the *Social Contract* should contain at least some vigorous apostrophes against that part of the social contract which Rousseau, in another work, sums up, thus: "You need me because I am rich and you are poor. Let us therefore make an agreement. I shall permit you the honor of serving me on the condition that you give me the little that remains for you in exchange for the trouble I take in commanding you." **

Indeed, inquiry in this direction leads nowhere. A single little note at the end of chapter nine of Book I shows us the broadest idea which Rousseau ever conceived of the division of property. He expressed it thus: "The laws are always useful to those who possess and harmful to those who have nothing, whence it follows that the social state is beneficial to men only as long as they all have something and none among them has anything in excess." ***

But did Rousseau apply this idea and investigate which political organization would best fulfill this condition? No, his *Social Contact* says nothing about it.

A small change in this note might have put him on the right road. If, instead of writing that the laws are always useful to those who possess, he had said: The laws are always useful to

---

* "Oh, Man! From whatever country you may be, and whatever may be your beliefs, harken. Here is your story . . . I feel that there is an age when the individual man would like to cease being. You will seek an age when you will want your species to cease. Discontent with your present state for reasons that proclaim to your unhappy posterity even greater discontent, you would perhaps want to retrogress, and this sentiment must incur the praise of your ancestors, the criticism of your contemporaries, and the terror of those who will have the misfortune of living after you." (*Discours sur l'origine et les fondements de l'inégalité parmi les hommes.*)

** "De l'Economie politique," an article inserted in the *Encyclopédie.*
*** *The Social Contract.*

those who make them, he could have added as a conclusion: Therefore, when the laws are made by and for the men who do nothing, they are harmful to those who work. And then he might have continued that if the workers made the laws, they would not establish property in the same manner and to the same end as the idle. But property was an institution born in the progress of civilization. Rousseau should not have condemned property without even seeking to perfect it. We do not want to be accused of ascribing to him sentiments that were not his. He made his position clear in this famous phrase: "The first man who, having fenced in a piece of land, took it into his head to say, 'This belongs to me,' and found people simple-minded enough to believe him, was the true founder of civil society. From how many wars, crimes, murders, miseries, and horrors would he have spared the human race who, tearing down the stakes and filling the dividing ditches, had shouted to his fellow-men: 'Beware of listening to this impostor! You are lost if you forget that the fruits belong to all and the land to none!' "

It would be very easy for us to prove with a large number of quotations that Rousseau hated the institution of property and the advantages which it procured for the idle, whom in *Emile* he very bluntly called thieves. But we are not afraid to say that it is impossible to find in all his work one phrase pointing to recognition of a means for distributing this land common to all in a manner useful to society.

The second-rate writers who have trudged along in the footsteps of Montesquieu and of the Genevan misanthrope have only commented on their masters and paraphrased them. They have attacked the structure of the past in detail and demolished it piece by piece, and when their task was fully completed in 1793, they showed the world their inability to build on new foundations.

When reading the *Encyclopédie,* that powerful crowbar of the critical philosophy, one should expect to find there some revolutionary ideas concerning property, that is, of the destructive principles of its old constitution. Far from this, the jurist who has edited the articles on this subject defends it ardently. But against whom? Against the partisans of the community of

goods, understanding thereby equal division. He ridicules Plato,
More, and Campanella. He does not resolve the dilemma: either
property as it exists is beneficial, or the community of goods is
preferable. As if one merely had to choose, as if there were only
two ways of conceiving the distribution of the instruments of
work.

Grotius and Puffendorf[7] could not fail to appear in such
articles. The editor thinks, as they do, that property is the result
of a social convention, but he does not examine any more than
they whether this convention is susceptible to improvement or
not, and whether it is the same in all epochs of civilization. That,
however, was the chief problem, for society was at the threshold
of a great revolution. The new conventions by which society
might consolidate its regeneration had to be prepared.

At last the great man to apply the political theories of the
eighteenth century appeared. Mirabeau had only to blow at the
past to make it disappear. But he did not go any further than
his masters, and even on his deathbed he respected inheritance.*
However, did the lightning of his eloquence in striking at the
privileges of families not also fall upon the privileges of society?
"Why," he said, "do you dedicate these privileged families to
idleness and licentiousness—which are often the same thing—
whose members often because of their fortune believe themselves
made exclusively for pleasure? Why do you have to prevent
several marriages that could be happy only to benefit one which
often merely flatters one person's vain pride? Why do you
destine several children of a family to celibacy, while letting one
of them devour the means of establishing all the others?" **

If the thinkers had not been preoccupied with the need for

---

[7] Samuel Baron von Puffendorf (1632-1694), the first professor in Germany
of the law of nature and the law of nations.

* This is what Mirabeau said in the speech read after his death by
Talleyrand on April 5, 1791: "There is nothing to prevent one, if one so
desires, from looking upon goods as rightfully returning at the death of their
owner to the public domain and then in fact being returned by the general
will to what we shall call the legitimate heir. . . . Society has felt that to
transfer the goods of a deceased outside his family would mean to deprive
that family, and that there is in this neither reason, justice, nor propriety."

** By substituting the word "society" for "family," one would have an
equally strong and valid criticism of the institution of property by birth.

destroying the inequality of privileges by birth, it would have been easy to recognize in Mirabeau's words a manifest condemnation of the principle of inheritance, which, according to him, is reasonable, just, and proper. Does not inheritance give birth to a class of men created merely for pleasure? Does not inheritance make a few privileged children of great families devour wealth which, if better divided, would serve to establish all?

Mirabeau's concern for the men who are forcibly condemned to celibacy recalls the efforts made by some economists (Malthus and Sismondi, for example)[8] to prove to creatures unfortunate by birth that they were not born to taste the sweet pleasures of family life. These writers make a case in defense of present day property which could be used to uphold the most inhumane institutions. They say: The present division of property condemns the proletarian (what barbarous derision this word implies!) to misery if he marries. Therefore, he should live in the world isolated, without a companion to share his suffering and without children who would teach him what hope is and bind him to a future.

When it proclaimed the right of primogeniture, the Middle Ages at least compensated those who had been disinherited with the richest portion for which a loving soul could long. It dedicated the purest and most indissoluble union when it consecrated disinherited virgins to the Church, and opened pious and peaceful retreats to the young sons of a baron, while the heir of his name won glory on the battlefield. It offered an unlimited future and an infinite hope to the cherished children of God and the Church. We shall furthermore say that it made them look without envy, with scorn and often horror, at this always greedy and almost always bloody worldly glory for which the privileged feudal nobility shed blood.

What do these men do today for the wretched proletarians disinherited for the benefit of the first born of the great and

[8] The linking of Malthus and Sismondi seems strange at first. "But there is indeed in Malthus—and even in Ricardo—an element of pessimism which brings him close to Sismondi. And Sismondi defines in Malthusian terms the evil created by the lack of harmony between population and total available wages." B186.

condemned by them to celibacy? Nothing. Misery, isolation, despair, and death are their destiny and future. But this is not yet all. Do Malthus and his students not prove that charity should refuse misery help and shelter?

Let us now leave the icy atmosphere of the economists and return to Mirabeau.

The famous discussion on property which took place in the National Assembly offers a large number of examples of contradictions similar to the one we pointed out. It should not be astonishing to find them among revolutionary or critical minds, since the principle which guided them was that of leveling and equality, a principle contradictory to human organization. But it is the role of the great epochs of disorder which we have called "critical" to bring confusion into all the minds, even those who most strongly uphold the disappearing social order.

Let us listen to the most brilliant and ardent defender of the past as he gives vent to his disdain and scorn for the ignorance of the inexperienced legislators of 1791:

"There is not one peasant," Cazalès[9] exclaimed, "who cannot teach you what you do not know. I mean the principle according to which he who has not cultivated does not have the right to harvest the fruits! Far from having its beginning in the feudal system, this principle is founded on the idea that property is based on work, a principle much too just and wise to be known by your committees." [10]

And what conclusion did Cazalès desire from this great principle? How did he apply it to the constitution of property? What laws did he demand for the regulation of its transfer? Roman law. With what purpose did this orator arrive at this great wise and just principle according to which he who has not cultivated does not have the right to harvest the fruits? He wanted to show that daughters did not have the right to inherit. But he did not consider that his principle, much more general than the particular case under discussion, barred from the division of wealth any man who was incapable of making it bear

---

[9] Jacques Antoine Marie de Cazalès (1758-1805), opponent of the Revolution in the Estates General.

[10] A very loose quotation. See B188.

fruit through his work, and divided this wealth among the workers alone, and only according to their ability, independently of their birth.

The inorganic reconstructions attempted by our first deliberating assemblies crumbled year after year. The champions of equality were always vexed by summits and ceaselessly strove to level them. Soon there appeared the absurd projects for the agrarian law and for equality of wealth. It must be said to their authors' credit that they were the most powerful logicians of their time. They carried the principle of the critical philosophy which had leveled all earlier social superiority to its logical conclusion. Once the social differences had been swept away, absolute equality was a logical deduction, since there was no theory which provided the means of instituting new ones.

We express ourselves altogether frankly on this subject. Having listened so often to dreams of equality, we understand how natural it is to think that when someone proposes a change in the constitution of property, he will end up by advocating the agrarian law. And although even a superficial examination suffices to show that Saint-Simon's doctrine cannot give rise to such absurdity, we believe it useful to reject it whenever an occasion arises.

Being tired of the efforts of the levelers in the Constituent Assembly, France soon fell back upon Roman law and feudal institutions. But we shall not dwell on this involuntary return to the past. Fortunately today it has come to be said that the imperial regime was merely a renewal of the old regime. Our publicists already look upon this epoch as a step backward which was necessary, however, to escape the revolutionary turmoil and to enter into the secure harbor of constitutional government.

We need now only to examine the doctrines of the liberal publicists on the constitution of property and there is little for us to do here. We do not know one work which investigated how property was to be organized to facilitate the wheels of the constitutional mechanism, that is, which went back to the principle of order that could make this last privilege of birth legitimate today. Nevertheless property plays a great role in our political life. In order to be worthy of representing the interests of

industry or to advocate successfully a good system of legislation
or public education better than that given by the Jesuits, one
must possess a considerable fief. To assist our judges, lest they
deceive themselves or deceive us, one must have at least a manor.
But we understand perfectly that in the Middle Ages, for example, when the true representatives of the nation were asked
only to give the best sword strokes, they were sought in the
castles and the manors, for there the good swordsmen were to be
found. Is the situation similar today? Is the criterion of wealth
in choosing political leaders really legitimate? We are merely
expressing doubt, and we think that we shall find among our
opponents many who try to prove to us that the idle owners are
excellent directors of a society of workers and that with a few
Jesuits less the Golden Age can be realized. But we congratulate
ourselves for having provoked this demonstration. At least an
attempt will have been made to justify one of our most important
institutions. As is desired of all sections of our law codes,
legislation relating to property will have been put in harmony
with the spirit of the *Charte*. Then we shall be able to say that
we know the principles on which the social utility of present
property is based within a constitutional system. Finally we shall
know that the transfer of property by birth, which was so natural
in the realm of feudalism, and whose consequence and mainstay
it was, is an institution suitable to a society which claims to have
triumphed over feudalism.

Without fearing to bare our ignorance, we declare that we
have not yet found anything of this kind in the numerous writings on legislation and politics which have been published during
the past fifteen years.

The work of the great English jurist who attempted to bring
all laws under the head of one principle will certainly be
brought to our attention. We are too great admirers of Bentham
to pass over his work in silence. He realized that it was only
through their utility that institutions could be legitimized, and
this realization was a great step, but it was not great enough. He
merely put the difficulty off, because what is meant by social
utility must still be explained. And indeed it will be realized, as
we have already said, that slavery was useful even for the slave,

when one considers that it replaced the barbarous destruction of the vanquished, even cannibalism.* Must slavery therefore be re-established?

Bentham believed that he had made the most valuable discovery when he said that the general principle of all laws was utility. We did not see that all societies in their most vigorous state appear to the citizens to be ruled by a legislation which is in perfect harmony with their needs, or in other words, that this legislation appears to the people as well as to their leaders to be the most useful conception of the social order and inspires the highest degree of love and devotion in all citizens. It would seem, when reading Bentham, that the legislators of the past amused themselves by making laws which they judged to be indifferent or useless. To say that the general principle of the laws ought to be utility is only to express in misleading words that now there exist a large number of useless and harmful laws that are no longer in harmony with the society moved by new needs and tired of the customs and sentiments for which these laws were made.

"Utility," says Bentham, "is . . . the tendency of a thing to preserve from some evil or to procure some good." What then is good and evil? What is pain and pleasure? Bentham answers: "It is not necessary to consult Plato nor Aristotle. *Pain* and *pleasure* are what everybody feels to be such—the peasant and the prince, the unlearned as well as the philosopher." These are the definitions which the English jurist gives us.[11] But a few lines later he takes it upon himself to avenge Aristotle and Plato for scournful frivolity with which he has just pronounced their great names. "If the partisan of the *principle of utility* finds in the common list of virtues an action from which there results more pain than pleasure . . . he will not suffer himself to be imposed upon by the general error," and so forth. Thus the opinion of the peasant and of the ignorant person regarding good and evil can be corrected. But those partisans of utility who are

* Saint Augustine confirms this fact in the *City of God* by the etymology of *servus, servare*. History moreover lets us easily verify this fact.

[11] *The Theory of Legislation* (New York: Harcourt, Brace & Co., 1931), pp. 2 f.

first to discover that a thing is harmful which has been thought of as useful until then are doubtless not ordinary men. They are the princes of the vast kingdom of the intellect; they are the Socrates', the Platos, and the Aristotles. Above all they are truly divine men who with their blood sign a new code of morals destined to regenerate the feelings of all humanity.

Has Bentham made comparable discoveries? The limits to which we must confine ourselves exempt us from investigating whether, indeed, this jurist has pointed out new pleasures, new pains, vices, and virtues unknown to the past. We shall limit ourselves to examining the application to property which he made of the principle of utility.

One example will suffice.

How shall an individual's wealth be distributed after his death? Bentham replies:

"In framing a law of succession, the legislator ought to have three objects in view: 1st, Provision for the subsistence of the rising generation; 2nd, Prevention of disappointment; 3rd, The equalization of fortunes." [12]

It is difficult for us to understand why the pains of "disappointment" appear in this catalogue. If a man expects an inheritance it is because the legislation of the realm in which he lives promises it to him. But it is a question here of drawing up legislation and defining its bases. Will legislation promise an inheritance to an immoral, selfish, incapable, idle man merely because he is another man's son? This is the whole question. Perhaps these words will be understood to mean that since the new legislation will annihilate hopes based on earlier legislation, it will be necessary to take this into consideration and to use a system of indemnities for persons whose reactionary hopes have been deceived. Indeed, nothing conforms better with the need for order. This procedure, however, is only for the sake of prudence and may retard the final adoption of a law but cannot modify it in its aim and principle.

The two other articles seem, however, fundamental and are directly applicable to the specific question of property. Well, we ask, is there in their wording the slightest indication that the

[12] *Ibid.*, p. 177.

children or relatives, of whatever degree of closeness, shall be the heirs? Does to provide for the subsistence of the next generation and to bring about the equalization of fortunes mean that a certain millionaire is to leave his whole fortune or the greatest part of it to his only son and the numerous children of the poor man are to enter the world even more miserable than their father was when he left it?

These are general assumptions, Bentham says. What! You assume that the children of a rich man experienced more difficulties of every sort than the sons of the poor man in finding their subsistence! Do you forget that the former are in a position to receive an education for which the latter have neither the money nor the time? Either education is not the most important prerequisite for well-being, or the rich give their children a poor education. But these two hypotheses stem from the same cause. Education is of no use when property is constituted in such a way that it can usually be acquired without work. And the rich give their children a poor education when the latter learn at an early age that with the gold of their fathers they will one day know everything without ever having learned anything.

But this assumption about subsistence is still more of a conjecture than the other. Indeed, if the legislator should have the equalization of fortunes in mind when dealing with inheritance, why does he let the wealth pass to the relatives of the rich and not distribute most of it among the children of the poor?

This discussion should prove to us sufficiently that Bentham himself, when trying to establish one of the general principles of legislation, could not defend himself against the influence of words. When speaking of inheritance he could not distinguish it from the peculiar meaning it has in our modern societies.

To succeed to, to inherit is, however, merely to replace. But whoever replaces a man who is occupied with a certain type of work should satisfy certain conditions of ability. To succeed a property owner, it is enough to be his next of kin. If the great partisan of the principle of utility had perceived this difference and had examined whence it springs, he would have seen that it resulted from the fact that an owner does not necessarily have to be able to do something. Then he would doubtless have defied

the general error. He would have torn that page of the common
catalogue of useful things to pieces, and would have declared his
prejudices on inheritance to have been vicious. For a man who
is fed in abundance, although he does not know how to do anything, must be harmfully superfluous in the eyes of a utilitarian.

The most elevated minds do not escape such errors when,
while fighting against an outworn political system, they are not
yet aware of the system that should replace it.

Thus Destutt de Tracy[13] is astonished* at what has constantly been taught as the process by which property came about.
"It seems," he says, "that according to certain philosophers and
legislators at one certain moment one conceived spontaneously
and without any cause of saying 'mine' and 'thine.' " If Destutt
de Tracy had recalled that one no longer says "my" slave, he
would be convinced that the processes undergone by the posses-
sive pronouns are not always purely philosophic diversions.
Moreover, those words "mine" and "thine" do not in any way
bias the question of inheritance. Why will the object which
today is "mine" be "thine" one day? Or why is that object
"mine"? Is it because my work has produced it or because my
father has made or stolen it?

De Tracy understood quite well that these questions deserved solutions. This is one solution he gave:** "One of the
consequences of individual properties is that if the owner does
not dispose of it at his will after his death, which is to say*** at
a time when he no longer has a will, the law determines in a
general way to whom it should pass after him, and it is natural
that it should be to his kin. Thus inheriting becomes a way of

[13] Antoine Louis Claude, Comte Destutt de Tracy (1754-1836), a disciple
of Condillac and one of the main Ideologue philosophers who went beyond
the school's merely theoretical concern that physics and physiology must be
the basis of the moral sciences to attempt to provide the classical economy
with a correct theory of value. Hayek credits him with having anticipated
by half a century the subjective or marginal theory of value. (*The Counter-
Revolution of Science*, p. 115.)

* *Economie politique*, chap. 3, Introduction.

** *Economie politique*, chap. 7, "Distribution des richesses."

*** We want to call attention to this "which is to say," because it is a
positivistic scholar that is speaking, a scholar who knows death and will,
and who is quite sure that the latter ceases when the former occurs.

acquiring, and what is more, or rather worse, a means of acquiring without work."

This phrase in its last part is, as can be seen, a rather distinct criticism of inheritance. A natural thing that produces an obviously bad result may be called a disease of mankind, a necessary ill, or as J. B. Say terms it when speaking of governments, one of those inevitable ulcers. But is this malady incurable? Is it really bound up, as de Tracy thinks, with human nature? We do not think so; and indeed to heal it, it should be sufficient to determine through law in a general way that the use of a workshop or instrument of industry always passes after the death or retirement of the man who used it into the hands of the man most able to replace the deceased. This would be as rational for civilized societies as succession through birthright seemed to barbaric societies.

Summary

We have shown that the economists, the jurists, and in general all political theorists have not produced one new idea which could serve either to justify the feudal transfer of property through birthright in our modern societies, so very different in every respect from those studied in history, or to reorganize property on a foundation corresponding to the present and future needs of mankind. It is important that we call attention to this fact while at the same time enunciating the views of the Saint-Simonian school on property. In this way we wish to put our listeners on guard against objections that may occur to them and that they may believe to have been suggested by doctrines more advanced than those that governed feudal society or the peoples among whom there was slavery. They are mistaken; the doctrines are the same. Our philosophers and publicists are still living in the past.

When we fight against property by right of conquest or birth, we struggle against antiquity and the Middle Ages on the side of the property of the future, that is, the property which will be made legitimate by ability alone and will be acquired by peaceful work and not by war and fraudulence, by personal

merit and not by birth. The new property right will be transfer-
able, but only as knowledge is transferred. It will be worthy of
respect and respected. For then antisocial customs and passions
will meet only with shame and misery while opulence and glory
will accompany work, devotion, and genius.

NINTH SESSION (April 22, 1829)

Education

Gentlemen:

We have just presented you with the most general views of the Saint-Simonian School on the transformation which property is to undergo and on the future organization of industrial work. We are far from having exhausted the subject and shall familiarize you with further developments.

But we believe that for the moment the best way to make you understand these developments most easily is to continue the exposition of our master's doctrine on other equally important points.

We have already said that the ideas pertaining to the future of property cannot be separated from the totality to which they belong. When this totality is presented, it will be easy for everyone to grasp these ideas and to complete them where necessary. We shall have an opportunity to return to them.

Today we shall deal with a new subject—education.

While devoting ourselves to the examination of this great social fact, we shall indirectly answer some of the objections addressed to us concerning property, namely those which do not question the justice and utility of an institution through which the workshops and instruments of work would be entrusted to those most capable of putting them to work, but are concerned merely with difficulties which the realization of these changes (that is, the radical transformation of the present social order from the economic point of view) would present. All these objections obviously stem from the difficulty of conceiving means by which the public may be made familiar with the social organization recognized as just and useful by the most moral and enlightened men most interested in the growth of society's wealth.

But education will furnish these means as it has always done in
the organic epochs of mankind.

In the widest meaning of the word, "education" must signify
the sum total of efforts undertaken for the adaptation of each
new generation to the particular social order into which it is
placed by the march of mankind.[1]

We have said that the society of the future will be composed
of artists, scientists, and industrialists. There will, therefore, be
three types of education; or rather, education will be divided into
three branches. One type will have the purpose of developing
"sympathy," the source of the fine arts; the second the "rational
faculty," the instrument of science; and the third "material
activity," the instrument of industry.

Society presents the triple aspect of the fine arts, science, and
industry only because the individuals composing it each possess
these three faculties and by the predominant development of one
become artists, scientists, or industrialists. Each individual, whatever his special inclination, is nonetheless always in love and
always endowed with intelligence and engaged in material
activity. Therefore everyone will be given instruction in all three
areas, from his childhood until his classification into one of the
three great divisions of the social body. And each of these divisions of the active generation will continue its moral, intellectual,
and physical education in accordance with its particular purpose.

Thus education of the nascent generation in the three
branches and the continuation of the active generation's triple
education in each of the three great divisions will be the principle that will serve as the basis for the future organization of
education.

At this moment we cannot take this principle as the point
of departure for our exposition without suddenly disrupting the
chain of ideas which your minds must follow to pass progressively from the present state of things to the future one and to
pass beyond the sphere of emotion, ideas, and interests amidst
which we live so that we may enter those which Saint-Simon has

---

[1] "The sociological tendency of this definition becomes clear if one compares it with the classical definitions, for example Kant's: 'The goal of education is to develop in each individual all the perfection of which he is
capable.'" B199.

outlined for the future society. We first must find the provisional language best suited to facilitate the understanding of the views we have to present on this important subject with which we are dealing.

Before doing so thoroughly, and indeed to hasten the time when this will be necessary, we shall examine education in terms familiar to you.

From this point of view, one of the two purposes of education is the initiation of individuals into society, the inculcation into individuals of sympathy and love for all, the union of all wills in one sole will, and the direction of all efforts toward one common goal, the goal of society. This may be called general or moral education.

The second purpose of education is the transmission to individuals of special knowledge needed to accomplish the various kinds of sympathetic or poetic, intellectual or scientific, material or industrial work to which they are called by the needs of society and by their own ability. This may be called special or professional education.*

Today attention is given only to this last branch. It is the only one which one usually has in mind when speaking of education. We shall have to show, however, in this limited field that the dominant ideas of today are false and incomplete. But first we shall deal with moral education.

Moral education is almost entirely neglected. It holds no place in the discussion in which the public takes an interest. There is immediately vigorous opposition whenever any intentions of reorganizing it become known. But this opposition does not spring from the fact that the existing attempts at reform are not adapted to social needs, but rather from an absolute prejudice against the very thought of systematizing and reorganizing moral education.

This opposition is easily explained. Every system of moral ideas presupposes that the aim of the society is loved, known,

* It can already be seen that we consider one of the greatest crimes against society to be the attempt to constrain individual inclinations. This constraint is inevitable, no matter how great one's love for liberty may be, when the highest social dogma does not urge classification according to abilities and remuneration according to works.

and concisely defined. But this aim is a mystery today, and it is not even believed possible for man to know his social destiny with certainty. There is general agreement that physical facts are interwoven, but this interlinking is not admitted in the human sphere. Facts concerning man, even the most general ones, are considered dependent upon chance and subject to fortunate or unfortunate accidents, but always to accidents and consequently to causes foreign to the sphere of predictability.

This belief does not always manifest itself in quite so explicit a form. From time to time we even observe political theories emerging, and it seems that the formulation of a theory is incompatible with the belief in complete disorder among social events. But if we take the trouble to go back to the source of these theories, and study their orientation, we shall always find the belief in social disorder which we have pointed out. Thus among present day political theorists, some boldly profess that history is a vast chaos where it is impossible to discover any law, harmony, or interlinking, while others think that every epoch of civilization has been subject to a law,[2] but that these laws, as numerous as the different people who covered or are covering the globe, have no common bond. They do not take into account the general progress of human society. If a few of the clearest minds seek revelation of what the future has in store in the advances accomplished up to this day, they come to the conclusion that systematization, organization, and regulation of moral education are retrogressions toward the most backward state of society: the barbarism of the Middle Ages or of Oriental despotism.[3] Hence we no longer need be astonished at today's indifference about moral education and the very terror which any attempt to systematize it causes. Having been convinced that it is impossible to foresee the future of society, one naturally is not concerned with prescribing a definite direction. And if one considers that it is widely believed that the men who have until now directed the masses have always hurt their development, one

[2] "Probable allusion to Guizot's course at the Sorbonne from 1828 to 1830 on the 'History of Civilization.'" B202.

[3] "An allusion to a passage from Benjamin Constant's *De la liberté des Anciens comparée à celle des Modernes.*" B203.

will understand that it is natural to reject guidance of this nature with horror since it, indeed, appears only as egoistical, ignorant, and brutal despotism.

If one should ask, however, whether man has duties to fulfill toward his fellow-man and toward the society of which he is a member, whether his personal position does not impose any particular duties upon him, like those toward his family or his profession, doubtless only a few people would hesitate to answer in the affirmative. But then ask how man is to acquire the knowledge of these duties, how to develop his love and determination for fulfillment. Ask our theorists, publicists, and philosophers, and they will answer you, according to the nuances distinguishing them, that the best rule of conduct for each individual in the various circumstances in which he is called upon to act is always clearly indicated by the very nature of the circumstances. Moreover, the equilibrium in which the individual forces directed toward a common goal, the improvement of their particular condition, work out among themselves ought to suffice in most cases to force each one to restrict his actions to proper limits. Finally they will answer that legislation can restrain those not kept otherwise within these limits.

It is worth noting that the men who refer to legislation in this way do not concern themselves with the origin of the legislator and his mandate. It is no less astonishing that they concede, on the one hand, that the legislators should be permitted to lead society into certain channels, negatively at least through legislation which corrects socially dangerous deviations. On the other hand, they are not inclined to admit that it is permissible to direct society through education.

Others will answer that every man is able by means of his individual reason to recognize his duties, and that the commands of his conscience constitute a sufficient sanction for the commands of his reason and a powerful enough motive to determine him always to act in accordance with justice and truth. It seems to them that man need only be put materially into contact with society to be able with the help of his reason, his conscience, and his liberty to embrace it immediately in its totality and in its details and to understand all the obligations it imposes upon

him. Moreover, he can feel in himself the desire, the will, and
the power to carry them out. They finally come down to claiming that the understanding and evaluation of the most complicated facts require the least education and apprenticeship.
Actually they require the most extensive knowledge, sustained
attention, and a rare disposition of heart and mind which permits
man to go beyond the limits of his individuality and place himself in the sphere of society and of all mankind.

We shall observe, furthermore, that these different opinions
that have been professed exclusively by the partisans of liberty
necessarily resulted in the introduction of violence as the only
means of establishing order in society. This consequence, directly
deduced from the belief that leaves regulations of each one's
action to the antagonism of individual forces and repressive
legislation, stems just as much from the second belief, which
considers individual reason and conscience as the only legitimate
sources of social morality. Since individuals are evidently incapable of spontaneously conceiving the general order of societies
and the duties resulting for each of its members, penal legislation, that is to say force and violence, is consequently the only
way to keep them in check.

We may determine the real value of these two beliefs, for
they have been applied in almost all possible ways. Indeed,
except for a few greatly weakened moral habits which are growing weaker each day, namely those which society owes to the
teaching of the Catholic Church but which today are transmitted
only mechanically, the only means of maintaining order are those
that result from the equilibrium of individual forces and, in
cases where disorder is too flagrant, from the sanction of the law
by fines, prison, and the hangman! But these means evidently
have only a negative value. They can sometimes prevent evil, but
only in a very restricted sphere. But they certainly cannot bring
about good.

However, while the old moral rule—the catechism—as well
as the old institutions—the sermon and the confession—by which
morality penetrated the minds, are being passionately and furi-
ously attacked, some philosophers are trying hard to find criteria

by which men's deeds might be judged. All their efforts have led only to the morality of enlightened self-interest. But for this principle to be considered efficacious, supposing it to be true, the moralists who established and preached it should have foreseen every situation in which man is called upon to act and should have indicated the conduct prescribed in each case by enlightened self-interest. The book containing all possible new cases involving matters of conscience should have been the law, the preacher, the confessor—in short, the guide of everyone into whose hands it would have been put. But in general, remarks were confined to such statements as: Understand your interest well, and all will be for the best. That would mean to presume that each individual was able and better able than anyone else to understand fully the relationship of his acts to the general interest, which is evidently absurd.

Will it be said that some men have gone further, that Volney and other writers have drawn up catechisms? We do not anticipate such arguments. The idols of the last century and even of the beginning of the present no longer are looked up to by the enlightened minds. And as for the masses, their common sense has dealt justly with these digressions from science.

The moral system of enlightened self-interest is the negation of all social morality, since it assumes that man's actions can and ought to be determined only by purely individual considerations or inspirations, never by the impulses of social sympathies; always by cold calculation, which is fortunately impossible most of the time, never by the irresistible ardor of men more moral than himself. Even admitting that this system can exert a real influence, this influence is limited to preventing men from hurting each other. But this is not man's only obligation. Men should help each other because their destinies are interwoven, because they are joint partners in each other's sufferings and joys, and because they cannot advance in the ways of love, science, and power except by ceaselessly widening this solidarity.

Moral education is completely neglected today, even by the men who are most deeply loved and most highly esteemed by the public. And it is remarkable that the defenders of the reaction-

ary doctrines seem to be the only ones who understand its importance.[4] Certainly they are mistaken about the ideas to be
taught and the sentiments to be developed, and in this respect
opposition to them is legitimate. But on the question itself, of
the necessity of a system of moral education, they show themselves to be infinitely superior to the more popular minds.

This part of education which is so very much neglected
today is, however, the most important. For if one should consider separately for just one moment that type of education
which regulates social relations and which presides over the de-
vision of labor, that is over the development of individual abilities, namely, general education, and compare it with special or
professional education, one will quickly be convinced that effects
in the former entail much more serious consequences than would
gaps in the latter. And, indeed, the sum of specialized knowledge can be preserved and even perfected without direct or regular instruction. It is transmitted, so to say, from individual to
individual, without any order or planning, to be sure, but after
all it is preserved and even grows. Thus we can explain the
progress achieved in our time in this type of knowledge, however
defective the institution given the responsibility of developing
it may be, even when all social foresight in this regard is lacking. It is not the same with the general or generous sentiments.
("General" and "generous" are synonymous in this case.) As soon
as moral education is first lacking, social ties are loosened and
soon break. Then mankind not only slows down or stops in its
forward march but to a certain extent turns backward, which is
to say regresses from social life to mere family life, and from
family life to savagery and the most debasing egoism. In these
critical moments man, no longer understanding devotion, calls
it folly, mysticism, weakness, and absurdity. Every generous feeling in his soul is extinguished, and yet he still works ardently
and passionately. But what is the goal of this work? Do the
industrialists and scholars exhaust themselves through hard work
and long hours so that mankind need no longer suffer from misery and ignorance? No, only to enrich and enlighten themselves,

---

[4] "De Bonald did not separate administration from education." B212.

to satisfy physical and intellectual appetites of a purely egoistical nature.

Our desire to recall man to the fullness of his existence and to the total dignity of his being alone should suffice to make us first of all deal with the reorganization of moral education. But this must necessarily also be done from the point of view of specialized work, for if each profession is to function according to the demands of any social order, all individuals must assent to this social order. In other words, the social rule must be formulated and taught in a systematic and orderly manner.

We shall add another consideration, which in itself seems to condemn sufficiently the indifference, and even repugnance, with which today all attempts at systematizing moral education are met today.

Laws regulate only that which has not been regulated by education. And indeed, how can the necessity for coercive action be conceived except as a triumph over resistance by the will? But the object of education is exactly to place the feelings, calculations, and deeds of each in harmony with social demands. The intervention of law hence becomes necessary only when there is a gap or a lack of intensity in moral instruction.

Doubtless there will always exist abnormal organizations opposing the influence of education, no matter how perfect it may be. At all times there will be men whose personalities will revolt against the generally adopted order, however favorable this order may be for the development of all. But fortunately these are only exceptions—otherwise, society would not be possible—very rare exceptions even in critical periods when they should be the most frequent, since neither is general order then known or loved nor does it influence individual deeds, for society knows no goal and its members no duties. The highest stage of perfection to be attained through the development of education would consist in reducing the need for coercive legislation to the cases of sinister abnormality only. Mankind ceaselessly converges on this goal. In proportion to its progressive development, moral education has become more direct and precise and has embraced more cases by reducing them to more distinct principles, and legislation as a coercive force has at the same time lost proportionally in importance and decreased in violence.

To oppose the organization of moral education today would mean to make society turn backward, since this would grant physical force a role which it is losing, a role which it had to play while there were warriors in the land and two societies in every society, namely masters and slaves. But it cannot keep this role, since mankind is called upon to form one family and to develop its strength only in a peaceful direction.

TENTH SESSION (May 6, 1829)

General or Moral Education

Gentlemen:

We have made it our task to make you understand the importance of moral education and to make you realize that it should be the object of a social plan and of a political function. We have shown how in this respect its progress is linked to the general emancipation of mankind. And finally we have proved that present day opinions which reject all systematization of this type of education necessarily lead to man's loss of dignity. We must yet explain our views on the nature, scope, and method of moral education.

The word "education" usually calls to mind the upbringing of children. Since this first epoch of life is, indeed, a preparation for the following ones, ideas on education relate to it particularly. Education, however, and especially that type of education with which we are dealing, is not limited to childhood. It should accompany man throughout the course of his life. If one considers that man's action is indeed determined at each stage of his life by desire and influenced by his sympathies, one recognizes how important it is to extend social foresight to all that is able to awaken and to develop within him sympathies in conformity with the goal that society has set for itself. And if man is susceptible all his life to benefiting from moral instruction, society ought to make sure that he never lacks this instruction.

Nothing can take the place of education during youth. Once thrown into active life, man no longer has the moral flexibility necessary for the assimilation of the culture he lacks, although he has twice as much need for it. Since his desires must be translated into action, the result is that when they are not directed toward the good, that is to say toward social progress, but are left alone, they lead to evil, namely egoism. Thus, lack of education must almost always be understood as education for evil, and someone whose early education has been neglected not only has to learn but also to unlearn. Only a very small number of privileged persons exist who, sustained and animated by the thought that they have a mission to fulfill, can triumph over an inferior early education.

It is true that history presents examples of entire generations somehow suddenly transported from one moral sphere to another. But first of all, these changes are never as abrupt as they seem at first sight. When we look closer, we shall always find that they have been in the making for a long time prior to the moment when they suddenly manifested themselves. It will then be seen that they appeared at first only in the most general order of feelings, ideas, and interests, and that it was only much later and by stages that they succeeded in invading the sphere of deeds and thoughts and secondary affections. Thus we also see that generations which supposedly were suddenly converted were for a long time unable to bring about completely the state of society for which the newly professed principles called. The peoples that were subject to the Roman Empire for several centuries had been prepared by the works of the philosophers to receive the word of the apostles, but nevertheless they remained more pagan than Christian for several centuries after the preaching of the Gospels, which they recognized as law. There was no truly Christian society until the guardians of the new doctrine could take hold of a man at birth, free him from the attitudes and customs of the old social order, and inculcate in him attitudes, ideas, and customs in conformity with the new social order.

The education of youth is doubtless the most important but it is not sufficient. If these impressions are not reinforced and renewed in later active life, they soon pass into a state of vague memories. Before long they are entirely wiped out by numerous considerations about one's individual position, which absorb a person's whole attention and monopolize his whole activity. Moreover, if the person should reflect on the moral precepts he was taught, he may conclude that he understands neither their suitability, purpose, nor utility, and he may consider them to be in conflict with the things which impress him and which he considers necessary. In order that early educational impressions retain their influence, they must constantly be reproduced. In other words, moral education must be extended through the individual's entire life.

The more civilization has progressed, the more moral education has increased in vision and extended the duration of its impact on the individual's life.

In antiquity each citizen—the numerous class of the slaves is, of course, not included under this heading—called upon to discuss the interests of the community in the forum and to take part in the enterprises undertaken in the public interest found himself in a position high enough to perceive the relationship between his personal acts and the general interests. But this awareness did not dispense with the early education that revealed to him the society of which he was a member. Without any doubt, the precepts of this education could have remained firmly impressed upon his mind even without the help of a special institution established for that purpose. And yet, look at the pomp of the Olympic games, the mysteries, the religious ceremonies, the numerous class of priests, sybils, and augurers. Everywhere a living instruction in the destiny of society awakened devotion and enthusiasm.

This situation has changed. Peoples are no longer confined to the interior of a city and no longer have room in a public place where the common interests can be debated by all. The division of labor, one of the essential conditions of the progress of civilization, which restricted individuals to increasingly more limited circles, also increasingly removed them from the direct consideration of general interests, and this at the time when these interests were becoming more difficult to grasp because of increasingly complicated social relations. As the division of labor became more extensive, it was necessary to put more emphasis on intensive and orderly moral education in order to realize the advantages which specialized education brought. In this way alone could man regain the general outlook which he had lost through the specialization of labor.

Moreover, more care has to be taken to see to it that the

impressions of early education are preserved and incessantly strengthened during the individual's life by outward, direct, and systematic action.

But if the division of work immediately resulted in narrowing the sphere of individual occupation, it also permitted privileged organizations to devote themselves more exclusively to the contemplation of general facts, and, through their action upon other men, to return with large dividends the same advantages to society which can be attributed to the confusion of all types of work in the hands of each.

We shall now examine which faculty makes man receptive to moral education and which faculty should dominate among those who are called upon to direct this education.

The philosophers, when comparing modern and ancient times, do not hesitate to ascribe superiority to the former and generally see it in the ever growing predominance of reason over feeling. They consider feeling as an attribute of mankind's childhood and reason as that of manhood. This opinion might perhaps have a semblance of accuracy if it were limited to explaining the progress made through the progressively felt separation of these two manifestations of human activity, which is to say through the direct application of each of them to the order of work with which each is particularly connected. This opinion would be accurate if its object were to point out disadvantages resulting from the confusion which, as we have said above, existed at the beginning of societies between poetry and science. But if, on the other hand, one perceives the decline of feeling in this useful division of labor, mankind is unduly mutilated. It suffices to hear the daily defense of reason and the violent attacks against feeling to be assured that such is the general opinion in our days. With what affected scorn they ridicule all that comes from that sublime source, love! How naively they imagine that an idea or an enterprise can be totally disproven or discredited by merely labelling it as "pure feeling"! Inspiration, which is to say genius, it seems, is the evil principle of our nature, and all our efforts must attempt to rid us of this formidable enemy. And this procedure, unfortunately, usually succeeds.

This opinion is doubtless not always expressed so frankly, but it is at the basis of all the systems which claim to be part of mankind's progress. When seeing us take up the defense of feeling against reason, one may be wrongly led to believe that we intend to apologize for spiritualism at the expense of materialism. These two opinions, when confronted, fight each other with the same weapon—reason. Neither of them knows what love is. Both analyze, divide, and break spirit or matter into their smallest form or tiniest molecule. Both reduce to dust the field they cross. Both carry death everywhere; neither of them shall have life.

Let us come back to reason's claim of superiority over feeling. Evidently this opinion must necessarily exert a great influence on the way the subject with which we are dealing is understood. From this point of view, indeed, the special, if not exclusive purpose of education appears to be the cultivation of man's rational or scientific faculty. It aims at enabling each individual to acquire for himself, by proof, the dogmas of social science, and to act only after having maturely calculated the consequences of an act for himself as well as for society as a whole. It is held that everyone would then be sheltered from the surprises and illusions of his sentiments and mainly from the influence of men who have the power to move him. And the belief that such a pitiful result is being achieved is a general source of gratification.

We need not now characterize those two great manners of being and of existence, reason and feeling, or describe the different forms in which the world and man appear to man himself and according to which he proceeds in his investigations in a rational or a sentimental way. This interesting analysis will always concern us. We shall be satisfied for the moment to expound dogmatically those ideas of the doctrine, which are particularly bound up with this problem.

The rational faculty does not become perfect in the development of mankind at the expense of the faculty of feeling. Both develop in equal proportion. If the rational faculty seems to dominate today, this shows only that there exists among us as little association and as little union as is possible among men joined in society. It should be easy to realize this situation fully if the characteristics we have assigned to the critical epochs are recalled.

Man lives and is sociable through feeling. Feeling binds us to the world and to man and to all which surrounds us. When this bond is broken, when the world and man seem to reject us, when the affection attracting us toward them is weakened and annihilated, life ceases for us. Without those sympathies that unite man with his fellow-men and that make him suffer their sorrows, enjoy their joys, and live their lives, it would be impossible to see in societies anything but aggregations of individuals without bonds, having no motive for their actions but the impulses of egoism.

Feeling makes man inquire about his destiny, and feeling first reveals the answer to him. Then doubtless science has an important role to fulfill. It is called upon to verify these inspirations, revelations, and divinations of feeling, and to furnish man with the insights to make him move rapidly and securely toward the goal discovered for him. But it is again feeling which, by making him desire and love this goal, can alone give him the will and the necessary strength to attain it.

Despite this great role which, contrary to general opinion, we assign to feeling, we are most assuredly far from wanting to curb or deprecate the efforts by which the present generation attempts to advance on the road of reason. If one wants to go back to our first sessions, one will recall that far from considering our century as having passed the limits of rational growth, we think rather that it has remained within limits. In this respect our age still has immense progress to make and in spite of its claims, it shows itself to be very much inferior to several centuries that precede it if its numerous elements are considered. If one returns to what we have said about the positive method, its value, the way it is to be used, and the use we ourselves have made of it in the study of the great phenomena of mankind's collective life, one will be convinced that we attach no slight importance to rational procedures, and we do not show ourselves to be less rigorous in applying them than those men whose work is regarded today as the most positivistic—namely as the product of the purest rationalism.[1]

But this should give us at least a right to repeat that man's total moral existence is not confined to the rational faculty, that he has other means of knowing than the positive method, and other sources of faith and conviction than scientific demonstrations; for as we have already said, all science presupposes axioms.

The general scholars—and from the point of view of our doctrine, we mean the trustees of the science of mankind, namely social physiology—these scholars can doubtless deduce the future from observation of the past and point out, with the aid of indications given them by the new conception and with the help of the method which it teaches them to use, at what stage the series of already achieved deeds will end. One can also easily recognize their ability to determine through continued investigation of secondary facts or through logical reasoning the social combination best adapted to the goal revealed to them by sympathy, consequently, also, their ability to describe the individual's obligations in terms of this proper place in the social hierarchy. But this place can only be assigned by love, which is to say by the men who are most strongly animated by the desire of improving the fate of mankind. And moreover, although one may attribute this ability to science, is there any reason to conclude that science ought to preside over moral education? However little one may reflect about this, one will realize science's powerlessness in fulfilling such a mission. This mission is beyond it.

And indeed, for the precepts of science to contain an obliga-

[1] "In the later development of philosophic thought in the nineteenth century, 'positivism' and 'rationalism' were often contrasted: rationalism laying down a priori principles based on reason; positivism subjecting facts to observation and thus coming closer to empiricism. Auguste Comte would not have accepted this juxtaposition; he spoke indifferently in the *Discours sur l'Esprit positif* of 'rational study' and 'positive method' (1908 ed., p. 38). He wants 'positivism' to become 'rational' (p. 70). And it is he whom the authors of the *Doctrine* criticize at this point. In fact, one wonders if this whole passage is not an answer to the first lesson of the *Cours de Philosophie positive* by Auguste Comte in competition with which the Saint-Simonians presented the doctrine of their master. In this lesson Auguste Comte no longer even ascribed to imagination an important although subordinate function, that of 'arousing the passions of the masses.' He absolutely neglected the role of feeling." B221.

tion to act, one must suppose that through demonstrations these precepts become the work and the creation of those who hold them. But such a demonstration would demand a perfect acquaintance with social science on the part of everyone. Yet supposing that all men were able to acquire it, they would still have to dedicate to this end all the time intended for special education which they need in order to fulfill their functions within society satisfactorily. This is evidently impossible.

The results of social science can be presented to almost all men only in a dogmatic form. Only the small number of those who devote their whole life to its study can prove these problems to themselves. These men are also the only ones of whom one may suppose that they will under all circumstances be guided by the precepts of science. But this is clearly only a supposition. Indeed, scientific demonstration can well justify the logical suitability of such and such an act but is insufficient to establish it. To do so, it would be necessary for scientific demonstrations to make us love these acts, and that is not the role of science. A demonstration does not contain within itself any necessary reason for action. Science, as we have just said, can indicate the means to be used in attaining a certain goal. But why one goal rather than another? Why not remain stationary? Why not even retrogress? Feeling, that is, strong sympathy for the discovered goal, alone can cut through this difficulty.

For the individual willing to restrict himself to a prescribed circle, it is not enough that the goal of the society and the means of attaining it are known to him. It is necessary that this goal and these means are objects of love and desire for him. The scholars can doubtless verify them and say what must be loved if one is not to go contrary to the march of civilization as indicated by the interlinking of historic facts. But they are unable to produce the feelings the need for which they recognize.

This mission belongs to another class of men, to those whom nature has particularly endowed with a capacity for sympathy. We most certainly do not claim that the men who are to be given the responsibility of leading society should remain strangers to science, but science takes on a new character in their hands. It is imbued with the life and sanction which only those men can give it who relate science to the destiny of mankind.

To convince ourselves of the preceding, we need only investigate what men and what means have always determined social volition and action and from what source the individual has always derived the satisfaction that follows the fulfillment of one's duties. One will find that the direction of society has at all times and in all places belonged to the men who have spoken to the heart; that the constructions of reason and syllogisms have always been only secondary and indirect means; and finally, that society has never been directly stirred onward except by the various expressions of feeling.

These expressions of feeling, called "cult" in organic epochs or "fine arts" in critical epochs, always result in arousing the desire for conformity with the goal that society sets itself in proving the actions necessary for progress. In this respect no difference is found between one state of society and another, organic or critical, except in the nature of the feelings that the cult or the fine arts are called upon to develop and the duties which they demand. In all these respects, the Middle Ages show themselves superior to the earlier times. Here we should speak of a means of education and of moral discipline peculiar to that epoch which we mentioned in the preceding session. We mean confession, which in recent times has been the object of unanimous censure. It has been viewed only as a means of seduction and espionage, as a practice put to use by the clergy to support ambitions and satisfy individual passions. This judgment was a logical consequence of the condemnation of Catholic doctrine in its entirety.

Since this doctrine has come to be considered a fraud, used as a sanction for a despotism for the profit of the few, evidently all that could have contributed to strengthening and propagating it, particularly confession, which is so effective in achieving this result, should have been rejected with mistrust and disgust. But if, from another point of view, Catholicism, that is Christianity as a social institution, is considered to have been at the time of its greatest power the moral doctrine best adapted to society's needs, it will be recognized that the institutions intended to make these needs penetrate men's minds were most eminently useful and moral as long as the doctrine itself remained in harmony with the needs of mankind. It was only when this harmony ceased that confession, except for the exaggerations that accompany every reaction, deserved the reproaches directed against it today. But at the time when the doctrine was at its peak and confession was one of its principal means of action, confession ought to be viewed only as a form of consultation by which less moral and less enlightened men came to look for insight and strength, which they lacked, from those superior to them in intelligence and morality. It was also a means employed by the latter to awaken and sustain the social and individual sympathies which they were to develop and direct. And if one reflects about the virtue of rehabilitation inherent in confession, one cannot help recognizing in it a moral power and an educational means of the highest order. While the sermon and the catechism, which were addressed to all, could only deal with general cases and were calculated for the intelligence and feelings of the average person, confession served as a commentary, made decisions in the many individual cases, and thus adapted the doctrine to each person's intelligence and sensitivity. No procedure so powerful in continuing and sustaining the first impressions of education was used by the ancients.

We have said that moral education was to teach through feeling, and that the guidance of this education should belong to the men with the greatest capacity for feeling. We may affirm that this is the first condition of any association; for no society exists where there is not a desired goal and where the collected individuals are not led, guided, and incited onward by those men who most ardently strive to attain the goal. This condition will be realized in the future as it was everywhere in the past. This does not mean that the same practices, and the same forms should be perpetuated, or that the catechism and the cult, which formerly passionately stirred the hearts of the faithful, should be kept. Nor should the form of consultation and rehabilitation known under the name *confession* remain the same. We merely wish to say that analogous but more perfect means should be put to use in the future to prolong the education of man during the entire course of his life.

Several questions are bound to be asked at this point. First of all, we shall be told that after having shown the importance of moral education and the need for conceiving its action in political and social terms and having defined the limits within which it ought to act and the faculties it ought to set in action, we must point out the practices, the ideas, and the sentiments that are to be the object of its instruction. For us, gentlemen, these practices, ideas, and sentiments result from the views we have already presented on the future of mankind, and from those which we shall yet explain. In other words, the doctrine that is to be taught in the future is the one which from this day on we have undertaken to make known to you.

Doubtless the following question will be asked. The men who were charged with guiding society by means of education in the past possessed as organs of a sacred authority a powerful sanction for their instruction. Will those who will fulfill the same mission in the future have a similar sanction? This brings us to the examination of a problem of the highest importance, which may be worded in this way. Has humanity a religious future? And if this question should be answered affirmatively, will the religion of the future be conceived as purely individual feeling without any fixed dogma or outward cult? Or must it be considered as the expression of a social theory and as having a dogma and a cult in the accepted meaning of these words? Will it occupy a place in the political order? Will it be called to dominate it in its entirety? How will it participate in the religious development of mankind?

It is impossible precisely to define the means that moral education is to use before first having answered this problem. We shall deal with it very shortly.

Specialized or Professional Education

Gentlemen:

In the preceding sessions we have dealt with general education. This time our subject will be special education, namely education intended to adapt individuals to the various orders of work in which they share in society.

All social facts may be expressed abstractly so as to relate equally to all times and all places. Without this abstraction, the human mind would not be able to rise to the idea of the interconnection of social facts and to trace their progress. And nevertheless, despite the identity of these facts, which represents the true picture of mankind's identity in the course of generations and over the various regions of the earth, it must be carefully noted that a social fact, when thus abstracted and transferred from one epoch to another, contains a new element of progress that cannot be understood by the direct and isolated observation of this fact and which only a general conception of the destiny of mankind can reveal.

This consideration becomes valuable above all, when a fact of the past is transposed into the future. The past in all its duration presents only one and the same state of society in which revolutions had only relative effectiveness but the future, without breaking the chain of human destiny, appears essentially as a new state.

When in our previous sessions we characterized the great differences separating the past from the future, we stressed particularly that all past societies were founded to a greater or lesser degree on the exploitation of man by man, and that the most important progress ahead of us today is the end of this exploitation in whatever form it may be conceived.

One cannot at first sight grasp the relationship between the decline in the exploitation of man by man and the question of education. However, a very intimate relationship exists. The realm of physical force, the principle, reason, and aim of every political organization of the past, necessarily resulted in the establishment of castes and clear-cut class distinctions which were perpetuated hereditarily. The further one goes back in antiquity, the deeper, more clear-cut and inflexible do these class lines appear. The closer we come to modern times, the more extensive but less rigorous these class distinctions become. But they exist none the less. However weak they may be today, these classifications nevertheless constitute a decree of fate for the privileged and the non-privileged, since the careers which the former or the latter are to follow are irreversibly determined by considerations other than their personal ability. When the time comes for them to take part in active life, no one asks about their inclinations, aptitudes, or talents: nothing is considered but their birth and the caste to which they belong, every possible effort is made to fashion them to the destiny to which they have been assigned by these circumstances. But this political order of the past is, after all, only one of the expressions of the exploitation of man by man. If it is true that this exploitation has reached its end today and that it ought to disappear entirely from the social order in the making, the assignment of individuals to particular branches of special education will evidently be made in the future according to individual aptitudes and talents rather than on the basis of birth.

Perhaps the partisans of the critical ideas will claim this state of things, for which we are appealing and which they doubtless consider as already attained, as achieved by the eighteenth-century philosophy and the political revolution that followed it. Let us examine the basis of their claims. The philosophy and the revolution of the last century doubtless destroyed the most apparent classification and, by freeing the lower classes from these fetters, proclaimed the right of every individual to take that place in society which he could claim on the basis of merit. But what have they done to make this right a reality? What have they done so that it would not be purely negative? They have overturned obstacles, but have they overturned all?

Doubtless not. Education, without which the most pronounced talents remain sterile, is not accessible to all without
distinction. Education is still a privilege granted by wealth, and
wealth is still a privilege almost always out of proportion to the
worth of those that possess it. And moreover, nothing has been
done to ensure to the few who can lay claim to an education that
they will be trained in terms of their aptitudes and talents. No
authority is entrusted with appraising and developing individual
tendencies. Here everything is left to vanity and to the ambition
of families or the thoughtless preferences of children.

In summing up: we may say that despite the political
triumph of the philosophical ideas of the eighteenth century,
education still remains inaccessible to the majority. For the
small minority which can obtain an education, the type of education is determined by chance, without any choice or foresight.

In the new association which men are called upon to form
and which will not tolerate any exploitation of man by man,
education will be provided for everyone, regardless of birth or
wealth, and will be determined on the basis of individual ability
and talent.

Will this classification of men through education give rise
to ideas of violence? At this time we should recall what we said
at the beginning, that in the changes we have proclaimed, one
factor, which one is apt to dispense with today, must always be
taken into account; namely, that moral education is called upon
to transform for every individual the obligations imposed by the
true leaders and legitimate heads of society into ideas of duty and
objects of love.

The appraisal of inclinations and aptitudes imposes upon
the future body of teachers a task that may be considered altogether new. The society of the past did not provide for this
appraisal, at least not on a sufficiently broad scale to enable
general planning. The assignment of types of education to individuals on the basis of ability describes the total social order
of the future, at least as distinguished from the past. Here,
indeed, each man will obtain all the power and well-being he
deserves in terms of his personality. Here that equality will be

realized which feeling has invoked for a long time without yet being able to define its composition.

We have described the general change education is to undergo, which will forever guarantee the complete emancipation of the greatest number. We can consider some of the particular advantages in detail.

Since the various functions and professions will be assigned on the basis of ability, they will be exercised more perfectly. Only, therefore, will progress in all branches of human activity be much more rapid than in any epoch of the past. The division of labor has been very rightly considered one of the most powerful causes of the progress of civilization. But evidently this division will produce all of its fruit only when it is based on the differences in ability among the workers.

The scheme we announce for the future offers a great new guarantee for the moral order. Feeling and reason both show us that missing talents, forced inclinations, imposed professions, and the resulting dislike and hatred have been the sources of almost all past disorder. But these sources will be eliminated in our scheme. We certainly do not claim to say that no error, accident, or even partiality will occur in this new division of education and of social advantages. We recognize human imperfection. Perhaps human societies will never be able to attain the conceivable limit of their progress. But if they only advance toward that limit and utilize all the intellect and forces at their disposal, if they only make progress real, one may correctly say that, humanly speaking, the true limit has been reached. From then on all the errors, accidents, and injustices are only exceptions. They constitute a steadily shrinking share, one of the less striking aspects of the totality of social facts.

We shall now deal directly with special education with regard to the subjects it ought to include and to its possible divisions.

We have said that the purpose of this part of education is to adapt individuals to the various orders of work that the state of society comprises. It remains therefore evident, by definition, that the system of specialized education can be conceived only as determined by social foresight and serving a political function. We do not propose directly to combat the opinion of those who would want to abandon specialized education in the future to un-limited individual competition,[1] and who see in this part of educa-tion only an industry that, like all the others, must be handed over to struggle, war, and consequently to fraud and charlatanism. What we will have to say about the indispensable conditions for a good system of specialized education will be sufficient to refute this opinion altogether.

The further one goes back into the past, the more limited and incomplete are the means of specialized education. To the extent that men were divided into castes, orders, and classifica-tions according to birth, this part of education was reduced to the state of mere tradition. It was transmitted from father to son, hereditarily within a family dedicated to one profession. When we come closer to modern times, we will see how societies tended more and more to make specialized education subject to political decision and social planning. At first this planning comprised only a small number of professions, but little by little it spread. It is sufficient to follow the sequence of advances made already in this field to convince oneself that specialized educa-tion, as a department of the public authority, should ultimately comprise all orders of work and all functions to which society can give rise.

Social foresight in this respect was shown clearly in the Middle Ages in institutions that were conceived and made real by men who exercised the great function of foresight. We shall especially dwell upon that epoch, because, despite the improve-ments education has undergone since that time, it has not given rise to any new general conception, at least to none which might lend itself to wider political application. In many, even in the most important respects, the old conception is still dominant.

If we justify its suitability at the time of its birth, we shall

[1] An attack against liberals like Benjamin Constant and the group around the liberal *Globe* who fought as ardently against control of the schools by the state—through the Université—as against control by the Church. The late 1820's also marked the beginning of the attack by Lamennais from a Catholic view-point against state control of education. Cf. B229.

have appraised the value it can have today, and we shall soon be engaged in making the changes and transformations this conception must undergo.

The first institutions of specialized education during the Middle Ages had the sole aim of training members for the clergy, secular or regular, according to the distinction established at that time. In these institutions, all of which were founded in monasteries and cathedrals beginning with the eighth and ninth centuries, all was taught which at that time formed the store of human knowledge. Instruction included dogmatic theology and what were then called the seven liberal arts. In these institutions, the store of knowledge was increased, and the works of the ancients and those of the Church fathers in which the Christian doctrine was scientifically elaborated were taken up again at the point where they had been interrupted by the great work of political reconstruction, which had engaged the most capable men for several centuries. The encyclopedic frame was extended, and rational theology, civil and ecclesiastic law, and medicine were introduced. The circle of instruction grew in proportion to that of science, and the teaching body itself took on a new form and a new organization. The revolution which had begun in the twelfth century was concluded in the thirteenth century with the establishment of the universities. It was then that the development of the content and method of instruction was definitely arrested. Since then they have undergone improvements in detail only.

In this system of specialized education, the only forms of applied knowledge commonly thought of were the works of the moralists, the jurists, and the physicians. All the industrial professions, including the military, which was then the most important in the temporal order, were outside politically organized instruction. It would be incorrect to reproach the body of medieval scholars with having neglected these professions. First of all, quite naturally the scholarly body would not endeavor to perfect the military profession since its principal mission was to fight and to destroy the state of things which made this profession necessary. And as for the industrial professions, the time had not yet come to appreciate their importance. Moreover, scientific theories were not yet advanced, and the practices of industry were too crude to be possibly related to those theories.*

Specialized education therefore then comprised all the professions it could comprise.

Here we must speak about instruction in the Latin language, which has held a very high place in the past and which is the subject of many discussions today which can be endless if its reason and origin have not been understood. In the Middle Ages the people of Europe were extremely divided from a temporal point of view. From a spiritual point of view, on the other hand, they were intimately united and formed the strongest association which until then had been conceived and realized, an association which assured them unquestionable superiority over the peoples of antiquity. The vast Christian community was represented and given reality by a guardian body of all the luminaries of the time, who spread it over all of Europe and acted everywhere in the same way. The unity of this body, the result of the unity of love, doctrine, and activity, had among other outward conditions of existence unity of language. How did Latin become the language of the spiritual body of the Middle Ages? It is useless for us to deal with this. It suffices if we recognize as a certain fact that this language was, if we may term it thus, the national speech of the Catholic clergy, and that it served through constant communication as a link to bring together its members, who were dispersed over the face of the Christian world. Through this bond of language, above all, the great association of intellectual work of the Middle Ages became a reality. Since specialized education included only the scholarly professions at that time, it is clear why it was based on the instruction in Latin, the language common to all these professions. But one will not find that Latin by itself was then considered a science, or a sphere of knowledge, forming a special branch of instruction.

* We shall later show how this negligence of industrial interests and physical sciences had a deep cause and was only a logical consequence of the Christian dogma in its entirety, which could not have and should not have understood the development of the material activity of man, because this epoch had to destroy, above all, the form in which this activity was practiced, namely war.

When in the sixteenth century the spiritual unity of Europe was attacked, the unity of language was attacked too. This had to be so. Unity of language and of doctrines were only different aspects of one and the same fact, which the instinct of the first reformers discovered first of all. Once the unity of doctrine had been broken, the unity of language was soon broken too. Little by little the use of the Latin language was abandoned. Already for a long time, the works of science, except for a few unimportant exceptions, have been produced and preserved in the various national languages of Europe.

However, since the intimate relation that existed between instruction in the Latin language and Catholic unity had risen from instinct rather than reflection, and since the clergy was not clearly aware of this relation, the same was true of the reformers when they attacked the unity. Despite the progress of the reform, the sway of Latin in the schools was not disturbed. Not only was it continued to be taught to those destined for the old scholarly professions, for which it became less and less useful, but as the classes that laid claim to a literary education became more numerous every day, it was taught to the artists, the military, the industrialists, and in short to all who could pay for it. It is remarkable that at the very time when the use of Latin had lost its usefulness and raison d'être one tried to justify its instruction in a thousand ways. It was recommended as a basic language. Its richness and harmony were praised, as well as the perfection of the works of its poets, orators, and historians. All these arguments in favor of devoting ten years to the study of a dead language are not worth our time to attack. According to what we have just said, the question of the suitability of Latin instruction can be resolved in two words. As long as it was the language common to European moralists and scholars, in short to the clergy, the clergy unquestionably had to learn Latin, which is to say its language, if its members were to understand each other. But today when scientific treatises in Latin are out of date; when the moralists and scholars use the modern national languages, when above all, the lettered no longer form one body, not only has the study of Latin lost its importance, but with a few exceptions limited to purely philological works, it has become more than merely useless: it is harmful, if the considerable loss of time which it involves is considered. Already for a long time it has been preserved only by university regulations.[2]

This digression on the instruction of Latin should make us recognize the false approach to specialized education. Moreover, it furnishes us with additional proof for what we said above, namely that no general conception of education has arisen since the Middle Ages. Of course, we are far from claiming that no improvement has been made in this respect. We recognize that the teaching of several sciences has kept pace with the progress in the sciences themselves since the Middle Ages. Special schools have been founded for the fine arts and the sciences, from which industrial instruction indirectly resulted. Some attempts have recently been made in France and England to establish such schools, but since these attempts were not connected with any general view of the needs of society and of the nature of the work required by these needs, they have remained almost fruitless. Finally education, which has been wrong at many points, has remained incomplete in others.

[2] "In declaring themselves so completely hostile to all teaching of the classical languages, Bazard and Enfantin are entirely faithful to the master's doctrine. See *Mémoire sur la Science de l'Homme* in *Oeuvres de Saint-Simon et d'Enfantin*, XL, 16: 'Such is the difference between the old and the new order of things, between that which existed fifty, forty or even thirty years ago and the present one, that if anybody had inquired in those days relatively close to our own if someone had received an outstanding education, he would have asked: Does he know his Greek and Latin authors well? Today the question would be: Is he strong in mathematics? Is his knowledge of physics, chemistry and biology, in other words, of the positive and empirical sciences, up to date?' Already three years before the sessions in the rue Taranne, Bazard insisted in the *Producteur* III, 526, 550, on the necessity of giving more space to the teaching of the special sciences, 'the only ones which are on the enlightened level of our century.' In current education they are 'subordinated to useless knowledge,' as 'in the case of the dead languages,' he added in a note. Here then is a point on which the Saint-Simonians disagree with the theocrats, the theorists of the restoration of order, and on which they are in agreement with the men of the Revolution. See Condorcet's *Second Mémoire sur l'Instruction publique*. . . . In accordance with this idea, the Revolution founded the Central schools as a reaction against the exclusively humanistic education linked with the Jesuit tradition. Destutt de Tracy, in drawing up the program of these schools, pointed out that the schools of antiquity did not teach languages and literature only, and that, therefore, to cultivate all of man's faculties one should also teach the physical sciences, mathematics, ethics, and politics." B230.

Today we can conceive of a complete and orderly system of specialized education only under the following abstract conditions: (1) instruction shall comprise all human knowledge in its most advanced state; (2) the teaching body will be organized in such a way that every advance will pass easily from theory to practice, from the hands of the scholars that perfect science to those that teach it, and thence to those that make immediate application of it; (3) specialized education shall comprise all the professions required by the needs of society; (4) finally, instruction shall be distributed so that each stage will at the same time be the consequence of the preceding step and the preliminary step for the following stage. Education, when taken in its totality, will present to each individual an orderly and homogenous course of study, which at its conclusion will immediately lead to a profession and a social function.[3]

None of these conditions is being fulfilled today.

(1) Specialized education does not include all human knowledge at the state of perfection which it has reached. On the other hand, some of the knowledge which it includes is useless or out of date. Useless within the reservations that we have set are ancient languages and literatures when they form the basis of instruction. Out of date, as they are taught now, are theology, philosophy, history, and (in its metaphysical aspects) legislation.

In these different areas, instruction not only is incomplete but contains an important gap, since each type of useless or outdated knowledge which it spreads could be advantageously replaced.

(2) The body of teachers is not organized in such a way as to take hold of progress as it takes place. What we have just said proves this sufficiently. In order that the teachers fulfill this condition, they must be directly related to the bodies in charge of

[3] "In the *Globe* of June 1 and 3, 1831, the Saint-Simonians described their plan of scientific organization more in detail. The *academies* are 'associations of scholars and theorists united for the purpose of perfecting one or more special fields of human knowledge.' The *colleges* 'are associations of doctors and professors united for the purpose of teaching one or more special fields of human knowledge.' The function of the *university* is to direct the academies and colleges, namely to harmonize the work of theory or of perfection, and that of practice or of teaching, in other words, to bring the scholars and the teachers together.' " B232.

the perfecting of theories. But today there are no bodies of this sort,[4] and those which might be considered as engaged in this task are in no direct relation with the body of teachers.

(3) Specialized education does not include all the professions it could include. We shall not speak about the fine arts, for which several special schools exist, although the character of the fine arts has not yet been understood, so that education in this field is as imperfect and harmful as possible. Neither are we speaking of the industrial professions which nearly all remain outside the sphere of public instruction. However, at the point which scientific theories and industrial processes have reached, a closer relation between them is conceivable. But it should be clear that industry, in its totality, must become the direct application of scientific theories. Nevertheless, nothing has been done to establish this link between science and industry, at least nothing of sufficient importance to be considered here.

(4) And finally, instruction presents no continuity or co-ordination at its various stages. There is no primary instruction, at least not in the proper meaning of the word. The first stage of instruction at which there is some regularity is "collège."[5] But the schooling, which consists primarily of languages and ancient literature, is, according to what we have already said, the primary instruction of the Middle Ages. Not only does it not introduce its students to the social applications of knowledge, but it does not even prepare them for the higher schools except in a purely legal way. Since the knowledge one acquires in the first school is almost useless for the second stage, each individual who wants to go to the secondary school must hastily acquire a specialized

---

[4] "Saint-Simon's judgment about the organization of science in his day was less harsh. It is true that he was speaking to the members of the Institute. See *Mémoire sur la Science de l'Homme* in *Oeuvres de Saint-Simon et d'Enfantin*, XL, 20: 'The scientific body is today divided into two distinct parts; or rather there exist two scientific bodies, of which each in its work embraces the total system of our knowledge. The one, namely the University, has as its purpose the teaching of acquired knowledge. The other, namely the Institute, works at completing the scientific system. . . . The organization of the scientific workshop is different from that which existed in the fifteenth century and very superior to it. There was then no scientific body except the University. As today, the University had as its purpose public instruction so that there was no body entrusted with perfecting the system of human knowledge.' " B233.

[5] A French secondary school.

education, the accomplishment of which is left to his own inspirations and effort. The higher schools, evidently too few in
number even to correspond to the most important divisions of
the various labors of society, are entirely insufficient to overcome
the gap separating theory from practice. The individuals are
left to their own resources to overcome this gap once they have
finished these schools. This they are not always able to do, and
when they can, it is only by paying dearly for their experiences.

We shall now be asked how the system of specialized education should be organized. To answer this question fully, we
should have to go into details and elaborations which would
exceed our scope and in many respects would anticipate what is
to follow. Moreover, since the criticism to which we just devoted
ourselves should be sufficient for the time being to give a general
view of the ideas of the doctrine on the institution of specialized
education, we shall add only a few more words.

The mission of specialized education is to enable individuals
to fulfill the functions to which they are called by their own
talents and by the needs of society. Shall we see what the subject
matter of its instruction and its principal division will be? It is
evident that one must begin by determining the works and
functions demanded by the state of society. The remainder
comes later. We have said that all manifestations of human life
can be brought under the heading of the three great orders of
principal facts: namely, the fine arts, the sciences, and industry.
This great division also furnishes a general indication of the goal
of instruction. Artists, scholars, and industrialists must be
trained. Innumerable subdivisions exist under this first division,
but as the latter rest on a reality that can be appreciated by
anybody, we need not discuss it any further.

We do not forget that independent of specialized instruction,
by which the artists, industrialists, and scholars prepare themselves for their particular kind of work, all shall first receive a
common instruction which will be offered as the basis and point
of departure for all later training. Here we want to speak of
moral education, which has already been discussed, and which is
offered to the rising generation as a preparation for any individual calling. This is indeed childhood's first initiation into the

fine arts, the sciences, and industry, within the limits within
which these different orders of knowledge are presented as a
necessary introduction to the exercise of all functions and all
professions.[5]

At the end of this primary education, which can be extended, shortened, or divided, the selection of which we have
spoken will take place. The aim of this selection will be to divide
individuals according to their various aptitudes and talents. In
accordance with this first selection, three great schools for the
fine arts, the sciences, and industry will be opened to students.
No matter into how many branches these schools may be divided,
the necessity for a common education for all artists as artists, and
similarly for all scholars and for all industrialists, shall be
recognized, whatever the subdivisions of the fine arts, science, and
industry may be. It is only in the course of this second preparation that the young people, now set on their future careers,
would be distributed among the various special schools for applied work, which would correspond to all the possible subdivisions of the three great orders of work which we have described
here in a general way. These schools would guide the students
until society considered them sufficiently prepared and would
consequently entrust to each his proper function.

We just used an expression which doubtless will be misunderstood, namely the term "artists." In any case it could be clear
that this word has a much wider meaning for us than is usually

---

[5] "This is how an ex-Saint-Simonian, Jules Lechevalier, was later to
judge tendencies of the system which has been presented in these chapters.
See *Etudes sur la Science sociale. Année 1832. Théorie de Charles Fourier*,
1834, pp. 362 f.: 'If one considers the goal which the Saint-Simonians set
for themselves in education and elsewhere, the promises and vows which
they made with their whole heart and soul, there is nothing to criticize.
But as soon as one comes to the means sought for and the results to
be obtained, one is forced to take the scepter of progress away from the
vague and flexible doctrine and to divest the pontiffs . . . of the halo of
liberty which they have tried to usurp. Indeed, for those who can see its two
sides, Saint-Simonianism presents on the one hand the annunciation of the
future and of new freedom, on the other the hideous spectre of the past
and of ancient despotism. To promise education to all, to develop all types
of activity, to give to each one the opportunity to follow his career is beautiful
and holy; but education by the government, classification exclusively on the
basis of function, and the determination of morality by the superior are all
still part of the old law.' " B236.

given to it. We shall later replace it by another word which we shall not yet use. This consideration obliges us to use the term "artist" provisionally to designate the men endowed with the sympathetic faculty to the highest degree, whether this faculty extends to all of mankind or is confined within the narrowest circle of social affections. This faculty should finally preside especially over moral education. Thus we arrive by a new road at the necessity of dealing with the religious problem, the terms of which were posed in the preceding session. However, before we approach this problem, we should quickly look at a part of the social order that is inseparably linked with the subject we have just discussed—legislation.

TWELFTH SESSION (June 3, 1829)

Legislation

Gentlemen:

Our last sessions were devoted to showing you the means by which a social idea can be applied to new generations to guide each individual to the function for which he is destined by his ability. We have said that education embraced a vaster field than that which we have been considering, that it accompanied man from the cradle to the threshold of the grave, ceaselessly developing the seeds deposited in the heart and in the intelligence of the child and of the adolescent. When dealing particularly with these first two stages of man's life (which are intended for his preparation and for his initiation into active life) we have pointed at the gap which leaves our exposition incomplete and which we shall soon bridge in order once more to cast a total view over the vast subject of education. It has been easy for you to gather from the kind of information for which we have been asked and from the discussions which have arisen from these questions that the basis of future moral education should be determined without delay. Then we could no longer be confronted by what we unhesitatingly call prejudices, by which we mean that the opinions with which we are often attacked are derived from an order of facts, ideas, and sentiments alien to the social order which we announce for the future.

And here, gentlemen, an observation is necessary which, we hope, will make the debates following each of our sessions more meaningful. If, as we think, the doctrine of Saint-Simon is the social doctrine of the future, and if it is to bring about in all mankind a renewal similar to that wrought by Christianity among some peoples, one should understand not only that we cannot devote our meetings to the detailed discussion of past doctrines, whatever their names may be, but also that we can be attacked profitably only on our own ground. A comparison will illustrate this idea. If a Greek or Roman philosopher, Emperor Julian, for example—and none of our adversaries will be hurt by this parallel—if, let us say, Julian, when discussing with the first Christians the brotherhood of man professed by the Gospels, had drawn his arguments from his conscience, enlightened by Greek philosophy; if he had fought the apostles by means of the distinction of the two natures, free and slave; if he had treated the doctrine of the Christ as a utopia, a dream, because it intended to destroy and replace the sentiment which until then had been the firmest support of the social order (since it hallowed the utility, the necessity, and even the justice of slavery), the discussion would not have been very profitable. It might have become very animated; it might have excited not the Christians, who had the firm conviction that they were bringing something new to mankind, but Julian, who was prompted by his conscience to fight against the opponents of the moral order of which he was one of the shining lights. The discussion would have been able to arouse hatred and anger, and history bears witness to this. But it would have served human destiny only by the spectacle of the martyr's faith. Let us thank Christianity that man shall be enlightened differently today.

By first considering the principal dogmas of the philosophy expounded to you only as hypotheses and then by examining whether they satisfy the various problems of the social order as the doctrines of the past have satisfied the needs of their times, you can consider this first idea: Is the Saint-Simonian social organization complete or not? And after returning to the sentiments which bind you to any other doctrine and comparing them with those called forth by our master's doctrine, you will either steadfastly adhere to the dogmas transmitted to you from the past, or you will join with us in desiring and hastening the realization of the future announced by Saint-Simon.

Let us proceed to the subject with which we will deal in this session.

We have just said that we shall have to expound the bases of the moral sanction with which no truly constituted society can dispense, and that there will be found the answer to several doubts which perhaps arose in your minds when we spoke of the constitution of property and its distribution on the basis of the right of ability, to be substituted for the right of birth, or when we indicated how social foresight prepared the coming generation to succeed the present without interruption.

However, before we approach this fundamental question, which sheds new light on all problems which interest mankind, and before we arrive at the core of the matter by seeking the principle of life at the collective being we are studying, we must terminate what might be called the anatomic work we have undertaken and which we are anxious to see completed. But, gentlemen, as long as one has not grasped the chain of sympathy which links man to what is not himself, which makes him a necessary function of the vast phenomenon of which he is a part, one sees only a being without life, a corpse, a fact devoid of morality. But being forced to stand, at least temporarily, on the arid ground where the men whom we wish to address are somehow immobilized today, we have had to examine the lifeless matter they deal with, if only to show its barrenness.[1]

Legislation, in which some of you have specialized, has not been directly the subject of any of our sessions. And at the point which we have reached, it would be difficult to pass over legislation quietly, although we would have preferred to have touched on this part of the social order only as a deduction from the moral rule which it is to defend. And, indeed, it is easy to see that legislation is always determined in its content and even in its forms by society's sympathetic or unsympathetic disposition for or against certain orders of facts, or by the manner in which it, according to the degree of civilization, expresses this antipathy and this sympathy by the punishments or rewards which it bestows. However, in its most striking aspect, legislation is too intimately linked with education, whose completion it is, for us not to present at least a rapid exposition of the principal ideas of the school on this subject. We shall reserve the right to come back to all the questions with which we have dealt in the preced-

[1] "The clearly vitalistic character of the passage we just read is new in the history of Saint-Simonianism. Toward 1829 Saint-Simonianism was transformed into pantheism. Nothing of the kind had taken place yet when Saint-Simon's disciples edited the *Producteur*." B240.

ing sessions after we shall have examined the ideas from which legislation itself draws the sanction it needs in order to exert the positive influence which it ought to have. The influence is purely negative when this sanction is missing.

Moreover, several questions which have been put to us also compel us to stop at this topic.

Without waiting for us to explain our views on the nature of sentiments in the future, people have wanted to know our entire opinion concerning the repression of certain things which we have declared ought some day to be considered immoral and harmful to the progress of society and socially disapproved. They have gone further and have assumed in advance that we were advocating harsh repressive methods. Forgetting that we announced the end of the reign of violence, they practically supposed that we were keeping the death penalty or at least police interrogation and bayonets in the back of our minds.

Such suspicions about an entirely novel social system are not surprising, and we are glad of them since they always give us an opportunity to explain the immense distance separating our sentiments, ideas, and actions from those of the men who, while they have the best intentions, strive to correct the vices of the past and cure the infirmities of the old man when it is a question of giving new life, of creating and animating the new man.

We are quickly going to examine the end and nature of legislation, the facts which it includes, the means which it uses, and finally the qualifications which should serve as the basis of the organization of the magistrate.

The end of legislation is to maintain the moral rule and to teach it in a particular form. It includes the exceptional facts of society, that is to say the abnormal facts whether progressive or reactionary: in other words, the moral or immoral acts which arouse most praise or blame.

Legislation is divided into two distinct parts: negative and positive, penal and renumerative. This division gives it a dual character deriving from fear and from hope. In the former role it acts as an obstacle to vice, in the latter as an encouragement, an incitement to virtue.

Let us stop for a moment with this proposition that we have just presented in three different forms. We ended with two words, "vice" and "virtue," which we must hasten to define because of their past ambiguity.

Any man can act by considering himself either as the center or at the perimeter of the sphere in which his action is to take place. In other words, he can subordinate the general interest, whatever it is, to his particular interest, or vice versa. The first case gives rise to egoism, the second to devotion (*dévoûment*);* the former corresponds to the so-called interests, the latter to duties. These two means generally lead to the same end in the epochs which we call organic, because then there is harmony between interests and duties which are equally loved and whose unity is felt by everyone. In the critical epochs, on the other hand, egoism dominates; and it alone is understood since there exists neither conviction in, nor the love for, what one thinks might be duty or general interest. Whatever may be the goal of society, whether it be organized to prosper through war or peaceful work, whether it hallows the domination of man over man or association, the preceding phenomenon presents itself always to the observer: the general interest finds itself in harmony with individual interest only among those men who seek by their actions to merit the esteem and love of those around them, in other words those who place themselves simultaneously at the center and at the perimeter.

Having failed to examine man from this twofold point of view, the philosophers of the eighteenth century revived in various forms the materialistic egoism of Epicurus or the spiritualistic, but none the less real, egoism of the Stoics. This con-

---

* It would be more exact to say "renunciation" or "sacrifice" than "devotion." This change of terms would contain the solution to the greatest moral problem with which mankind ever confronted itself. But it would demand elaborations which will be presented in our second volume when we arrive at the religious dogma of the future. For the time being it suffices to point out that devotion (*dévoûment* or *dévotion*) always carries with it the idea of renunciation and sacrifice, while in the future devotion (*dévotion*) will consist in harmonizing general and particular interest in such a way that renunciation as well as egoism will disappear. This can occur only in a society in which everyone, regardless of birth, is classified according to his ability and remunerated according to his work.

fusion is as evident in the "enlightened self-interest" of Helvétius as in the duties toward oneself of the spiritualistic metaphysicians. Helvétius reduces man to a passive mass, beset by immediate and purely individual appetites. Spiritualistic metaphysicians attempt to raise him in their own eyes by pronouncing the sacred word "duty"; but this duty is not imposed by the general needs of mankind. It is not the voice of God or that of the peoples which the metaphysicians seek to understand: they listen to their own voice. From their individual consciences they ask revelations.

Therefore, let us hasten to remark that all these philosophers, arrayed under two great banners of different color, divided by imperceptible lines into groups in which all treat each other as enemies on the philosophic battlefield, amicably join hands in matters of morality and politics. The atheist d'Holbach, the deist Voltaire and Rousseau, in short all the philosophic sects which have rallied to Protestantism, or better to Gallicanism, jointly profess the same social doctrine.

This formidable unanimity of all the defenders of individualism on questions of politics should suffice to prove to them that their social beliefs are not logical deductions from their so-called philosophic doctrines and should make them doubt the value of their beliefs for this reason alone. And if it were not contrary to the dogmas accepted by the various sects to go back to a source higher than individual conscience, our philosophers and publicists would easily recognize that they are students of the same master.

This digression has been useful to us. Lest we fall into the errors we have just pointed out, we wish, before completing what we have to say concerning the words "vice" and "virtue," to show by an example that the meaning of these words is necessarily determined not by individuals like Locke, Reid, Condillac, or Kant consulting their consciences, but by the revelation of individual conscience being confirmed by the general needs of mankind according to its particular stage of civilization. The masses express these needs in such a confused manner at first that they are understood only by the men who have the deepest sympathy for the masses.

No code of morality—it is repugnant to us to call mystic conceptions of egoism in critical epochs by this name, and all of mankind adequately justifies our repugnance—no code of morality has considered the individual as the center, that is to say, has preached egoism. All the institutions of the organic epochs exist, rather, to lead the citizen back to the perimeter from which he may have been diverted by particular circumstances. They have always aimed at recalling him to his duties by inspiring him to fulfill them or by making him fear neglecting them.

At this point, gentlemen, we must call to your attention that it is not our intention to offer you today a regular course in morals. All that we have said up to now is independent of the nature of the social duties imposed on man at one or another stage of his development. However, it is important for you to recall here some of the general ideas of our school concerning the development of man, ideas which will now find their application.

At each social renewal, developing social sensitivity discards from penal or renumerative legislation certain elements which have ceased to be harmful or useful. But at the same time, it introduces others which then take on this character, in other words, which become the objects of its repugnance or admiration.

Thus, under the aegis of Christianity, not only in the bosom of the Church did virtue lose the ferocious character of violence and trickery which it possessed in antiquity, but in the warrior himself it took on a form wonderfully tempered by love. The brilliant manners of chivalry would have rejected as criminal and discourteous all the heroes of Homer whom Greece and Rome admired as the sublime types of mankind.

In the great periods of regeneration, a transformation of the moral system takes place like that of the political system. Old terms receive new meaning and new words appear to designate equally new impressions.

We feel that this warning is necessary for us to avoid the criticism arising from the fact that the words "vice" and "virtue" are associated with different things today than they will be in

the future. It suffices for us to say that we intend to designate by
these terms, on the one hand, all the facts which seem likely to
favor the march of society towards the goal it proposes to attain,
and on the other hand, those which seem to present obstacles to
its development. For example, making a game of death, braving
it laughingly without passion or devotion, confronting danger
merely to show courage, a prime virtue in former times, may well
be considered some day a mad bravado, ridiculous, or even
dangerous in an age when it will not be necessary for man always
to be ready for struggle and war. Doubtless one will still admire
power, that of Watt, for example, as one used to admire that of
Achilles; but it will not really be the same power, for it will be
applied toward a very different goal from the one which used to
inspire it. Finally, cowardice will certainly still be ostracized
with shame and dishonor, but it will not be that of the past. The
idle will be the cowards of the future. Power and courage, the
virtues of the future, will certainly consist in increasing man's
scientific and industrial domain and perfecting human sentiments. By these means will personal nobility and glory be
deserved some day.[2]

Legislation, as we have said, is divisible into penal and
remunerative parts. The double sanction, embodied in the institutions of penalties and rewards, corresponds to the division
established among human acts on the basis of their morality into
vices and virtues. The courts are then the organs through which
society expresses censure and praise.

Although it seems that these two parts of legislation should
be treated at the same time, we shall try as much as possible to
limit our examination to one of them, and you will easily understand why. All the works of the jurists and of the publicists
really dealt only with penal legislation, despite the efforts of

---

[2] "The Saint-Simonian doctrine does not question the right of force since
it assigns remuneration in proportion to work, or more strictly it does not use
right and force as two mutually exclusive terms. It ignores abstract speculations about right and restricts itself to announcing the coming of a social
state in which forces, no longer defined as destructive but as productive, will
be brought into harmony and will pursue a common goal according to a
common moral doctrine." B245.

Beccaria[3] and Bentham, who have dared, unsuccessfully however, to approach this question directly from the dual point of view. This was quite natural, since the only institution which for several centuries had had a moral existence of remarkable strength was losing in influence each day, without being replaced by an analogous institution which could bring a sanction of equal weight to bear on the judgments of human justice, and which could proclaim the rehabilitation of the guilty and crown the genius.

Sad deities of the doctrine of individualism, two creatures of reason—conscience and public opinion—soon received the homage which mankind refused the Church; and then all re-munerative legislation was reduced to one dogma which the metaphysicians expressed thus: "The virtuous man is rewarded by his conscience": and the critical publicists say: "Public opinion rewards a good man." This, as we pointed out above, leads to one political result: opposition to any attempt at organization from a center of direction for the moral interests of mankind, to hatred of power.

Before confining ourselves to the examination of penal legislation, the only instrument of order of which the politics of a critical age can conceive precisely because it is as devoid of morality as possible, let us consider for a moment this vast gap which the social organization of our days offers and which gives such great opportunity for the attacks by reactionaries who dream of a return to the institutions of the past. We shall come back to this topic again after having indicated our views con-cerning the moral future of mankind. But a quick glance at the degradation of society in this respect will for the present prepare the ground for what we shall have to say later.

Note, gentlemen, that this gap of which we are speaking, this widowhood of society deprived of the moral force which sustains the weak, doubles the strength of the genius, and alone can reconcile the repenting criminal with the society which he

---

[3] Cesare Bonesana, Marchese di Beccaria (1734-1794), author of *Crimes and Punishment*, published in 1764, in which he condemned the common theory that penalties should be made as horrible as possible to deter crime and called for a humane penal code and for prison reforms.

has hurt—note, we say, that this gap is not only felt by the lack of that part of legislation which we have called remunerative. The generally accepted distinction between justice and equity gives us proof of this. After having repudiated the moral order, the legal order, deprived of the former's support, remained powerless to counteract the harm caused by this distinction. But that is not all: a new and more obvious injury lay in store for it. This injury, the harsh reward for the attempts of the jurists to destroy the political foundations of the moral order of the past, but a just punishment for their lack of foresight in not constructing a new structure, was expressed in the institution of the jury.

Indeed, gentlemen, is the jury not a consequence of the distrust inspired by the presumed immorality of the law or by the fear of corruption or at least of ignorance in the magistracy? One wanted to be judged by his peers as soon as superiors were no longer recognized in morals as in politics. Then by a happy instinct which man never loses entirely, he wanted to return to the words of the law the force of opinion which they had lost—a futile endeavor, for the ballot box from which regularly a few unknown names come forth is neither the source from which reconciliation flows nor even the source of social reprobation.

And yet, gentlemen, this is the only guarantee claimed today for the moral order in legislation. Few minds deceive themselves sufficiently not to recognize that such institutions are poor, cold, and colorless. However little one reflected, even if only to criticize, about the judgments pronounced by the Christian Church at the apex of its power; about canonization, which commended Christian virtues to all the faithful and their posterity; about excommunication, which even in earthly life placed the guilty in a sorrowful purgatory; (and we do not hesitate to add) about the indulgences, as long as the Church did not traffic with them shamefully, one cannot help feeling pity for the society which does not hesitate to celebrate the destruction of these great instruments of order without being concerned with replacing them for the future. One understands the look of contempt and of despair which the great minds of our day cast on this society. One understands de Maistre ardently wishing to return to the past and Goethe and Byron covering the ruins, on which we miserably vegetate, with a shroud and poisoning the atmosphere.

No, gentlemen, mankind has not been eternally condemned to this state of moral nullity and consequently of immorality, for man cannot long remain left to himself without falling into egoism. The day will come when the words spoken by the organs of social justice will carry true joy or deep sorrow into all hearts. The day will come when men devoted to mankind can lay claim to a new crown of sanctity, when vice will be punished by the sorrowful spectacle of the pains which it inflicts on virtue. The day will come when repentance will know hope.

May this last idea always be present in your minds, gentlemen. Then you will appreciate the real significance of the powerless efforts of the philanthropic jurists when they seek to re-establish in the hearts of men the peace which has been disturbed through their lack of foresight. They apparently want to begin society's moral regeneration in the penitentiary. They are shocked by the eternal suffering which accompanies the man who has once been cursed by the terrible and miserable instrument of social justice, which closes forever the path to repentance and reconciliation. All bemoan the abject condition into which continual contact with crime leads the weak, who are helpless at the sight of the disorders caused by egoism. And none of the philanthropic jurists have realized that these beings themselves, whose misfortune they deplore, come from our civilized cities where they lacked moral support and where they left many souls, weak like themselves, to follow them soon to be lost in the prisons and perhaps to say farewell to earth from the scaffold.

But let us return to the question which we have promised to discuss. We want to speak of the theory of punishment and of the organization of the body instituted to apply this theory to the various social facts.

We cannot repeat too often what we have already said several times, that one of the great laws of development of the human species consists in the constant decrease of the rule of force, or better yet—for the word "force" presents an apparent contradiction with the political growth of industry—of the rule of violence and of the exploitation of man by man. Applied to the subject with which we are dealing, this law shows us on the one hand that vice takes on less and less brutal forms, on the other hand that punishment assumes a more and more humane character. In this respect, despite the progress that may have been made up to now, it would be wrong to imagine, when hearing us use the word "repression," that we meant the methods used by the Chinese or the Greeks, for example, in repressing population growth by exposing children or hunting slaves, or by the Christian church in its decline in repressing impiety by autos-da-fé.

No, gentlemen, although it is impossible for us to determine in advance in detail the repressive means to be used in the future, we could be accused of a contradiction manifest in our very principles if one supposed that in a social order in which we recognized only morality, ability, and work as conditions of power, we could permit the existence of a magistracy which would not sympathize greatly with the guilty and not see in their punishment a beneficial correction, a genuine means of education rather than of vengeance.[4] This misconception would be even more unpardonable if it were applied to the repression of moral delinquencies and, for example, to questions which are so highly inflammable today: freedom of instruction, of the press, and of worship. But, since you want to know all we think on this subject, here it is.

We think that in a society constituted as we foresee that of the future, punishments inflicted on the propagators of anti-social doctrines will aim above all to protect them from public animadversion. By punishing them severely, the authorities will mitigate the punishment demanded by the public, whose hatred is so easily aroused against the men and the things which hurt

---

[4] "In defining punishment as the expression of society's repugnance against certain kinds of deeds, the Saint-Simonians seem to have rehabilitated the old theory of 'public vengeance' while giving it a positive meaning. The idea of vengeance is indeed too negative and antisocial for them to maintain. But in presenting punishment as a 'means of education,' as a lesson given by society to the guilty, are they not proposing the rehabilitation of an old theory belonging to the 'organic' epoch which preceded the philosophy of Enlightenment, namely the definition of punishment as expiation?" B254.

the feelings of the masses. But to understand this idea, do not forget, gentlemen, that our first hypothesis, our only goal, is to attain the organization of a power loved, cherished, and venerated. But whatever prejudices you may have at the moment, could you, when confronted by the generally believed dogma of perfectibility, think that the human species, after having for so long felt the respect which links the weak to the strong, the admiration which makes intelligence bow before genius, the love which joyously devotes itself to the man to whose life the destinies of a people and those of the entire world seem tied, could you think that mankind was entirely disinherited of these noble elements of its happiness? If these elements were supposed to have perished, they doubtless did so at the moment when revolutionary anarchy seemed to have dispelled them forever from the human heart. And didn't we see them then come back to life, at least partly, to give France the amazing strength which during twenty years so astonished and frightened Europe?

Reassure yourselves, gentlemen, about the severity of punishments in the future. When the authorities inflicting them enjoy the confidence and love of the people, you may be sure that the people will celebrate their clemency more often than they bemoan their severity.

Now that you know what we think about the severity of punishment, we shall turn your attention to the social purpose which they ought to attain, or, in other words, to the usefulness which society can expect from them and consequently the character which they shall take on.

At a time when, as we have already said, almost no direct means of education is in the hands of the authorities, that is, in the epochs when there really exists neither ability nor mission to teach the peoples, penal legislation is the only arm which the government possesses—not to lead society on the good path toward the future of which it is ignorant, or to prevent it through wise foresight from embracing the evil path and returning to the barbarism of the past, but only to deter society from vice, conceived in its crudest forms, by the spectacle of the punishment of the guilty. This means of education, the weakest of all in organic epochs, since it acts only indirectly, is the only one remaining in critical periods. It seemed, therefore, of great importance to the modern publicists, who have sought to discover the moral value of legislation. True, these publicists are few today; and Bentham, who indisputably occupies the first place among them, could not fail to recognize that we were not happier than the Greeks and the Romans in the selection of punishments, and that Catholicism alone had known how to utilize this terrible means of effectively impressing men's minds. This observation might have put him on the path of a great number of truths which his critical orientation made him ignore, and which we are going to develop before you.

Yes, the Catholic Church[5] knew how to use even penal legislation as a means of popular education. She knew how to do so since everything was a means of education to her, so great was the faith in the mission to teach the world which Christ had given her. And while she left to the earthly powers the task of applying the temporal punishments, she exercised her influence there, too, by giving these punishments the moral character which they lack today. The dreary ceremonies which today have been reduced, so to say, to a surgical operation seem as brutish and void of life as possible. However, gentlemen, one breath still animates them. See the man who appears on the scaffold between the hangman and the victim. He carries hope and love into the theater of death. Is not all of life there?

Unlike Bentham, we are not astonished at the moral nullity of our penal laws. However, we may say with him that most punishments under our legislation, at least those where blood does not flow, are really judicial parodies.

We now know the cause of this poverty and consequently are not far from the means of making it disappear. We know that where there are no common moral beliefs, set forth by those who are most fervently motivated by them, brutal force is the only means of order at the disposal of the authorities. So it is worthy of note that when the peoples are dazzled by the fear of

[5] "Compare what Saint-Simon, in criticizing Protestantism, had to say about the preacher, who, if he wants 'to have the greatest and most useful effect' and 'create in the minds of the faithful feeling of terror, joy, and hope,' must have the help of poets, musicians, sculptors, and architects." B257.

despotism and arbitrary government, they consent most easily to leaving the most terrible weapon of despotism, material force, in the hands of a mistrusted authority. We point out this inconsistency in order to make felt once more the vicious logic happily presiding over all the deeds of a critical era.

Let us say clearly and frankly that when education of the social sentiments has been reduced to repressive action, that is, when it exists only in penal legislation and the hangman is the only teacher of morality certified by the authorities, then only can despotism reign and then only can mankind be reduced to a most real and degrading form of slavery.

Let us not leave this topic without learning an important lesson from the opinions of the great English jurist. You hear repeated every day, *ad nauseam,* that the human mind must no longer be satisfied with incomplete solutions, with facts contradictory to principles, and with incomprehensible explanations of effects without causes: in short, that all that seems amazing and miraculous to man is only the expression of his ignorance, an indication of the work still to be undertaken to discover truth obscured by poorly observed phenomena. We are merely expressing a scientific belief which is too popular in critical periods for us to fear contradiction on this point. Well, gentlemen, how does Bentham explain that the Greeks, the Romans, and we are equally unable to profit from the body of penal laws, while Catholicism, on the other hand, used it advantageously to inspire the fear and the hopes with which it wanted to imbue men's souls? The problem would have been of interest to the man who wanted to establish a link between antiquity and us. Bentham passes over this point without scrutiny, and it is impossible not to be convinced, knowing his political opinions, which are those of all our publicists, that this superiority of Catholicism over us and over the Romans is a truly incomprehensible miracle for him, as for all men subject to the influence of the critical spirit. Indeed, how could one admit that the barbarous Middle Ages knew the great secrets of the conduct of peoples? How could one admit that they were skillfully using means which produced an effect on the masses calculated, so to say, in advance, while we, the wonders of civilization, do not know what civilization is, or, at least, can do nothing to facilitate its development?

As our personal experience permits us to affirm, the same embarrassment appears in all general questions, however one may try to resist the blindness of the education which the eighteenth century has bequeathed us. Put your antipathies against the Middle Ages aside for a moment; forget temporarily that the doctrine of the social leaders at the epoch of human life is repugnant to you; and you cannot help but recognize a very remarkable harmony between that doctrine and the acts of the authorities at that epoch. But it is precisely the harmony between thought and acts which forms the healthy state of the human spirit, as their disagreement is the sign of folly. Bentham's comparison of the Middle Ages with the present epoch is one of clearest proofs of the vicious circle in which the critical doctrines hold mankind imprisoned.

We must still speak about the magistracy, that is, about the choice of the men charged with applying the moral doctrine to the exceptional vicious cases, for we deal here only with penal legislation.

Let us first establish a subdivision which will permit us to pass over a part of the question which we can treat usefully only after having expounded to you directly the ideas of the school concerning the moral or rather sentimental future of mankind.

The exceptional vicious cases can be divided into three classes which correspond to the threefold point of view from which man and mankind can be envisaged. We wish to speak of the three aspects which we designate by three words: the fine arts, science, and industry. There are three types of crime: crimes* against the sentiments or against the moral relations of

* Let us remember, as we have already indicated, that to commit a crime always means to commit an act of a *reactionary (rétrograde)* character, to reproduce a practice from the past, or, in other words, to prove that education has not attained its end. The guilty is for us, therefore, merely a son of the past, and all present efforts must aim at making him a child of the future.[6]

[6] "An interesting attempt of the Saint-Simonians to incorporate their theory of progress into their sociological theory of punishment. According to Saint-Simonian theory the delinquent is therefore socially 'retarded' and represents within a given society a society already passed by history. It

men among themselves, crimes relating to science, and crimes
against industry. The same division exists among virtuous acts
which appear as progress of the sympathies of sociability, scientific discoveries, and finally conquests of industry; but for the
moment we have nothing to say in this regard.

According to this classification, the magistrature, from the
standpoint of penal law, is divided into three orders, as is also
the penal code; and these three orders correspond to the three
great social orders, which for us are not monarchy, aristocracy,
and democracy, but the artists, the scholars, and the industrialists.
We repeat that we are using the term "artist" provisionally, since
the term which we want to use would doubtless be misunderstood
today.

Which persons within these three great classes of society shall
judge whether certain deeds are vicious; that is, whether they
offend the sentiments; whether they are injurious to the progress
of the teaching of science; and finally, whether they are contrary
to the development of wealth and its distribution according to
the worker's ability?

You will understand, gentlemen, that the abstraction to
which we have just exposed you does not mean that there are no
abnormal and complex facts. Certain cases under the present
organization of the judicial order fall under two different
jurisdictions. That will also occur in the future, but this abstraction is nevertheless necessary, precisely in order to establish
the special prerogatives of each tribunal.

After these preliminaries, you will see that we should for
the moment omit the discussion of the order of the sentiments
and limit ourselves to an investigation of the other two classes.

We, too, gentlemen, agree with the critical publicists that

---

foreshadows the kind of objection often made against Durkheim's theory of
punishment, which is so close to the Saint-Simonian theory in many respects,
but which finds some difficulty in defining wherein progress consists; so that
the individual who anticipates social development, as well as the one who
stays behind, undergoes and consequently deserves public reprobation and
therefore punishment." B260.

See also the article in the *Globe* (September 13, and October 3, 1831), in
which the Saint-Simonians called for the transformation of prisons from
punitive detention places to work camps which aimed at the moral and the
professional re-education of the criminal.

one should be judged by one's peers, provided that one means that industrial crimes should be judged by industrialists and crimes against science by scientists. But this is a long way from jury by lot; and to avoid our being led there, we hasten to add that if one is to be judged by one's peers, it shall be under the condition that among these peers the superiors will judge. Without this condition, this principle is rather a cause of disorder than a guarantee of order, since in adopting it one declares that one can leave to chance the task of deciding whether immorality, ignorance, and incompetence will judge.

To judge a particular deed, one must be placed on a higher plane than its doer. One must have a broader understanding and broader interests than the latter. To know whether a fact is abnormal, one must know the general fact to which it corresponds.

Who then, for example, can carry on the scientific magistracy if not the men who know best the general needs of science? And do not hasten to conclude from these words that we wish to give such prerogative to the French Academy, or to the Academy of Medicine, or to the Faculty of Law, or to some other existing institution. No, gentlemen, if we expect a social regeneration, these institutions, which are only infinitely small, specialized branches of our organization, will consequently undergo a radical change. However, we recognize that men often raise themselves to the level of the circumstance for which they do not consider themselves to have been made, and that happens, above all, when the habits of their lives lead them naturally, instinctively, so to say, to the new mission entrusted to them. A recent example will make you understand the full truth of this proposition. We wish to speak of the commercial courts.[7]

No principle which we have put forth so far is contrary to the composition of commercial courts. This institution, as well as the establishment of the commercial code, seems to us the only testimony of the progressive element in our legislation. And we do not hereby mean to say that the code and the commercial

[7] In its discussion of commercial courts, the *Doctrine* rests heavily on ideas developed by Saint-Simon in *L'Industrie* (*Oeuvres de Saint-Simon et d'Enfantin*, XIX, 116 ff., 127 ff.) Cf. B263.

courts will not undergo great modifications in the future, but
merely that they will contribute more efficiently than any other
part of our judicial apparatus to the general reform of our
legislation. Thus something has been observed which seems
miraculous to a jurist: men dedicated to work seemingly foreign
to legislation make decisions about the most delicate questions
relating to commerce with a promptness and an exactness unknown to other tribunals. The astonishment, moreover, was
quite natural, since it resulted from the false idea necessarily
brought about by the spectacle of legislation which, except for
commercial law, related to facts outside the knowledge and habits
of each citizen.

It was, therefore, recognized that the commercial magistracy
could be entrusted to industrialists and that this tribunal could
serve as a first level of jurisdiction. But admittedly one acted as
if the power of these industrialists were not to be trusted. One
becomes convinced of this when reflecting about the importance
of the areas remaining under the jurisdiction of civil legislation,
which, nevertheless, relate directly to the production and distribution of social wealth, or, in other words, to the operation
and organization of society viewed from the industrial point of
view. Thus questions relating to real property, those serving to
regulate the distribution and transfer of the instruments of work
(that is of leases, sales documents, inheritance, and dowries),
questions which have been determined only in terms of the social
doctrine of the past, have remained in the domain of so-called
civil legislation. But if you will recall the sessions in which we
spoke of the constitution of property, you will understand how
the legislation of an industrial society would include the regulation of landed property as well as acts relating to commercial and
today, particularly, to movable property. And then, profiting
from the attempt to make the commercial courts into higher
courts (called by their true names, industrial courts), we shall
have all deeds harmful to the progress of wealth, that is, to the
development of industry, be judged precisely by the men who
contribute most effectively to its progress. And let no one object
to us by mentioning the ignorance in which almost all industrialists are today in regard to the civil laws, since this ignorance

proves nothing but that the civil code is not in accord with the present state of society and was not conceived in accordance with a general view of the real needs of our epoch and, above all, of those of the future. But let us not overemphasize the knowledge of the jurists and the ignorance of the industrialists. For if it were a question of judging the usefulness of almost all our laws in regard to the material prosperity of society, the judgment of the industrialists would carry at least as much weight as that of the jurists. The former suffer at every step from the evils of the law, since these evils are precisely the element in which the jurists live and find their reputation and, above all, their clientele.

But what particularly characterizes the progress of which we see proof in commercial legislation—that happy development of the attempts made by industry since the first establishment of the communes to constitute itself as a social force—is the way in which the industrial judges constantly view all disputes. While form is important to other judges, the industrial judges are interested in getting to the bottom of things. Where the jurists seek to stress the points of conflict, the commercial judges attempt to discover the elements of conciliation. Finally, friendly arbitration, the consultation of experts, and the personal knowledge of the judges concerning the subjects under discussion are greater guarantees of the quality of commercial judgments than the power of appeal. And this procedure seems so true to us that there would undeniably be more equitably invalidated decisions if appeal operated in a manner contrary to present day practice, that is to say from civil to commercial judges.

Note, gentlemen, that the motives which serve as bases for the institution of the jury could have no application here precisely because the commercial judges decide on matters which, in all probability, they would know much better than juries named by chance.

We have extended our discussion to the commercial courts in order to resolve the doubt which must have entered almost all minds exposed to a new social doctrine. For the most difficult thing to understand in this case is the change which the present must undergo to assure the characteristics announced for the future. Moreover, Leibniz and many others have said that the present is heavy with the future. Consequently, if our future is to be realized, it exists already, even if unperceived, as a germ in the facts we see. We have discovered it already in regard to industrial organization in the development of credit through the banks and through the increasingly rapid mobilization of property titles, even including real property; in the constant lowering of the interest rate; in the slow, to be sure, but inevitable fall of commercial prejudices which separate peoples; finally, in the increasingly important role which the leaders of industry take in the administration of political affairs. In this connection, we must still discuss with you the progressive seed contained in that part of present day legislation which is intended to regulate property and to avert attacks against property.

We have said that to judge a deed, to call it a crime, one must know what is not a crime, namely the regulations of the particular order, or perhaps the industrial, scientific, or sentimental code of society. From this we concluded that one should be judged by the superiors in the hierarchy to which he belongs. Similarly, we shall state that all changes in the various codes should be made only by these superior men, and we shall have explained what we understand by the legislative power, something so important today and yet so inadequately understood.

The determination of who is able to make and apply the laws is the basis for all good legislation and for every social order, since the determination assumes the desire to entrust the drawing up of the regulations for the particular order and the care of enforcing its observation to the individual most able to appraise their justice and utility. If this is true, gentlemen, it is difficult not to be astonished when one sees our publicists extol the profundity of their political doctrines and at the same time seek the guarantee for legislative ability in qualifications most alien to this ability and to ability in general. From the fact that in the state of barbarism, in which we still are, certain men have the power to live abundantly without producing anything, without working, in the most complete idleness, our publicists seem to conclude that it is among these idle that the men must necessarily be found who know best the interests of a society which lives by work alone. We are far from saying that they are wrong in measuring legislative ability today by tax contributions, but one must admit, if we may say so, that these contributions are largely a matter of luck. When war was the real support of the body social and the soil was the property of the warrior, when military habits were those which suited everyone best and the lords were the most perfect models of these habits, a count was the natural judge of his vassals, and logic was as satisfied with this dogma of feudal legislation as was all of society. But as soon as the counts and the barons had destroyed their turrets and had let their swords rust, the property of the land was merely a title to idleness by choice, and no longer an obligatory social function. The conditions of legislative ability were soon to be changed. However, before they had arrived at this new basis, we saw unprepared legislators rushing from everywhere to the tribune's chair, involuntarily restored by the "parliaments" which had destroyed seignorial or military justice. These invasions were not of long duration, and soon one man and a few bayonets sufficed to force these legislative intruders to abandon their place. But this man, also ignorant of the future, turned violently back to the past and placed legislation again on the foundations of feudalism, that is to say, on property by right of birth.

Since then some fortunate innovations have been made which will confirm what we have already said about the seed of the future being contained in the present.

The patent, the only brevet which society gives today to the men who nourish it, has been included in the electoral census, and professors, physicians, and lawyers appear on the jury lists. The practice introduces an intellectual and personal condition, very vague, to be sure, where there had been only a purely material condition, completely independent of the individual.

If the earth were today the appanage of the industrialist on the basis of personal ability, as it was that of the warrior by hereditary right, one would understand how a peaceful society could adopt a principle in use in a military society, because, as in the case of feudalism, there would exist a union of men having a common goal: in short, there would be a society. And the

counts and barons of industry, organized hierarchically according to merit, would be the natural judges of the material interests
of that society, as the lords in the Middle Ages were the natural
judges of the military society.

After recalling what we have told you in other sessions concerning the constitution of property, it will be easier for you now
to understand the organization of the industrial magistrature.
Each of the special workshops—and by the term "workshop" we
do not understand one room or even a four-story house, but a
commune, a village, a city, an entire nation, since society, however numerous, has always an industrial function to fulfill—each
of the special workshops or each industrial municipality needs
a set of regulations and, consequently, men capable of judging
whether certain facts harm production or whether they are advantageous. These are the men who impose the industrial magistrature.

Gentlemen, in order that the word "magistracy" does not
create false ideas in your mind or, rather, does not awaken those
which the present state of society has put there, do not forget that
the future, as we see it, will ignore these endless, bitter discussions about property. If a dispute arose among some industrialists concerning their right to use a certain instrument or workshop, the institution in charge of the direction of material works
would be the natural arbitrator which would explain the obscure terms in the charter of infeudation issued by it to every
producer at the time of his industrial investiture. Similarly, the
fate of widows and minors, assured by communal protection and
not by the direct and often blind foresight of individuals, will
not require guarantees against any third party. Finally, since the
transfer of property during life or after death will take place only
in the form of a new lease (granted to a new manager), sales, auc-
tions, wills, transfers, securities, mortgages, expropriations, and
so on will be unknown.

Thus there will disappear from the future social state the
multitude of archivists and notaries, and that army of fighters,
the lawyers, admittedly businessmen, today ceaselessly occupied
with maintaining, attacking, and defending rights which will
give place to arbitration by the leaders of industry. Legislation

and the procedures relating to property will be reduced to this arbitration, since the distribution of products, like the discussions about the ownership of the workshops, that is to say about the administration and exploitation of real property, will never be appealed to any other tribunal.

But here, gentlemen, as we know in advance, that formidable objection will reappear with which we have already dealt when speaking about the organization of the banks. It is formidable because it uses terms producing an effect like that of a Medusa's head terrorizing men's minds. They will say that we are predicting corporations and their retinues, the jurisprudence of consuls and syndics, the mixed councils of master-tradesmen and workmen and all their rubbish, of which the revolution has freed us for all times. For people who follow this line of argument, no way of establishing order is possible today, because all instruments of order have their analogies in the past, even if they may have been used for different purposes then. We know well the shackles which the old corporations put on industry. But these shackles, true limitations on the industrialists in the early days of their social existence, did not make for co-operation among them once they had become of age, for not all of them were equally strong and enlightened. Because there were institutions, called corporations, repugnant in their forms, it does not necessarily follow that industrialists should not organize. Finally, because the former association of labor no longer serves its purpose, it must not necessarily be concluded that a general attitude of "save-himself-who-can," called competition, is the superlative of industrial well-being.

Observe that this inclination not to understand a man because he is dressed in a way which at first seems Gothic is the prejudice most to be feared when one's dress is not Gothic but tailored after a patron of antiquity; not feudal but Greek or Roman. Let us reject this dangerous prejudice, gentlemen, and try first to look dispassionately at the former order as well as at the present liberty, and if, like us, you decide for the Saint-Simonian order, it will be because you will have recognized, as we did, that through it alone can true liberty exist.

This promise on our part will doubtless not suffice, and you will expect from us more positive assurance of our lack of affection for the past. Indeed, some may claim that we might wish to re-establish the past without mistrusting it and believe that we were making something new of it. Well, gentlemen, Saint-Simon has made something new. He has really announced good news; you will be persuaded of this, as we are, when you examine whether the goal which he assigns to the future society is really new, that is to say, whether the regenerating or co-ordinating principle of all the facts of this renewed society is different from the principles which presided over the organization of the Middle Ages and the societies of antiquity.

If this difference exists, even if we predict for the future corporations, a hierarchy, directors of moral, scientific, or industrial activity, even if we speak of nobility and even utter those terrible words *clergy* and *priest* (as we have already spoken of *confession, excommunication, canonization*), you will not want to pass over this lightly. You will seek to penetrate to the core, and you will find no fiscal corporations of the seventeenth or eighteenth centuries, no feudal hierarchy based on war and for war, no fiefs, functions, or coats of arms transmitted by inheritance. Finally, above all, you will not find social directors, priests, and warriors constantly fighting and involuntarily bringing confusion into a society which has hesitated until now to free itself from its primitive barbarism, that is to say from antagonism, from slavery, and from war, in order to embrace freely and irrevocably the peaceful path of universal association.

All that we have told you until now should be repeated to you in summary, giving the ideas already expressed a general color reflecting the broadest principle on which all our views of the future are founded. This principle determines at every epoch of civilization the affection of the citizen for society and for the entire universe of which he is a part and makes him cherish them everywhere, because everywhere he finds the principle again manifested in a thousand different forms. It is to this principle that the industrialist, the scholar, and the artist relate all their deeds and all their thoughts, because it alone definitely sanctions or condemns, because it alone presents mankind to us not as obscure chaos, but as the execution of a plan, of a harmoniously conceived will imposing duties of man which, if carried out by him, bring about his happiness.

Yes, gentlemen, the social principle of the future discovered by Saint-Simon, in other words, the soul and sentiments of the new society, will be different from those of the past. And one thing also will convince you, namely, that with our words we constantly disturb the consciences of men attached to the past. Examine whether the war which we wage against all birth privileges, for example against the transfer of wealth through inheritance, as well as our pronounced opposition against the military regime, are not direct condemnations not only of feudalism but also of the sentiments which alone seem to unite these men today.

No, gentlemen, we do not hesitate to say that the defenders of inheritance, even if they condemn the right of primogeniture and the *majorats,* are still subject to the influence of the doctrines from which we have been completely emancipated by Saint-Simon.

But, we repeat, only after we have spoken about the sentiments and about the morality which is its theory can we directly approach the antipathies which have arisen from the critical position of our age, antipathies tending to see despotism and arbitrary government wherever there is one direction, as if we did not know ourselves from our own experience that people let themselves be led joyfully and carried away when marching in the footsteps of men whom they venerate and love. Will mankind never benefit as fully as it might from the privileged souls, from the ardent hearts, from the keenest minds? Will it let them emerge painlessly and risk seeing them extinguished in the languor of hereditary idleness or in the debasing works to which misery condemns? No, gentlemen, we are weary of all political principles which do not aim at returning the destiny of the peoples to the hands of devotion and genius. We shall cast off our fearful mistrust when we reflect calmly for one moment about the pitiful results it brings about. And we shall joyfully return to that great virtue, so disregarded—we may even say, so misunderstood—to that easy and gentle virtue among beings who have a common aim they wish to attain; a virtue so painful, so revolting when it stoops to egoism. We shall return lovingly to obedience.

Introduction to the Religious Question

Gentlemen:

In presenting to you most of the principal ideas of Saint-Simon, we have tried particularly to make you understand that society is to be organized according to a general idea and ceaselessly to be guided in its entirety and in its details according to this idea.

In our last sessions, we spoke of the means of social direction, and above all of education, the first and most powerful of all. We said that education was destined, on the one hand, to put individual wills in harmony with the general goal, to make them concur sympathetically towards this goal and, on the other hand, to distribute among the members of society the special knowledge needed to carry out the various types of work and fulfill the various functions of society at the particular stages of civilization.

We have also spoken of another great means of social direction, namely legislation, which in organic epochs is at once penal and remunerative. We have shown that when deprived, like all social facts during critical periods, of the moral sanction which alone can give it a positive value, legislation is reduced to a negative role, namely the purely material and entirely brutal repression of vicious and retrograde abnormalities.

We have said that all these ideas have remained incomplete, since we were unable to present them to you in their entirety as long as we had not raised you to a sufficiently elevated point of view to evaluate their full importance. We could not yet approach the tremendous problem which comprises all the others and whose solution gives all human facts a new meaning.

We may be asked why it was not our first task to pose and

answer this great problem which we claim to be indispensable to
the understanding of all the others.

This delay was intentional. Considering the moral disposition of our age, we thought that we should first of all develop the
ideas of our master to the point where the necessity of examining
this problem would be understood by everyone. This procedure
is necessary to draw adequate attention to the problem under
discussion, the terms of which are such as to arouse the strongest
antipathy.

This problem can be expressed thus: Has mankind a religious future? And if so, can religion be reduced to a conception or to purely individual contemplation? Should one not conceive of it as inward thought, isolated from the totality of the
sentiments and from each person's system of ideas, without any
influence on his social action and political life? Or shall the
religion of the future not appear as the expression, as the outburst of the collective thought of mankind, as the synthesis of all
its conceptions, of all its modes of being? Should it not take its
place in the political order and dominate it entirely? These,
gentlemen, are the important questions which we must examine.
This is the vast field which we shall enter; for the moment, we
do not claim to explore it to its fullest extent but shall at least
survey its principal directions.

Doubtless, courage was needed by the men who first dared
to trouble mankind in its religious beliefs when all, princes and
subjects, artists and scientists, warriors and industrialists, unanimously recognized the existence of one God, of one providential
order.

Times have changed greatly.

We certainly do not claim to be heroes for introducing the
foundations of a new religion to you. In this indulgent, or rather
indifferent, century, all opinions, as we know, can appear without danger, especially when they seem not to go beyond the narrow confines of a philosophic school. But we also know that
we are speaking to men who consider themselves superior because they are unbelievers, and who smile scornfully at all religious ideas, which they relegate to the dark ages, to what they
call the barbarism of the Middle Ages, and to the childhood of

mankind. We do not fear to brave this smile. Voltairian sarcasm and the arrogant scorn of modern materialism can dispel from some men's hearts the vague sentimentality common today. They can frighten away and confound that type of individual religiosity which in vain seeks forms to express itself, but they are powerless to destroy deep conviction.

Yes, gentlemen, we have come here to expose ourselves to this sarcasm and scorn. For following Saint-Simon and in his name, we come to proclaim that mankind has a religious future; that the religion of the future will be greater and more powerful than all those in the past; that it will, like those which preceded it, be the synthesis of all conceptions of mankind and, moreover, of all modes of being. Not only will it dominate the political order, but the political order will be totally a religious institution; for nothing will be conceived of outside of God or will develop outside of His law. Let us add finally that this religion will embrace the entire world because the law of God is universal.

These are the propositions at which the school of Saint-Simon has arrived concerning the great problem occupying us at this moment. We have such confidence, or rather such deep faith, in the truth of these propositions that we do not believe that we are taking any risk by acknowledging that if their falsity were successfully demonstrated, the structure we have erected would be overthrown.

We repeat that we are far from exhausting such a vast subject in one session. Keeping in mind the prejudices prevalent in an age when religious questions are considered to have been judged once and for all, we are at this moment concerned only with combatting this preconceived disfavor and with destroying the arguments presented against even hearing an examination of these vital questions.

Religion, we are told from all sides, is a fruit of the childhood of societies, a product of the times when imagination was their only torch. Why should one concern oneself with it today? The advances of science and its astonishing discoveries have emancipated the human mind in this respect and should preserve it from ever again falling prey to the illusions of earlier times. Science has undermined the very foundations of religion. It has reduced the priests to their true roles of dupes and impostors. It has demonstrated that their teachings were mere illusions if not lies.

Gentlemen, what does the magic word "science" mean to those who use it with such assurance and arrogance? Science! But which one? Astronomy, physics, chemistry, geology, or physiology? We acquainted ourselves thoroughly with the sciences to learn what they taught, but certainly became neither pagan nor Catholic. This confused agglomeration of bits of isolated knowledge, however, without link or unity, furnished us no proof, no argument of any value against the two great foundations of the entire religious structure: God and a providential plan.

True, the European societies have become irreligious. This, at least, is the general character which they present at their peaks today. But it isn't science, or rather, to use the anarchic language of our epoch, "the sciences" that have brought about this passing phenomenon. It is the philosophic ideas of the last three centuries whose origin and character we must presently determine. The scholars have doubtless ardently participated in the destruction of the religious ideas. But it was not as scholars and in consequence of their previous works in this connection that they were led to direct their research toward giving an irreligious interpretation to the facts which they observed. They did so in the capacity of fervent disciples of the critical philosophy. And with little reflection, indeed, it will be seen that nothing less than the philosophic faith that inspired them was necessary for them to find (in their systems on spontaneous generation, for example) an unchallengeable demonstration against the existence of God; for them to find above all, as they claim, a proof of disorder in the existence of facts which they could not classify and whose functions they could not explain—which discovery should only have proved to them their own ignorance. It is not from their positive works that the scholars have drawn their irreligious faith, as they seem to believe, but from a hypothesis, the critical hypothesis which in one form or another has implicitly or explicitly proclaimed that no love, no intelligence, and no force governs the world; that all is left to chance; that man, the incidental product of some general fermentation, has no destiny in the chaos in which he lives, a chaos which doubtless will some day blindly annihilate him as it has blindly created him.

No, gentlemen, the sciences have not brought about the irreligion which we witness. And if one reflects about the nature of the sciences, he will see that the tribute paid by the scientists to this critical hypothesis is the result of a manifest violation of their mission, of the mission which they have assigned themselves with just pride. And, indeed, what do they propose? What do they claim? What is their goal? To co-ordinate the phenomena according to the laws governing the universe; to relate all isolated laws as far as possible to one single law.

But, gentlemen, mark the entire significance of the word "law." Consider the disposition which leads all scientists to link all phenomena, a disposition without which science would be impossible. Indeed, to be able to study the world, the scientist above all must believe that a certain order presides over it, that his environment is not an immense chaos, that his predictions will not be deceived by a secret and unfathomable fatalism. Yes, gentlemen, this is the faith indispensable to the scholar. He must adopt as his first hypothesis that all is interlinked in the universe if he wants to draw any conclusion whatsoever from his observations.

Yet even if through this inevitable hypothesis the scientists were not unwittingly bearing witness of the existence of a providence, their authority in religious matters could at least be challenged by means of the method which they claim to be using exclusively, and to which they attach the positive character of their works. What do they really claim? To be limiting themselves to observing phenomena, to classifying them impartially, passively, according to the order in which they occur, without worrying about their cause and their end in relation to man and his destiny. It is, therefore, evident that in the present state of scientific claims any investigation by scientists in the field of religion can only be a digression from and a formal contradiction to the rules which they have laid down for themselves and in which they glory.

Take the religious standpoint, but one more elevated and broader than any mankind has yet attained. As long as science preserves its atheistic character, which is considered essential to it, science will not give expression to man's faculty to know successively and progressively the laws by which God governs the world: in brief, the providential plan. None of the discoveries upon which atheism, when threatened, relies will be able to escape the formula: "This is how God manifests himself."

No, gentlemen, it is not the destiny of science, as many seem to believe, to be the eternal enemy of religion and constantly to restrict religion's realm in order some day entirely to dispossess it. On the contrary, science is called upon to extend and constantly to strengthen the realm of religion, since each of science's advances is to give man a broader view of God and of His plans for mankind. And have not the illustrious leaders of science felt so, even those men in whose footsteps the scientists of our day glory to follow? Behold Newton, raising himself to the idea of gravitation and humbly bowing before God whose will he has just discovered. Hear Kepler render thanks unto God in a hymn full of enthusiasm for having revealed to him the simplicity and grandeur of the plan upon which He has founded the universal mechanism. Listen how Leibniz, according to de Maistre's pronouncement the greatest man in science, declares that if he attaches any value to science, it is above all in order to have the right to speak of God. You will then recognize that the higher science rises, the more it approaches religion, and that finally scientific inspiration in its highest state of exaltation becomes one with religious inspiration.

We have said, gentlemen, that one must go back to the critical philosophy to explain the atheistic deviations of science. Let us attempt to explain the origin of this philosophy, of this moral state of societies, which is not a new phenomenon in this world.

In our first sessions we showed at various points that mankind successively passed through organic and critical epochs. In the organic epoch, mankind moved with regularity, under the sway of a common belief, toward an ardently desired goal. During the critical epoch, all forces were engaged in destroying the principles and institutions which had guided the preceding society.

We said at that point, without developing the idea further, that the critical epochs had always been irreligious. It is easy to explain this, their dominant characteristic.

The work of destruction until now has been a special task provoked by the present general feeling of uneasiness and has been undertaken without a plan for reorganization, at least without an idea which could serve to this end. When the time of the critical epochs or the epochs of destruction arrives, new realities arise. Society experiences new needs which cannot be admitted or understood by the overly narrow and now inflexible framework of the established belief and of the political institution based upon it. However, these new realities, these demands of the future, seek to come to light and to assume their rightful place. At first they unsuccessfully batter the old order, but by their repeated shocks they end in shattering and overthrowing it. Society then presents the picture of embittered war, of complete anarchy, where sentiments of hate alone seem to be able to develop. Frightened by the confusion which they observe, no longer able to perceive the order to be established, experiencing nothing but repugnance for the order which has just perished and in which they see only a long, oppressive deception, men of thought soon arrive at the conclusion that the world has been abandoned to disorder, and that it is the plaything of chance and of blind fatalism. When all the hopes which had first animated the struggle vanish after some futile attempts to create a new harmony, man delights in contemplating all the facts which seem to give evidence of disorder. If he looks at the past of mankind, if he studies history, he does so to tell of murders and betrayals, to assign base and shabby causes to events and treacherous intentions to deeds, and to combine his examples in a way leaving no hope for the future. And when he looks at the world which surrounds him, he at once wants to deprive it of life, to treat it as an inorganic entity, as a being without morality, that is, without destiny. But soon he does not even perceive an ingenious mechanism. He sees everywhere a picture of disorder without providence, and he reflects about all that surrounds this society which repeals and hurts him. And just as history appears to him as merely a series of bloody revolutions, nature appears to him as the sphere of tempests and storms, of volcanoes and floods. Everywhere he sees disorder, and it seems to him that Mirabeau or Byron alone speak the language of genius.

But, gentlemen, when man has arrived at this moral state, the necessary consequence of the critical epochs, God withdraws from his heart: for God and order are two identical conceptions to him. But as soon as God ceases to dwell in the heart of man, all morality disappears too, for there is morality only for him who conceives of a destiny which can be conceived only in God.

This sad picture which presents itself to our eyes is not occurring for the first time. The period which separates polytheism from Christianity offers a similar one. Is this not a reason for hoping that the exhausted beliefs of Catholicism will soon give place to new ones?

We have just said that the necessary consequence of organic [*sic!*] epochs has been the loosening, or rather the breaking, of all moral links. We need to explain what we mean.

We have shown previously that critical epochs can be divided into two distinct periods: one forms the beginning of those epochs during which society, united by a fervent faith in the doctrines of destruction, acts in concert to overthrow the former religious and social institution; the other comprises the interval separating destruction from reconstruction during which men, disgusted with the past and the uncertainties of the future, are no longer united by any faith or common enterprises. What we have said concerning the absence of morality in critical periods refers only to the second of the two periods which they include, but not at all to the first, or to the men who figure in it and who, through some sort of inconsistency, preach hatred through love; call for destruction while believing to be building; provoke disorder because they desire order; and establish slavery on the altar they erect to liberty. Gentlemen, let us admire these men. Let us pity them merely for having been given the terrible mission[1]

---

[1] "De Maistre had already pointed out the kind of providential mission assigned to the revolutionaries. See *Considérations sur la France,* 1822, chap. 11." B283.

which they have fulfilled with devotion and love for mankind. Let us pity them, for they were born to love and their entire life was dedicated to hate. But let us not forget that the pity with which they inspire us should be a lesson to us; that it should increase our desires and confirm our hopes in a better future— in a future in which the men who are capable of love will cease-lessly be able to apply their love.

No, gentlemen, the men who have delivered mankind from the beliefs and institutions which arrested its progress after hav-ing aided it could not be without morality. From the height upon which the doctrine of Saint-Simon places you, look down on the careers of those who just accomplished for the last time that terrible task, and you will see that they merely put the finishing strokes on the work begun by Christianity and through their acts bore witness to their faith in the divine word which eighteen hundred years ago proclaimed the day of human brotherhood to the slaves.

We have just shown that the sciences cannot offer a single valid argument against religious ideas; that those arguments supposedly found in the sciences were in obvious contradiction to the nature and purpose of the sciences and to the ideas which served as the foundation of science; that one must attribute the atheism of the scientists of our day to the influence of critical philosophy alone and to the antipathies aroused by it against Catholicism and not to their specialized works, as has usually been done. But, of course, it is not enough to have refuted the testimony brought against religion in the name of science. In-deed, whatever may be the source of atheism, one can at least confront us with it as a fact and ask us if this fact has been pro-duced in vain and if it is not rather imposing in view of the number and above all the authority of the men who testify to the impossibility of a new religious future.

We know, gentlemen, that to the superior men of our time, deep faith is only blind fanaticism, and religious beliefs are nothing but absurd superstitions. But we also know that at the same time when this change in outlook was taking place in modern societies, egoism became dominant. The noblest feelings are daily denounced as prejudices. We know that despite the work of philanthropic political economists (*philanthropes éco-nomistes*),[2] the immense majority of the human species sees in the minority merely idle exploiters, not protectors and leaders who sustain and guide them. And because we know all this, we do not despair for the religious future of mankind, for we believe not only in the return but also in the progress of the general sympathies of devotion and of association.

Doubtless, Christian ideas have lost their force, and we shall not seek to hide this fact by showing the temples still filled with the faithful today. But, gentlemen, you have not forgotten that when Jesus appeared on earth, faith in paganism had also been shattered in the world. The first families of Rome were already refusing to let their daughters fill the functions of vestals, formerly always reserved for the highest nobility, which had guarded this privilege jealously. In order that the priesthood could maintain itself yet for a while, an edict of Augustus was required which opened the order to the daughters of the emancipated.

Among us, too, the social superiors have left the ranks of the clergy which formerly had attracted all the men of great ability. The disciples of Voltaire have laughed at the priests. Did not Cicero ridicule the augurers? We have skeptics and epicureans, but those of Rome were as good as ours. We flee from the Church to run to the theater, and we thereby act like the Romans when they fled to the circus.

But perhaps you will say that we, at least, have no magicians, no sorcerers, no soothsayers; that the credulity of the people is less great today; that the people would reject beliefs which the barbarians would have accepted.

But first of all, it is not a question of the future of beliefs which captivated the peoples of eighteen hundred years ago, nor of keeping the external forms which these beliefs took. Moreover, we must call attention to the fact that it is not right to

[2] "We believe that, as context and even word order indicate, we are here concerned with these philanthropists who strive to show that true philanthropy consists strictly in respecting the 'laws of political economy.' One would be tempted to conjecture that the authors of the *Doctrine* were thinking of T. duchâtel. whose thoroughly Malthusian work had just appeared in 1829: *De la Charité dans les rapports avec l'état moral et le bien-être des classes inférieures de la société.*" B285.

make us seem more unbelieving than we are, for we have deep faith. You say that we have neither sorcerers nor magicians, and you conclude that we are not believing. This is a false conclusion. It proves only that sorcery and magic are too crude means to deceive the men of our day; that our charlatanism is more elevated, our juggling more refined and subtle. Nor are examples lacking here. We could show you enough stages, pulpits, and rostrums surrounded by an openmouthed and often duped public. By command we could mention the hotheaded convictions which often make an egoistic bourgeois[3] seem like a devoted citizen. Mankind never lacks faith. One will no more have to ask whether man has the inclination to believe than whether he will some day renounce love. Rather, it is merely a question of knowing on which men and ideas he will bestow his confidence and for what guarantees he will ask before abandoning himself to them.

You may be certain, gentlemen, that we are as believing as the Romans. We should be ashamed of our credulity if it delivered us defenselessly to egoism, but let us thank God for this precious gift if it makes us confidently embrace the inspirations of devotion.

Our incredulity is not an obstacle to the appearance of new religious ideas. It is rather in our credulity that these ideas find an obstacle.

After having refuted this opinion, we should not hide that there is another, almost opposite opinion which merits examination and which we had to neglect while we rejected the first.

Thus, we shall be told that we paint the present period falsely in antireligious colors, and that society includes many men highly endowed with true piety. And we shall be confronted with the example, which we have just quoted, of the church doors being besieged by masses of faithful.

To the first part of the objection, we reply first of all that the importance we attach to what merits the name of a religious system prevents us from attributing any significance to the more or

---

[3] "The first occurrence in the Saint-Simonian writings of the word 'bourgeois,' which was to acquire such great importance among the socialists." B286.

less mystic contemplations which, at mankind's expense, absorb some individuals with beliefs of their own who through the process of abstraction seem to have forgotten that they are not alone in the world. Moreover, if one intends to speak of the men who are still connected with formulated, public beliefs, with the various sects of Catholicism and Protestantism, we shall point out that Gallican and Jansenist Catholics, Ultramontanes and Jesuits, Lutheran or Calvinist Protestants, Socinians, Episcopalians, Presbyterians, Independents, Quakers, Methodists, and others have as rallying points only dogmas which, despite the significance which they seem to attach to them, are so insignificant in their own eyes that the difference existing between these dogmas, differences completely separating them in their religious practices, introduce no distinctions in their individual or political conduct. They are in agreement not only among themselves but also with the atheists on the things which interest mankind most. Their so-called religious beliefs tend rather to separate them from society than to bind them to it. And finally, if these beliefs are considered only from a practical, which means from a moral and political standpoint, they constitute veritable atheism; for their religious opinions, having so to say only a purely speculative meaning, are almost foreign to society and separate the believers from society rather than uniting them with it. They contain the seed of atheism instead of being the expression of a truly religious sentiment.

But we shall call your attention to the second part of the objection we have just raised. Yes, gentlemen, the temples are still full. Without stopping to take into consideration those who are believers because it is the thing to do or from idleness or calculation: does this fact not prove the ineffectiveness of the critics who claim that they have been able to destroy the most irresistible need of man? Haven't they used all forces at man's disposal to arrive at this goal? Haven't they closed the churches? Haven't they substituted the entire library of the eighteenth century for the holy writings? Gentlemen, if the temples of polytheism had been closed a century before the coming of Jesus, the Greeks and Romans would have returned to fetishism rather than to have lived without religious beliefs and worship. And, similarly, the peoples of our day would return to polytheism if the word of Christ would no longer be preached to them. We do not hesitate to say with you that what is not atheism today is ignorance and superstition. But if we want to heal mankind of this wound, if we want it to abandon the beliefs and practices which we consider unworthy of it, if we want it to leave the Church of the Middle Ages, we must open the Church of the future. Let us stand ready, as de Maistre has said,[4] for a tremendous event in the divine order toward which, as all must notice, we are marching at an accelerated speed. Let us say with him that there is no longer religion on earth and that mankind cannot remain in this state. But more fortunate than de Maistre, we shall no longer wait for the man of genius whom he prophesies and who, according to him, shall soon reveal to the world the natural affinity of religion and science. Saint-Simon has appeared.

[4] Cf. de Maistre, *Soirées de Saint-Petersbourg in Oeuvres complètes,* V, 231, 237, 242. Cf. B288.

Objections Stemming from the Alleged Irreligion of the Positive Sciences

Gentlemen:

The questions we are going to discuss before you today are to such an extent alien to the thinking habits of our epoch that the men dealing with them seem strangers to our age of enlightenment. There is little interest in the question of whether these men are alien to our time because they are ahead of our age, even if at first sight it must be admitted there are good reasons to consider them as belonging to an earlier time.

Most of your hesitations about the ideas of Saint-Simon stem from a cause known to us, because we ourselves were long subject to its influence. Moreover, we do not expect a single significant objection from our audience which we did not raise ourselves when we first came intô contact with the doctrine of Saint-Simon. We wish to cure you of the prejudices which perhaps affected us more than others, but we know that this very delicate cure is impossible when the patient has no confidence in the physician's insights. Consequently, as long as you believe Saint-Simonian science to be faulty and accuse us of falsely presenting the facts serving as our arguments, we shall try to prove to you that your point of view prevents you from seeing clearly and that the doctrine which you follow disfigures and discolors the sublime picture of mankind's development.

We congratulate ourselves on the results of our meetings during the past six months. After having devoted almost all the sessions to developing our historical method for you and to showing you how one could read mankind's future from its past, we have reached the point in our discussions where you are trying to use our own weapons to fight us. You know now that the chain of human destiny is continuous, that the future, whatever it may be, can only be the development from the realities of the past; that only in this way can a positive character be given to the dogma of perfectibility, of which a few superior minds had a premonition toward the end of the last and the beginning of this century. Finally, you are convinced that any foresight which does not rest on a rigorously ascertained tendency of mankind should be rejected as the product of a sickly, weak, and dreamy imagination.

We repeat, gentlemen: the first result of our efforts has been of great importance to us. You have now at your disposal the instrument with which to leaf through the annals of mankind. We need only discuss with you the applications of this method.

However, gentlemen, note that this method will be useless unless you are convinced beforehand that the ground to be exploited contains a gold mine, that is, that the development of mankind is constant progress. You would not even take the trouble to study the past and to investigate history in this way if you did not think that you would have to conclude from this ever increasing wealth that a new and even richer vein would be unearthed by your works, if you did not strongly feel that mankind has not reached the end of its progress, if you were not filled with the desire and hope of bringing humanity a step closer towards happiness.

Yet this is not all. The feeling which guides you would be powerless, the instrument you possess would be useless, if you did not put some order into your works, if you traveled haphazardly through the labyrinth of history. You need a guiding thread. You must know in advance how to classify the materials which you are observing, in order to distinguish those belonging to exhausted parts of the soil and those, on the other hand, which are to lead you to soil containing new and more abundant riches. Then, and only then, will you march with as much fervor as assurance.

To attain this goal, we have tried in our first meetings to make you sense that to understand mankind, even to know man, one must study his *feelings*, his *reasoning*, and his *actions*. Translating these three words belonging to all the philosophies of the past into Saint-Simonian language, we have pointed out to you the historic facts which should be subjected to observation. We told you that the poet or religious, the theoretic or scientific, the practical or industrial development of human societies should be studied.

The fine arts, science, and industry—there is the philosophic trinity of Saint-Simon which we have opposed to that of Plato. There the difference lies for us between the positive philosophy of our age and the so-called metaphysical philosophy which originated over two thousand years ago. This difference, which does not seem considerable at first sight, is tremendous: it gives us the secret of mankind, but Plato had only a premonition of the secret of man and this only in an imperfect manner since he entirely lacked a general view of man's relation to mankind in its totality. This difference is tremendous because Saint-Simon's philosophy is to serve as the foundation for a social morality, while on Socrates', as developed by Plato, only an individual morality could be established, which has not been perfected during eighteen centuries and cannot be without the new conception of the destiny of mankind.

We ask you to think about this idea because at our last meeting one of the objections raised was founded on the supposed philosophic perfection of Plato's doctrine, a doctrine which has been rightly considered the seed that soon was to give life to Christianity. Our admiration for Socrates and for the two men who shared the work of elaborating his doctrine is extremely great. But Saint-Simon, in teaching us what they did for the progress of mankind, showed us what they left undone. There would be a definite contradiction in the thinking of a person who would recognize that social science reached what is called the positive stage only in our days, and who, at the same time, would claim that the philosophic doctrines of Greece have not been surpassed. Indeed, if such a change in mankind's way of viewing the realities affecting it most had neither been discovered nor foreseen by Plato, must it not be concluded that the analysis made by this philosopher of the operations of the human mind, as well as of its moral, political, and religious views, necessarily had to reflect this omission or, rather, ignorance; but that the moral, political, and religious views of Saint-Simon ought to give evidence of the influence of this new conception? The transcendental perfection of the Platonic doctrine should not be used as a weapon against us under the pretext that Christianity was the only religious result of this philosophic doctrine—the most perfect man could have conceived—and that once Christianity was destroyed mankind could not hope or fear for the appearance of any new religious belief. No, gentlemen, Saint-Simon has come to plant on this earth, turned topsy-turvy by the revolutions of the last three centuries, a new philosophic seed of which the future will gather the fruits.

When we told you that one must study the sentimental, scientific, and industrial development of the human race, you must have realized how we were making every effort to place ourselves on the plane occupied today by all men engaged in serious work. We were careful not to have you apply the historical method to the series of the sentimental development of mankind. We spoke principally, we might almost say solely, of the scientific and industrial progress of societies, and we dare to speak of the progress of the sentiments only in terms of the decline of exploitation of man by man and of the increase in the spirit of association. We knew that many of you would vigorously reject this method if we first presented those of its results which would most strongly hurt prejudices acquired by our critical education, and we did not need to mention the word religion to create this effect.

Today, however, the problem which this word raises should be solved. Whatever your personal inclination may be in regard to religious ideas, it is impossible for you not to notice the important place which these ideas occupy in the development of mankind. You cannot deny that facts of the highest importance can be related to these ideas to form a system, and that the law underlying their relationship would furnish a clue for understanding the future of mankind in this respect. You will have discovered the constant progress of the industrial class and the decline of the military spirit and habits. You can similarly demonstrate to yourself the growth and decline of religious feeling.

But here, gentlemen, an objection is raised which, if justified, would save us from wasting time by examining an insoluble problem. We may be told that only that can be observed which is in the realm of observation, and that religious beliefs, being only more or less ingenious hypothetical conceptions, fruits of thoughtless imagination, cannot be subject to rigorous scientific examination and consequently can never be formulated in terms of scientific laws. One might say, moreover, that since religious feeling is characteristic of weak minds, the roles such minds will play will be of little interest once ever developing intellect and reason have assigned them to the lowest ranks of the social order.

Note that this refusal to discuss the subject would grant the singular privilege of judging the question while saying that one did not want to examine it. Is it certain, for example, that in the past the weak men have been those upon whom religious ideas exerted their strongest hold? Is it not evident, on the contrary, that these ideas have had the strength to lead mankind onward on the road to progress which man has followed?

But the first objection appears more real. If religious ideas are beyond observation, why, indeed, observe them? What, gentlemen, does one understand by these words? What about the ideas which are beyond observation? Are those the things which cannot be seen, touched, smelled, heard, or tasted? In that case we should excuse ourselves from speaking about the past at all. No, we will be told that observable facts are certain facts not subject to debate, whether they occur before our eyes or are affirmed in an irrefutable manner. Well, what is more certain, for example, than the facts represented by these words: "fetishism," "polytheism," and "Christianity"? What ideas can be more easily studied than those of Homer, Moses, or Saint Paul? What phenomenon is more real, even for the man who has no religion, than the existence of certain individuals whose happiness is brought about by these ideas?

Suppose for an instant that you would experience no sentiments of affection or love which play such a great part in the lives of most men. You would, however, definitely consider it possible to determine the effects which various sentiments have on the individuals animated by them. For example, because music does not give you pleasure, it does not follow that you cannot observe the pleasure it provides for others. All that you can do in such a case is to regret your imperfect and defective organization, which deprives you of a large number of joys and keen emotions. But you would not claim that the sensation of music could, therefore, not be observed by means of the actions which it called forth, even if it did not act upon you. You certainly would keep from saying that this sensation did not exist.

We do not ask you, gentlemen, at this moment to be sensitive to the great harmony of the universe. That isn't necessary for the calculation and the rational inquiry with which we approached the past. On the contrary, we ask you to remain cold towards religious ideas, to ward off beforehand all sympathy for, but also all antipathy against, these ideas; for we are not seeking to find first whether these beliefs really constitute the happiness of mankind, but simply whether they tend to disappear or, on the other hand, if they are spreading and growing firmer at each of the great revolutions the human race undergoes. Moreover, and we cannot repeat this too often, we do not claim to demonstrate to you the material reality of the facts professed by this or that religious faith. We do not want to confront you with the tangible realities which will inspire the religious beliefs of the future. In brief, we do not want to prove God: axioms cannot be proven. Such pretension loses all foundation as man moves further away from idolatry and the religious sentiment develops. At this point, we do not even wish to seek with you the external forms of the religious dogmas of the future. We shall limit ourselves to establishing the historical facts relating to the successive beliefs of mankind and to deduce from them the law of their disappearance or of their progressive growth.

Later, when we shall have completed this first task, when we shall have shown you that each development of mankind has been marked by a development in the extent and the intensity of religious ideas, when we shall have formulated the law of social progress in this connection according to the historical method, when, finally, we shall be able to recognize that these ideas tend to become even more extensive, then we shall first appeal to you and to your sympathies. If you persisted in believing that such ideas are sinister, that they are attributes of

weakness and ignorance, you would be boldly asserting that instead of being perfectible the human race was becoming weaker
and more degenerate every day.

We can say in advance that such a conclusion would be
revolting to you, gentlemen, for it is precisely because you are
convinced of perfectibility that you reject religious beliefs today
as incompatible with this idea. You deprive the future of religious beliefs because you consider them an obstacle to the
greatest development of human faculties, before having examined whether they were not always and increasingly their
greatest driving force.

We shall, therefore, have to examine whether religion was
not the most active stimulant in determining the actions necessary for social transformation in all epochs when mankind made
great progress and when new social forces appeared. We shall
at the same time investigate if this feeling did not become greater
as did the actions it called forth, and if the Christian faith was
not stronger, more active, and consequently a greater civilizing
force than all the beliefs preceding it.

Indeed, gentlemen, it seems to us that one can make his
problem clear without a long demonstration. We do not believe
that it is necessary to compare minutely and from all aspects the
sentiments of a Christian with those of a pagan, or even with
those of a Jew, or with those of fetish worshippers, to recognize
that the will of God, revealed by Jesus, embraced a much wider
order of things than that revealed by Moses to a single people
for the conduct of this exclusively cherished people. We do not
think that one can doubt even for an instant the superiority of
the religious ideas professed by the Church to those taught by
the priests of the protective divinities of Troy, Athens, Sparta, or
even Rome. Moreover, we think that the entire world will agree
with our comparison of the powerless attempt made by Julian
the Apostate to revive the pagan cult with those being made today to return to the Catholic cult the pomp and influence it possessed several centuries ago. However, the prejudices of a critical
age are so difficult to uproot that we shall often return to past
events which support the propositions we have just enunciated.

But, first, let us stop for a few moments at one of the principal ideas of the doctrine, an idea we have already presented to you and which is indispensable here. We wish to speak of the division of the past into organic and critical epochs.

This first classification of history is already considered by most of you not only as possible but also as very useful and even indispensable for explaining the progress of human societies; a constant, often unnoticeable progress, but sometimes, although rarely, strikingly marked by a terrible struggle between progressive endeavors and retrograde resistance.

When one has adopted such a dogma, it is not sufficient to apply it to a few isolated facts in the development of mankind. It must be considered as the point of departure in any verification of a view of the future. Thus when we seek to solve the problem of whether mankind has a religious future, we are certain in advance that since we have an organic future in mind, we must find our proofs in the chain of organic states of mankind. And, it is indeed evident by definition that since every critical epoch has as its aim the destruction of the organic system which preceded it, all these epochs should be devoted to atheism as they are to egoism and, in general, to the negation of any idea of order. They have come to struggle against the principles of devotion, devotedness, and duty (these three words have a common origin), which served as a link in the society they wish to destroy.

Gentlemen, after this comparison you will realize how one would be prone to commit errors by neglecting to distinguish between these two very different states of mankind. And indeed, such neglect never occurred even on the part of the men to whom our doctrine was most alien. Note, indeed, how European societies during the past three centuries have turned sympathetically to Greece and Rome and have scornfully bypassed the Middle Ages.[1] The eighteenth century fought Christianity.

---

[1] "Condorcet's philosophy of infinite progress and that of his immediate successors met with two difficulties. It assumed continual progress, and yet on the one hand it considered the whole Christian Middle Ages as deprived of any value in the series of progressive stages. On the other hand, it spoke a language which gave one to understand that classical antiquity was for a modern republican an ideal for the resurrection of which one should strive. The Saint-Simonians attempted to do away with this double confusion by

222 THE DOCTRINE OF SAINT-SIMON

It was, therefore, natural that it took its models and drew its strength from the societies in which polytheism had breathed its last, and that criticism was for it the normal and healthy state of mankind as belief in organic unity was its sick state. The difference between the eighteenth-century philosophers and us does not derive from the division of human life into two states but from our way of conceiving these two states. However, gentlemen, as a student of Saint-Simon says, let us abstract the advantages and disadvantages of the system of the future. For the moment, the principal and only question for us as for this student is which social system, on the basis of the observation of the past, is destined by the march of civilization to be established today? But like this student of Saint-Simon, we shall soon add, while changing one of his terms, however, that if this new system is verified (and not, as Comte has said, determined) in this spirit, it will not lead society to its final stage in this rational form. For this rationality will be powerless to drive back egoism, which has become predominant with the dissolution of the old system, since it must pull mankind from its apathy; in brief, must impassion the masses in order to organize them.[2] We repeat again that for the moment it matters little to us to know whether mankind is on the verge of recovering its health or of becoming sick. We wish to discover how its organs will interact in the future. We do not worry about the more or less happy lot mankind will enjoy. Whether healthy or sick, this being will perform certain functions. We must foresee these functions in order to apply medicine or prescribe hygienic rules.

---

putting first classical antiquity and then feudal society in their proper places in the history of progress." B299.

[2] "We have already pointed out many of the often veiled allusions to the doctrine rival to theirs taught by that other disciple of the same master. Here the polemic becomes direct. The substitution of the participle 'verified' for the participle 'determined' marks the distance which separates the 'Saint-Simonian religion' from the 'positive philosophy' of Auguste Comte. According to Auguste Comte, positive science 'determines' our moral goals; feeling has no other function than the entirely subordinate one of 'impassioning the masses.' According to the Saint-Simonians, the determination of goals is a matter of feeling, and positive science fulfills the function, which in the final analysis is subordinate, of 'verifying' the hypotheses of feeling." B301.

You see that in order to place ourselves on the ground from which objections are raised against us, we do our best to put aside for a moment all sympathy for the organic epochs and all antipathy against the critical ones. We are neither religious nor atheist, neither devoted nor self-centered. But we ask this same abandonment of your feelings and the same indifference from you, gentlemen. Try hard to abstract yourselves to the point of not preserving a single human faculty within you. Reduce yourselves for an instant to mere passive instruments of observation. Forget that you love the philosophy and politics of the Greeks and Romans more than those of the Church and of feudalism. Try to remain impartial judges between de Maistre and Voltaire. Examine solely if the course of the past announces an approaching reconciliation of the genius of these great men, as Christianity once brought about the reconciliation between the students of Cato and Julian and those of Epicurus and Lucretius. See if, according to Ballanche's expression, we are not at the end of one of those palingenetic crises in which the passage from an exhausted critical epoch to a new organic epoch takes place: that is to say, when a society, tired of living without a moral link, discovers a new one, stronger than the one which has been destroyed, to which criticism itself slowly submits.[3]

But, gentlemen, another objection has been raised, and we shall hasten to answer it immediately because, seemingly founded on the rigorous application of Saint-Simon's method to the study of the development of mankind, it would ruin all our foreknowledge of a religious future.

First, let us congratulate ourselves again on seeing our opponents invoke the name of our master. Saint Augustine noted similarly in his time that by placing themselves under the standard of Christ, the pagan philosophers struck a few last blows against the Church. With an isolated and consequently misunderstood part of the doctrine, they attacked its totality and unity. The Christians no longer had to fight against philosophers when

[3] See Enfantin's letter to Ballanche, April 1829 (*Oeuvres de Saint-Simon et d'Enfantin*, II, 39), in which he discusses the great impact which Ballanche's *La Palingénésie Sociale* had on the Saint-Simonians. Cf. B303.

they were crushing heresy. Our task will be more advanced when
we shall be fighting only with admirers of our master's genius
and with the disciples of his students.

We have been told that social science, when it reached the
positive state with Saint-Simon, had taken a step which all the
other sciences had taken before; in addition, that all sciences had
been in the theological, then in the metaphysical, and finally in
the positive state. In the first case, man linked phenomena by
supernatural causes; in the second he joined them by means of
personified abstractions (which were no longer entirely supernatural and yet not natural); and finally, when the positive state
arrived, facts were linked according to ideas or laws suggested and
confirmed by the facts themselves. From this development it is
concluded that theology should disappear from the future that
will no longer acknowledge God.

Gentlemen, before examining whether this objection is
founded historically, which we admit with one reservation, let us
carefully consider the meaning of the words expressing this
objective. For example, what is meant by ideas "suggested by the
facts and verifiable by them"? If, as we have mentioned above,
you see a religious man or people, does this fact not suggest that
there are men who believe in God? And if you wish to verify
this idea, are the facts or the men who have suggested it not there
to attest to it?

Now, what is meant by supernatural and by natural causes?
If the belief in God stirred a man, a nation, all of mankind, and
even if you did not share this belief, would it not appear to you
as the very natural cause of a large number of acts? Would it be
more supernatural than the coarsest appetite, than electricity or
magnetism?

Well, look at the past. Does man not seem to you as an
eminently religious being? Is there a more positive fact than
this? Is this not the general and thoroughly natural fact which
best explains and co-ordinates all acts and best permits you to
link them?

Gentlemen, the threefold division of scientific development,
which is quite exact within the boundaries which we shall set,
is false and incomplete in the application used to attack us. We,

too, claim that science—this name referring to the totality of human knowledge—passes through three great different stages. In the first, it presents a confused collection of isolated phenomena. Each fact is its own explanation, reason, and cause. In the second, it is composed of more or less numerous groups of facts, subject to some distinct laws but independent of each other and almost always in conflict. The third, finally, is the complete association of all observable facts obeying one single law. In other words, we recognize that, simultaneously with mankind, science has passed through fetishism, polytheism, and monotheism. This manner of viewing progress is applicable to the development of the human species from earliest times to ours.

The classification which is opposed to ours is, on the contrary, applicable only to one given state of civilization. It is only the explanation of the movement of the human mind in its passage from an organic epoch to the succeeding critical epoch. And yet, we must modify the terms used to present this classification. It indicates the steps made by science from the moment when science, by rejecting a dogma which does not include it, in other words which has not given birth to it, gradually sheds a backward theology and prepares the building materials for a new dogma. Thus one can say that in every organic epoch science has been theological because it was cultivated in the temple and by the priests. It became partly theological and partly atheistic and was divided into sacred and profane science whenever outside protests or often even protests within the temple arose against the former beliefs. Finally, it became completely atheist, and then the name "negative" might have fitted it much better than the name "positive," when the anarchy which corroded the Church began to exist also in the Academy, when science disappeared and only sciences remained. Human knowledge finds itself in such a state today. It had reached the same situation at the time when Lucretius was mechanically building a world and when Aristotle, outside polytheism, compiled an encyclopedic work in which all the sciences were, so to say, put together materially but not united.

These two ways of viewing the development of science, gentlemen, are, in our opinion, applicable to the dual aspect under which we see mankind. Now we can observe man passing through the centuries from an infinite number of causes to one sole and infinite cause. Then again we see how, in order to go through this long development, mankind stops at certain beliefs and gradually abandons them to take us new ones. In this suc‹ cession of religious and irreligious epochs, science, which is only one side of man's being, has followed this course. It has passed from theology to atheism, from pure synthesis to exclusive analysis, from an incomplete and provisional order to an even less enduring anarchy. By not taking this dual aspect into account, one commits the error of confusing alternating facts with constantly progressive ones; of putting heterogeneous facts into the same sequence; of considering transitory progress brought about by criticism as a growing reality, although it must disappear completely in the following organic epoch.

We have just uttered two words, "synthesis" and "analysis," which remind us of an objection raised against us. Its refutation will aid the development of the preceding ideas. Always armed with Saint-Simon, our opponents quote the following passage of the *New Christianity*: "From the establishment of Christianity until the fifteenth century, humanity was principally"—remember this word, gentlemen—"concerned with the co-ordination of its general sentiments, with the establishment of a universal and sole principle and with the foundation of a general institution which had as its purpose to superimpose the aristocracy of talents on that of birth, and in this way to subject all particular interests to the general interest. During this entire period, direct observation of private interests, of particular facts, and of secondary principles was neglected. They were decried by the great majority of minds and the opinion dominated that all secondary principles should be deduced from general facts and from a universal principle. This is to be sure, a purely speculative opinion, considering that human understanding has no way of establishing generalities precise enough for the deduction of specialized knowledge as a direct consequence of the general principle."

Let us for a moment examine the words "purely speculative," for they have given rise to a grave error. Yes, gentlemen, it is a purely speculative opinion to claim that one must deduce all particular facts logically from a general principle, for what mankind could deduce logically in one day could never be transformed into reality in all the centuries. This opinion remains speculative as long as it is not coupled with another idea. Thus Saint-Simon hastens to demonstrate the influence of this second fundamental idea in order to make understood the necessity of using both synthesis and analysis equally in the future. Let us follow him as he continues: "Since the dissolution of the European spiritual power as the result of Luther's insurrection, since the fifteenth century, the human spirit has been cut loose from the most general views. It has been given over to specialization. It has been occupied with the analysis of particular facts, of secondary principles, of the private interests of the different social classes. During this period, the opinion became established that considerations of general facts, general principles, and the general interests of humankind were only vague and metaphysical and could not effectively contribute to the progress of the intellect or the perfection of civilization.

"Thus, since the fifteenth century, the human mind has followed a road contrary to the one it had pursued up to that time, and certainly the important and positive advances which resulted in all spheres of our knowledge have proven irrevocably how our ancestors in the Middle Ages were mistaken in considering the study of particular facts, of secondary principles, and the analysis of private interests to be of little use.

"But"—note this *but,* gentlemen—"it is equally true that a great wrong to society resulted from the state of neglect in which the study of general facts, general principles, and general interests was left since the fifteenth century. This neglect gave rise to the feeling of egoism which has become dominant in all classes and all individuals. This feeling made it easier for Caesar to recover a part of the political power which he had lost before the fifteenth century. To this egoism the political malady of our epoch must be attributed, a malady which has inflicted sufferings on all the workers useful to society, and which allowed the kings to absorb a very large part of the poor's wages for their courtiers and soldiers. This malady has brought about an enormous tax placed by royalty and by the aristocracy of birth on the earnings rightly belonging to the scientists, the artists, and the leaders of industry for directly and positively useful services rendered to society."

But, gentlemen, what conclusion did Saint-Simon draw from this broad view of the Middle Ages and of the last three critical centuries? The following:

"It is, therefore, highly desirable that those works having as their goal the perfection of knowledge about general facts, general principles, and general interests be promptly reactivated and henceforth protected by society equally with those undertakings aiming at the study of particular facts, secondary principles, and private interests."

Thus you see that Saint-Simon's idea is precisely the one which we just expounded to you when we spoke of the organic or religious stages of science in the past and of its critical or irreligious epochs. What Saint-Simon says here about the Middle Ages and the centuries that criticized them is equally applicable to the Roman Republic and to the Empire, to the ancient beliefs of Greece and to their criticism under Pericles, as well as to the Mosaic law in its age of splendor and to the epoch when the Hebrews were divided into Pharisees, Sadducees, and Essenes. This passing from general to particular facts, from general to secondary principles, from general to private interests is throughout the past the same as the transition from religion to atheism. And science, which is nothing but mankind viewed from the products of one of its faculties, has never been excluded from these alternatives, which it has ceaselessly formulated in its language by the terms "synthesis" and "analysis."

Well, gentlemen, we know now from Saint-Simon in what ways these alternating movements have been useful. We know that only when particular facts are neglected, does the contemplation of general facts or their purely synthetic arrangement become a vague and purely speculative metaphysics. The future will, therefore, avoid the mistakes of the Middle Ages in this regard. But we also know that analysis is a cause of disorder when it scorns general facts and the habits of synthetic thinking, without which all works would be only an immense chaos. The future will, therefore, escape the dangers of criticism and domination by egoism. Thanks to Saint-Simon, we have precise knowledge of the causes of mankind's progress. It is up to us, therefore, to establish the future on such foundations that progress will take place with regularity and without interruption.

We hope to have made clear the inadequacy of the three terms "theological," "metaphysical," and "positive" when applied to the three stages of science, whether one has in mind the complete development of science from the origins of society to our days or only the modifications science has undergone each time mankind has been entirely transformed and regenerated. In the most general terms, science, like mankind itself, has been fetishistic, polytheistic, and monotheistic; and secondarily, at each perfection of the general idea, it has been religious, semireligious, semiatheistic, and finally completely atheistic. As you must easily perceive, neither of these two formulas can lead to the conclusion that mankind has no religious future. They instead confirm our foresights in the most positive manner—the former because from fetishism to monotheism the growth of the religious sentiment in intensity and extent is evident; the latter because if science is atheistic today, we must attribute this only to the critical epoch in which we are, which, if the experience of the past is to be believed, proclaims the approaching appearance of a social state in which science will again assume the religious character it has always had in organic epochs.

If our development of these ideas was too involved to be easily understood, we ask you to give your attention for a moment to our more precise formulation of these ideas in the subsequent summary.

In all organic epochs, science is theological because all scientific discoveries come from the temple.

When the laity—and we apply this term to all those who were not of the priestly caste in antiquity as well as the non-clergy of the Middle Ages—when the laity, we say, made advances in science, and the Church did not assimilate their discoveries; that is to say, when the brightest lights of human intellect were not found among the clergy, then the sciences took on a hybrid, partly atheist and partly religious character. These are the epochs which can rightly be called superstitious, because in them the priests themselves fall into ignorance and drag the masses with them, while the scientists, subjected to the yoke of former beliefs, do not yet carry a thoroughgoing atheism into the domain of science. Finally, the day arrives when the chairs of philosophy and science dare rise in open insurrection against the chairs of theology, under whose authority they were first set up. Then theology is silenced. Only outdated dogmas still come forth from the church, and they are branded with ridicule when they dare appear in their Gothic attire.

We repeat that these three so very different aspects of science and of the clergy are observable not only in the course of the last centuries. The same phenomenon has appeared before Christianity; and the pontiffs and sibyls of polytheism, the rabbis of Judea, as well as the druids and bards, had not taught the people anything for a long time when the Christian Church took possession of the mission which they had abandoned. For a long time their scientific influence had been destroyed, and the clergy of the gentiles had been dethroned like ours by scholars and philosophers and by atheists when a new clergy, crushing atheism under the weight of its arms, took science and philosophy into its powerful hands and led them back to a new sanctuary. From there they spread over the entire world and especially among the slaves[4] the light of which the Alexandria museum had shed only a few feeble rays on the idle youth of Greece and Rome.

[4] "In the same way as Christianity crept into Graeco-Roman society through the slaves, the Saint-Simonians anticipate that their 'New Christianity' will creep into the modern world through the 'slaves' of our industrial society, the wage-workers. They will proceed, as did the early Christians, not by calling for revolt but by moral persuasion and by religious preaching." B307.

A Digression on the Work Entitled The Third Book of the Industrialists' Catechism, *by Auguste Comte, a Student of Saint-Simon*[1]

Gentlemen:

In one of our last sessions, the authority of a student of Saint-Simon was invoked against us, a student who, in a work published by his master, had scientifically expounded some parts of the doctrine. We were confronted with quotations, definitely worth examining, and with protests in the name of Comte and of Saint-Simon himself against the religious future which we proclaim—we, the disciples of the same master, who have heard him reveal on his death bed his most comprehensive thought, the *New Christianity.*

[1] "Read by Olinde Rodrigues (H. Fournel, *Bibliographie saint-simonienne,* 1833, p. 70). Apparently the Saint-Simonians are discussing the first *Système de Politique positive* by Auguste Comte, written in 1822 and published in 1824. Actually they discuss the 'Course in Positive Philosophy' which Auguste Comte had just begun on January 4, 1829, before an audience very superior in quality if not also in numbers to the group of young enthusiasts who listened to the lectures in the rue Taranne. The mathematician Fourier, de Blainville, Poinsot, Broussais, Esquirol all were in Comte's course. The 'heretic' thus threatens to exert more influence than the 'orthodox' from whom he had dissented several years before. When Saint-Simon published Comte's work called *Plan des travaux scientifiques nécessaires pour réorganiser la société* under the title *Système de politique positive* in the third number of the *Catéchisme politique des Industriels,* he added a preface in which he expressed his reservations about the orthodoxy of his collaborator and so-called pupil. Saint-Simon, to use his own terms, subordinated 'Platonic' or sentimental and religious ability and 'Aristotelian,' meaning scientific, ability to 'industrial ability.' But he put both of the former on the same level. Comte, on the other hand, granted imagination only a role inferior to that of science and placed scientific ability first. Comte was therefore already at variance with the group when the *Opinions* were published without his collaboration. He only consented to contribute to Cerclet's *Producteur* because of that collection's eclectic character, although protesting against that very eclecticism at the same time. He ceased to collaborate, thus interrupting the

Auguste Comte's work, which we have already had the opportunity to introduce to you, has served for several of us as an
introduction to the doctrine of Saint-Simon. Who, therefore,
could judge its value better than we? If it is considered from the
author's aim in writing it, that of basing political science on the
foundations upon which the observational sciences rest today, no
purely scientific enterprise can be compared to it.

But if, from the point of view to which Saint-Simon has
raised us, we propose to link all the sciences by a new general
conception, to lead them out of the state of isolation and egoism
into which they as well as the men who have cultivated them
have fallen; if, viewing the progressive march of mankind
simultaneously from three aspects (the fine arts, the sciences and

---

publication of his 'Considérations sur le Pouvoir spirituel,' when Enfantin
took over Cerclet's place as editor. It is also difficult to discover in the
Producteur indications of the future 'Saint-Simonian religion.' Enfantin
speaks only of 'political economy.' Bazard's articles only develop the theme
which is dear to Comte, that of the 'necessity of a general doctrine.' Rodrigues, after two articles entitled 'Considérations sur l'industrie' only contributed a series of articles on the life and works of Saint-Simon. In these
articles he defined religion in terms which would have satisfied Saint-Simon,
as 'an applied science which serves as intermediary between the scholars and
the people.' (*Producteur*, III, 290.) Cf. Saint-Simon, *Introduction aux travaux
scientifiques du XIXe siècle* (*Oeuvres Choisies*, I, 213): 'Religion is the collection of applications of general science by means of which enlightened
men govern ignorant men.' *Id., ibid.*, II, 247: 'Luther was not at all a first-
rate genius . . . he only occupied himself with religion and religion is only
an applied science.' Unfortunately the *Producteur* ceased publication before
Rodrigues began the analysis of the *Nouveau Christianisme*. One can trace
in Enfantin's correspondence the slow year by year transformation of the
'dogma' into a 'religion.' Enfantin is the true founder of this 'religion.' If
Olinde Rodrigues now became the spokesman, it was probably because in
his role of last confidant of Saint-Simon he was in a better position than
anybody else to excommunicate Auguste Comte. One year later Rodrigues
played the role of intermediary between Bazard and Enfantin, to use Saint-
Simon's term between the 'Aristotelian' and the 'Platonist,' and received from
both an agreement to an arrangement according to which the scholar and
the priest (or artist) as the two popes of the 'New Christianity' would stand
side by side and be of the same rank." B308.
The five persons referred to as members of Comte's audience were outstanding scientists. The famous Jean Baptiste Joseph Fourier (1768-1830)
and Louis Poinsot (1777-1859) were mathematicians; Henri Marie Ducrotay
de Blainville (1777-1850) was a naturalist; François Joseph Victor Broussais
(1772-1838) and Jean Étienne Dominique Esquirol (1772-1840) were physicians,
the latter an alienist.

industry), we ardently desire to know and to bring about the universal order on this earth; then the man who is absorbed in his love of science, who in writing the history of man almost forgets to speak of the progress of man's sympathies, is, it seems to us, not getting to the heart of the matter. And if this man, even further blinded by his predilection for rationality, wants to disinherit the future of its happiness and glory; if he tries to prove that devotion will be subjected to cold calculation, that imagination will soar upward only with the permission of cumbersome and obstructive reason, and that the words of the poet will go forth from his mouth only after having been commented upon, weighed, and hacked to pieces by the measuring stick, the scales, and the scalpel of science, then we shall say that this man is a heretic, that he has renounced his master and thereby mankind.

However, we repeat, gentlemen, that we are happy that the objections against our doctrine rest finally on ground over which several of us have passed on our way to the master. We are happy since it will be easier for you to discover after this first step where to find unity of doctrine and where heresy.

Let us state the objection.

There is no religious future for mankind, for Saint-Simon himself has said through his student, A. Comte, that since all the sciences have passed through three states (the theological, the metaphysical, and the positive, which is their final stage), it should be the same with the science of social phenomena, and that thus the social future would be entirely extricated from theology.

To admit the contrary, they say, would be unwittingly to regress. It would mean to return through religious ideas to where we began and to make inevitable the return of that critical epoch, from which we all suffer today and which we want so much to leave; for history shows us that all theological epochs are destined to undergo the criticism of the following epochs. Here, gentlemen, are the words of Comte on this subject:

"By the very nature of the human mind, every branch of our knowledge is, in its course, necessarily subject to passing through three different theoretical states: the theological or fictive, the

metaphysical or abstract, and finally, the scientific or positive
state.

"In the first, supernatural ideas serve to link the small number of isolated observations of which science is then composed.
In other words, observed facts are explained, that is to say, seen
a priori, in terms of invented facts." * This state is necessarily
that of any science in its cradle. However imperfect it may be,
it is the only possible method of establishing relationships at that
stage. Consequently, it furnishes the only instrument by means
of which one can reason about facts and stimulate mental activity, which above all needs some rallying points. In other
words, it is indispensable to further progress.

"The second state is destined to serve merely as a transition
from the first to the third. It is hybrid in character. It connects
facts according to ideas which are no longer entirely supernatural
but not yet entirely natural. In brief, these ideas are personified
abstractions in which the mind can see at will either the mystic
name of a supernatural cause or the abstract enunciation of a
simple series of phenomena, depending on whether it is closer to
the theological or the metaphysical state. This metaphysical
state supposes that the now much more numerous facts have
been more closely related by extended analogies.

"The third state constitutes the final form of any science, the
first two having been intended only to prepare gradually for this
last stage. Then the facts are linked by general ideas or laws of
an entirely positive order, suggested and confirmed by the facts
themselves; often these laws are only simple facts general enough
to become principles. One always tries to reduce them to the
smallest possible number, but without ever imagining anything
hypothetical which is not of such nature as to be capable of
eventual verification by observation. These laws are regarded in
all specific cases only as means of generalizing about phenomena.

* If Comte had observed that the phenomenon which he points out here
occurs even in the most positive sciences whenever a new conception is first
introduced into that science in a hypothetical form, then all his conclusions
against what he calls the theological or fictive state would have fallen, since
hypothesis is always the first necessary step in proceeding towards each new
co-ordination of facts.

"When politics is considered as a science and the preceding observations are applied to it, it will be found that it has already passed through the first two states and that it is now ready to reach the third."

Comte presents the same idea in another form:

"Imagination dominates over observation in the first two states of every science. The positive state towards which the sciences ultimately tend is one where imagination plays only a subordinate role to observation."

Approaching this idea from the one the author has just expressed concerning the laws which serve each science in co-ordinating observed facts, one arrives at this conclusion: there is nothing finally admissible in the realm of human intelligence except observed, or better, experienced facts; imagination has no other role to fulfill but that of inventing more or less fitting nomenclatures or facts which can serve temporarily as principles which possibly some day themselves will be verified by observation.[2]

This last expression of Comte's idea clearly illustrates where the scholars stand today in their philosophic conceptions. This can easily be confirmed by running through the preface of the principal works recently published on various theories of physics.

But what is meant by some day verifying a provisionally accepted principle or hypothesis? If it were merely suggested that the hypothesis and the theory derived from it would be upset the day contradictory facts appeared, and that after all means of validating the various applications of the theory had been exhausted a more general theory and a broader hypothesis would be needed, nothing would be truer and more in conformity with all the facts testifying to the progress of human science as well as to the very nature of the mental processes of the individual. But if observed facts can be related only by a principle which itself is subject to eventual verification in the

[2] "Not quite exactly. Auguste Comte attributes another role to the imagination, although this role is usually subordinated to the role of observation in science. See also in this connection the observations presented toward the end of this session." B311.

same way as the facts over which it presides (and here Comte sees a difference between natural and supernatural principles), the realm of experience is unwittingly confused with that of observation; and one concludes by reducing certainty to an immediate and external sensation and finds means for relating even provisionally only those facts which can be experienced.

Thus we believe, for example, with all scientists that the phenomena of tides are caused by the combined action of the sun and the moon, and it is indeed with these data that one arrives at the formulae of celestial mechanics. But is it not evident that this hypothesis can never be verified in the same manner as, for example, the heights of the tide in the port of Brest on a given day?

And is it not the same with the movement of the earth, the discovery of which caused such great alarm among the clergy in its decline, whose authority had been broken for over a century? Experience proves that this hypothesis is applicable to facts which happen before our eyes, but the hypothesis itself cannot be sub-jected to experience.

And is it not the same with the observations transmitted from the past on the various states of human society? And if the globe presents at several points analogies of these various states which have vanished and which are unverifiable for us now, should this analogy, which we accept to help us in perfecting our understanding of human relations, therefore be rejected simply because it is unverifiable by observation?

To the extent that the field of each science broadens beyond immediate experience, the conception which serves it as a link becomes less and less verifiable in the positive sense of the word. And its provisional character in turn disappears before the extent of the generality of the facts included in the hypothesis, an extent and hypothesis which become limitless when no science is conceived as isolated, when all sciences lead to one single dogma which assigns each science a rank, and when all brute and all living bodies are understood as linked to a common destiny. Then the supreme hypothesis becomes the first of all axioms, and man says: God exists. But before going on, we must note that in reasoning about observed facts, we cannot dispense with a hypothesis, no matter what its character may be, and that this hypothesis always precedes and does not follow reasoning.*

You cannot reason about observed facts except by means of an idea adopted beforehand with which or by means of which you compare them. One seeks to demonstrate only the theorems one has formulated.

Thus what characterizes the various stages of science is not the position which a hypothesis holds in relation to observation but, rather, the character of the hypothesis itself. Each science tends to relate all the facts of its special field to one single principle or hypothesis by which these facts are co-ordinated. But once all these special hypotheses are related and sub-ordinated to a general hypothesis, they become various expressions of the general hypothesis which serves as dogma or as the basis of the general science and of human knowledge. They reflect this general hypothesis in the various paths which man's mind must travel so that the most individualistic works will always converge on a social goal. This unity occurs in all organic or religious states of mankind. At some times the anarchy existing in society appears in the scientific realm. The tree of science dies. All its branches are detached from the trunk that gave them life. The special sciences, now isolated, no longer possess the bonds which may unite them. Similarly the scientists become isolated. They no longer carry out general works requiring the co-operation and effort of many. Egoism finally dominates them because they no longer feel a common destiny, and each special field is split more and more. There are as many systems as there are men, and, consequently, no science; similarly, from a different point of view, there are as many religious beliefs as there are men, and, consequently, no religion.

In organic epochs, we say, all sciences are related to the general science or dogma.[3] At least this is the trend the scientific

* We say here "which precedes reasoning," and not "observation," because in all epochs the perception of facts of our environment has been an indispensable condition for the formulation of hypotheses, for reasoning and acting. But the difficulty does not lie here (see Session III).

[3] " 'Dogmatism is the normal state of human intelligence, the state toward which human intelligence constantly tends even when it seems to reject it most strongly. . . . The modern peoples have obeyed this imperious

development of mankind has been taking. But progress can be observed in the succession of dogmas to this day, for through Saint-Simon alone did mankind become conscious of its destiny. Hence none of the successive dogmas of the past were as general and universal as the new dogma. Each dominated men's minds for a time and enabled society to make great progress under its protection. But none has been able to understand and govern facts unforseen by its laws, and entire sciences developed outside its temple. Soon the generally held beliefs are disturbed; and the already outdated dogma can no longer reinstate them, for beliefs forge ahead on ground yet unexplored by dogma. Disturbance is followed by resistance, hatred, and struggle; and in this struggle, the assailants are at first still united in the name of a new but anarchical hypothesis. The defenders of the old dogma are challenged by a desire for independence. However, a separation takes place between the scholars of the dogma under attack and those united under the banner of independence. Fiery Luther raises the standard of revolt and later Galileo formally refutes the scientific language which the Christian clergy believed itself unable to abandon without deserting the faith of Christ.

Then the special sciences tend to become organized separately. The academy like the Church becomes a prey to heresy and Protestantism. The scholar no longer has a master as the believer no longer has a pope. In vain will the leaders of this modern science, those who enrich it by great discoveries, attempt to come to terms with the belief of their fathers. In vain will Leibniz spend part of his life corresponding with Bossuet. The old dogma is exhausted and needs a new transformation. It must directly undergo the test of a new general conception which will systematize all the scattered sciences and all the isolated works that have been playing less and less of a social role, and which inevitably have thrown the scientists into the abyss of egoism. This is, indeed, the last stage of criticism. Once the so-called

---

law since whenever they really had to act, even if merely to destroy, they were inevitably led to give their essentially purely critical ideas a dogmatic form.' (Auguste Comte, 'Considérations sur le Pouvoir spirituel,' *Producteur*, III, 359 f.)" B312.

positive sciences* have reached this point, it would be vain to seek in them and in their method, which has so powerfully facilitated their disunion, the regenerating conception that will restore unity and life to the sciences and will give the scholars a new consciousness of their lofty ministry. And yet, at the end of these periods of anarchy we have just depicted, some minds, tired of disorder but ignorant of the new order which mankind has not yet proclaimed, try to reimpose unity in the works of the intellect. Their efforts are powerless, for they do not reveal to man what he seeks. They can only recall to him what he already knew. Thus the revived materialistic or spiritualistic theories (mere reprints of Epicurus and Lucretius, of Plato and of Proclus,[4] augmented by a few commentaries made necessary by the discovery of additional details) are the products of this fruitless attempt. But they proclaim, at least, that the genius of discoveries will soon appear. Whence does this genius spring? From the inspiration of social destiny. To this destiny alone is reserved the glorious mission of revealing to men what they all desire, what they all call for, what a single one among them first knows how to express. Deeply moved by the sorrows of mankind and ardently wishing to put an end to them, he is leading mankind out of a world it no longer understands, which hurts mankind and where it destroys itself. At his word, this world, already reduced to dust, disappears. A new world is created, for in these new regions order and harmony prevail. All those phenomena which were daily becoming increasingly isolated and individualized are united by a common chain and point to one goal. All are interdependent where once they were merely reflections of the same passions which stirred the scholars and like them seemed to move toward independence.

Gentlemen, let our rationalism merge with admiration and love for this divine faculty of man by means of which he binds what has been disunited and recalls love and order where discord

* They are so called in opposition to the old dogma which has ceased to be considered positive.

[4] Proclus (411-485), a Neo-Platonic philosopher. Victor Cousin had shortly before published an edition with commentaries of Proclus and a translation of Plato. Cf. B313.

and hatred have reigned. Let man adore this faculty which creates new relations of attraction and affinity where he formerly saw only rejection and antagonism. For this faculty, which manifests itself to us everywhere in the progress of mankind, is truly generative and primordial.

Thus men have all been enemies, but some day they shall be brothers. Each phenomenon has had its cause, or rather had contained within it its own cause for being. But one day all shall have only one cause and one end. Families, cities, and nations have been isolated, but there shall be only one human family, one city, and one fatherland. Similarly, every phenomenon has had its own science, and each group of phenomena has constituted a special field. But one universal science will come to be, the link of all the special sciences, of all phenomena, giving all a common cause and end.

Indeed, progress in the political as well as in the scientific order is due to the same faculty, to genius, to inspiration, to the love of order, of unity; that is, to sympathy: for it is sympathy which binds us to the world around us and makes us discover the link among all the parts of this world in which we live, and thus reveals to us in this world a life similar to ours.

This is the mission of the men whom we have called artists* because of the prejudices of some of our listeners. To us, the artists are the men who ceaselessly impress on mankind the progressive movement which has made man come up from the crudest brutality to the degree of civilization we have attained. At this very moment, the men who deserve to be called poets are those to whom the secret of social destiny has been revealed only because their love of mankind made it an imperious need for them to discover it. But only when the artists have spoken, only

* If one has attentively read the parts of the doctrine already expounded, he will understand that two designations from the past fit particularly well the function of which we are here speaking. These designations are *poets* and *priests*, the former corresponding to the critical epoch, the latter to the organic. And indeed the mission of the poet, like that of the priest, has always been to incite the masses towards the realization of the future of which he sang or preached and of which the poets and priests were the most powerful interpreters because they were the most deeply animated. The future will combine these functions into a single one, for the most sublime poetry will be the most powerful sermon.

when they have pierced the veil separating us from the future, does science, departing from this revelation as from a great hypothesis, justify this revelation through the interlinking of all past events which it has established in accordance with this hypothesis, and through the predictions which this new conception of universal order permits it to formulate for the future.

Comte does not conceive of the role of the artists in this way. According to him the scientists transmit to the artists the coldly contrived plan for the social future in order to have it accepted by the masses. The artists, he says, can then use all the means suggested to them by their imagination. Their ways can and should then be free of outside intervention. He even adds that help from the artists is indispensable because the impartial work of the scientists, who must search for and find the law of the development of humanity according to historic facts, would in their minds produce only a stubborn conviction without being able to turn back egoism, which is no less predominant among them than in the rest of society.

It is difficult to understand in this system how the artists can become impassioned with the icy demonstrations of science, and yet this is the first condition the artists are to fulfill in order then to communicate to the masses the fire consuming them. From another standpoint, one cannot see why the industrialists are to put them into practice. But what would then become of the necessary intervention of the fine arts?

It is time to sum up our opinion of Comte's work. As a scholar he has given a perfect description of the development of science in its transition from each organic epoch to the immediately following critical epoch. He might have said that the sciences, religious when they are united by a general conception of human destiny, as occurs in the vigor of the organic epoch,* become little by little completely irreligious when criticism has reached its peak. But this observation may in no way be applied

---

* We shall see later why Catholicism has considered certain sciences profane. It must not be concluded from this that the way in which the sciences were conceived was not a consequence of the dogma. On the contrary, this consequence is easy to ascertain when one remembers that the physical sciences had to be excluded from a temple where the anathema against the flesh resounded daily.

to the transformations the organic doctrines themselves undergo, that is to say, to the progress of the sympathies or of human sociability. Viewed from this standpoint, science, like all of mankind, has passed successively through fetishism and polytheism to arrive at monotheism, which itself contains three great organic epochs in its development: Judaism, particularly materialistic; Christianity, particularly spiritualistic; and the one we are announcing, in which matter and spirit, industry and science, the temporal and the spiritual, will be subject to the rule of one law of love. This last epoch, which is to unite all the past epochs among themselves and with the future by a single conception, is truly final and consequently safe from all future criticism. This answers the last part of the objection raised against us.

We have shown that the claims of the most positive thinkers about the subordinated value of hypotheses are vain. What greater proof is there than Comte's book itself? He conceives of, or rather accepts, since his master has already revealed it to him, a new general idea of human societies, a new classification of historical facts, that is to say, of the various aspects of man's and society's activity. Saint-Simon has shown him all the elements of civilization divided into fine arts, sciences, and industry. Comte, following him, proclaims that the human species is subject in its general development to one invariable law. He even adds that if this idea is accepted, any attempt to account for the development of society must be given up. Does he try to prove this very law? No, he is satisfied with stating it in this way: "When in the study of an institution or of a social idea, or rather of a system of institutions and of an entire doctrine from birth to the present epoch, it is found that at a certain moment the power of this institution or idea began to decline, it may be concluded that it is slated to disappear, and vice versa." [5]

"It can be concluded . . ." But why this conclusion? Why should not what has been diminishing until now take an upward course? Why have we not reached a moment of rest when this

[5] "Auguste Comte's phrase is even more dogmatic, and one wonders why a weaker expression is given here. One reads: . . . has always been diminishing or always been increasing. One can, after this series of observations, foresee with complete certainty the fate which is in store for them.' (*Système de Politique positive,* 1822-24, p. 110; ed. 1912, p. 99.)" B317.

decline will cease? Why then this faith in the perseverance of mankind's efforts? Well, do not hesitate to admit this faith. Say clearly that you have confidence in your love for your fellow-men and in their love for you. Say that you believe in the progressive will of mankind. Say that you believe that the world, in which this will is exerted, favors its development. And say, moreover, that one bond of love unites man closely and indissolubly with what is not himself, and that these two parts of one single whole advance together toward a common destiny and aid each other mutually in their love, their wisdom, and their efforts. Then fearlessly name this law, which you have just stated; this law which the scientist has not created and which he can justify only by his faith in it; this hypothesis of order; conceived by genius, which serves as the basis of science, this universal law which rules man and the world; this powerful will which sweeps him ceaselessly toward a better future. Name it without fear: it is the will of God.

A Letter Concerning the Difficulties Which the Adoption of a New Religious Belief Faces Today

I sympathize with you, my friend, in the difficulties you experience in attempting to deliver your brother[1] from the critical prejudices warping his great ability. This is a conversion worthy of your zeal, for it would certainly bring fortunate results for the doctrine and also for this dear brother who would share with us the hopes Saint-Simon has implanted in us and the happiness he has given us. Tell me all you did do to attain this goal. For my part, I shall try to give you some advice on where you should direct your attacks, because I have taken all the steps which your brother would have to take to leave the narrow road which I, too, once traveled.

In speaking to you of myself, I shall have your brother in mind. You know that it did not take me long to see the insufficiency of my studies at the Ecole Polytechnique. I felt their lack of scope quite soon. And political economy, philosophy, the works of Cabanis,[2] Gall,[3] Destutt de Tracy, and Bentham, made me understand that mathematics and the so-called positive sciences in general were only preparations for higher studies. My almost exclusive admiration for the men whom our century calls scientists par excellence, those who are occupied with matter and movement, was disturbed; or rather, abandoning inorganic bodies, I ardently acquainted myself with the general ideas concerning organic beings.

There I was still in the midst of the "inorganicists." Like

---

[1] "A brother not by blood but according to the doctrine." B320.

[2] Pierre Cabanis (1757-1808), a leading Ideologue philosopher who attempted to approach psychology primarily from the physiological aspect.

[3] Franz Joseph Gall (1758-1828), strongly influenced by the physiological approach to psychology and the founder of phrenology.

them I took a scalpel and began to "anatomize," to dissect the body social. The economists, above all, had seduced me. They worked on matter; I had always something positive in front of my eyes. However, I felt a gap, an immense void to be filled. The dreams of Say on "immaterial products," [4] the unfortunate endeavor which has tempted Storch[5] to analyze these products and compose a theory of moral and intellectual wealth, led me astray. Moreover, I viewed with some distrust the digressions of a science which until then had only claimed to comprise facts resolvable into material products. I also did all in my power to bring together the hybrid views of moral economy, those of equally moral physiology, and those of always moral philosophy, professed by the men I had just named. But I easily perceived that the principles, the dogmas at which I had thus arrived, could not inspire me with a generous confidence, and that I was unwittingly led to doubt about almost all fundamental questions.

Doubt or indifference[6] is a consuming sickness which cannot be endured for long. For man is an eminently sympathetic[7] being who cannot remain completely cold to his surroundings unless he dies. In such a state he would have no incentive for attachment and only those motives for action necessary for the maintenance of his physical forces. He would be reduced to the state of a mere beast; or rather, would be "disorganized" and entirely like the minerals. His life would present a phenomenon similar to that of crystallization.

I was weighed down by doubt. I freed myself from doubt by unwittingly renouncing the scientific habits that had led me there. Educated by our "inorganicists" in complete indifference to the search for causes, I denied their existence. My teachers had told me—and I had even ceaselessly repeated it—that science

[4] Unlike Adam Smith, Say considered services such as those of a doctor, lawyer, administrator, or actor, for example, as products. Cf. B323.

[5] Heinrich von Storch (1766-1835), a German-Russian classical economist.

[6] Lamennais in his *Essai sur l'Indifférence en matière de Religion* had seen in indifference an even greater social evil than in religious error. Cf. B324.

[7] "Note again the difference from the attitude adopted at the same time by Auguste Comte. For him doubt is a disease because man is essentially a 'dogmatic' being; for Enfantin, because he is a 'sympathetic' being. On the idea of sympathy in the Saint-Simonian doctrine, see Session X." B325.

should stop where phenomena can no longer be observed. Well, I forgot this great principle and sought to prove the nonexistence of things which I could not experience.

I recall with what complacency I dared to believe that I was proving the absurdity of all these beliefs which established a link between the finite existence of man and the infinite existence of the universe; with what mathematical rigor I believed myself able to deny immortality, for example, as if my geometric compass or my scalpel had taken eternity apart, as if a corpse had answered me: "All is finished." Fortunately I stopped; Saint-Simon held me back at the edge of the abyss into which I was about to plunge. He came to tear me away from the complete moral dissolution which threatened me.

Perhaps, my friend, at first you will not understand why I am saying that an abyss was opening under me, and that by abandoning passive doubt to deny one of the two hypotheses which dispel this doubt while I adopted the other, I was approaching complete moral dissolution. Nothing is truer, however, and my demoralization would have been greater had I been more competent. The common people alone can obey good sentiments which their reason rejects. They have, if I may say so, an organic heart and a critical mind. They experience sentiments which unite them and bind them to their surroundings; and at the same time, they follow a rationalism which detaches and isolates them, and always leads them back to their individuality. We see them as devoted parents, fairly steady friends, almost ardent citizens, and lukewarm patriots. They are philanthropists who need charity balls and spectacles if they are to give alms.

Yes, my friend, atheism leads to immorality because the sublime synthesis "God exists" is of the same nature as those which serve as bases of all moral ideas. From this it follows that in rejecting this synthesis, one must, with a little logical rigor and perseverance, go further in the ways of egoism.

If at first sight you do not perceive the intimate union between the great axiom of the science of the universe and that of the science of man, if you believe that morality rests on more solid and more material bases than religious sentiment, then examine the works of the men who have analyzed morality, who have calculated devotion, and tell me whether these rigorous logicians, these severe materialists[8] who ridicule the reveries of the sentiments have not also been satisfied with pure hypotheses. Ask them what end morality serves. They will answer that morality strengthens the social bond. But what reason is there for a united society or even for the savage state extolled by Rousseau? What reason is there for the human race? What difference does the strength of the bond uniting men make to me? What does their existence and mine mean to me? What does it matter to me to give life to children who doubtless will soon watch it unfold with the same indifference with which I see it approach its end?

Thus would the man speak who has shut himself off from the vast field of hypothesis. But does this impassionate, cold, marble-like being exist? He lacks imagination and feeling; nothing moves him. He loves nothing, desires nothing, and hopes for nothing. Is that a man?

Now, listen to the makers of hypotheses. One type is represented by Byron, Goethe, or any other critical demon. He plunges not into chaos but into hell. He is not struck by the monotonous uniformity of things human. His soul is not numb with indifference, and the weariness of doubt does not paralyze him. His choice is made between two hypotheses: he sings of disorder and his imagination finds colors to paint vice and crime.

Conversely, the other type believes in a happy future. He hopes and ardently desires to communicate his dearest hopes. Order and harmony make his heart beat. He desires them and this desire dominates his hope to such an extent that he would even give his life if this harmony, for which he prays, so demanded.

Yes, my friend, the words "order," "religion," "association," and "devotion" are a sequence of hypotheses corresponding to the sequence "disorder," "atheism," "individualism," and "egoism." You may perhaps find that I treat the organic series poorly in ascribing to it the same foundation as to the critical series and

[8] An allusion to the eighteenth-century French materialist philosophers, Helvétius and d'Holbach; possibly also to Bentham. Cf. B326.

relating the one as well as the other to two conjectures. Rest assured if I say that two hypotheses exist. I affirm at the same time that mankind rejects one with horror and lovingly embraces the other. I affirm that mankind becomes irresistibly attached to that one of the two hypotheses which promises a happy future. I dare say that it reserves for the pupils of Saint-Simon, if they fulfill the hope, an even more beautiful crown than the one which adorned the heads of the first Christians.

But what have I just said? "A crown, glory, and immortality —there you have our religion," your brother will exclaim with all the atheists of our epoch. And they will ardently hasten to prove their belief. All generous feelings, as Chateaubriand has said, take refuge under the flag.[9] The republican soldier will thus die for his faith and also know the value of the martyr's suffering.

This is the happy contradiction which I just pointed out to you. God, the great God, the only God, who lives in all things, is denied, but they dedicate themselves to the worship of the secondary deities. They call themselves atheists or are pagans. *Liberty, reason,* and *fatherland* are their altars, or at least basically rule their hearts, while the great fatherland—the only one where true liberty resides, because there, only, intelligence and strength are subordinated to love—is not worshipped.

But let us come back to me, my friend. I may say let us come back to you, to your brother, to all of us, children of the eighteenth century, for the same trials are in store for us.

I had thus left cold skepticism in favor of hypotheses. Unwittingly I became concerned with causes. I saw that they had perennially interested men who had always said with Virgil: *Felix qui potuit rerum cognoscere causas;* and finally, I saw that the existence of God and the immortality of the soul, always adopted or rejected, could not be considered as idle questions, indifferent to the welfare of mankind. Doubtless feeble minds, mediocre men, above all those absorbed by narrow specialties, have been able to bypass these immense problems. But on the other hand, have the great men, under the philosophic names of spiritualists or materialists (or rather under the religious names

[9] An inaccurate quotation. Cf. B328.

of believers or atheists) not made these problems, so to say, the occupation and goal of their entire lives? Could they escape the necessity of taking a stand in the affirmative or the negative?

Well, I have made my choice. Neither Leibniz nor Pascal nor Newton could restrain me. I did not confine myself to saying with Montaigne: "What do I know?" I repeated the famous *post mortem nihil,* and I strove as hard as possible to find proofs for it.

Reread the letters which I wrote you at that time. Do you understand how I, who believe in saying what I think and feel, could plead a case without conviction and faith? The reason for this is simple. I sought my proofs in science, but, as I have already told you, what is called science today is not concerned with such questions. It can consider their solution only as axioms, for they are beyond its reach.

However, these efforts of atheism helped me, because I soon came to realize the impotence of scientific verifications for or against the ideas of God and immortality. I reached my conviction through Saint-Simon; and, once penetrated by his doctrine, I felt sufficiently strong to prove to all scientists that they could say nothing satisfactory against religious beliefs and that they were revolting against their own method, about which they made so much fanfare, when they dared to declare war on God. I had taken the great step and thus regained my quality as a man. I had given science its true place and could believe in the inspiration of my sympathies.

What admirable progress, your brother will say, to congratulate oneself on entering the realm of illusions of believing what cannot be materially verified, on deluding oneself with dreams and sinking into vagueness. Scientists, he'll say, will have their romanticism, too.

Well, what is classical science? Has it despite the progress of which it brags succeeded in producing a treatise on morality which even remotely approaches the Gospels? In order to reproach us with having abandoned ourselves to the illusion to which our sympathies led us, the scientists would have to prove that, if man is a calculating and reasoning being, he is not also a sympathetic creature susceptible to the most passionate and even unreflected devotion. We, on the other hand, say that he becomes impassioned and reflects, that he foresees, invents, discovers, imagines, and verifies, that he conceives of desires and calculates means of satisfying them.

But let us go further. Why do you speak of these illusions scornfully and contemptuously? "Because they have created unhappiness in the world," say the critics. "Because they have imposed absurd and horrible beliefs; because they have given power to a few privileged cheats who have used them to exploit the masses; because they have incited cruel wars between peoples." Well, so be it. Let us reject all the beliefs of the past. They have maintained antagonism, you say. They have permitted the exploitation of man by man; they sanctified slavery and war. That is enough for us to be horrified, for we believe in the final association of humankind. We hope for this happy future. We feel that this is our destiny, and we shall do all we can to attain it. Reject, therefore, the egoistic "sympathies" which bring about struggle and disorder; we shall join you in combating them. But respect and worship those "sympathies" which make men believe that they will find happiness only where peace and delightful harmony rule.

You see that I am condemning the beliefs of the past in order to make our opponents' game easier. But is it possible that those who rise in opposition to these illusions are themselves blind at this point? And who has constantly fought antagonism? Who has destroyed the bloody customs of mankind's childhood? Who has sustained the weak and aided the peaceful in breaking the iron yoke weighing them down? What? We delight in celebrating the glory of Aristotle and the power of the syllogism, the works of Archimedes, the discoveries of Galileo and Kepler, the calculations of Newton and of La Place, and we find only insults and hatred in our hearts for those sublime dreamers, for these divine men who have only had to proclaim their faith in a better future and their belief in the purest of destinies to hear them repeated enthusiastically by all of mankind, to tear man out of barbarism and bring him ever closer to the future.

Therefore, you who show haughty contempt for religious reveries, try, if you can, to write out your articles of faith, or rather of unbelief, your moral theory, the cathechism of egoists. See whether even a hundred persons will consent to learn them by heart, to recite them and to comment upon them joyfully every day. Try it, sing "Te libertatem laudamus," and tremble if there is an echo to your hymn.

I can say such things only to you. God keep me from speaking today about the "Credo," the "Lord's Prayer," and the "Te Deum" to your brother—to your brother who knows Homer but hasn't read the Bible; to your brother who knows Virgil and several passages of Cicero by heart, but who has not opened Saint Paul or Saint Augustine; in short, to your brother who has read Helvétius, Dupuis,[10] Volney,[11] and even Dulaure,[12] but who knows the Gospels and the Catechism only through Voltaire and boasted the other day in my presence of never having looked at such books.

Let us smile at our impulse of pity, or rather let us sigh together at seeing the sad products of our classical education and the sad conceit of these men who are such experts on man's past, who know basically only one or two centuries of Greece and Rome and their beloved eighteenth century, and who do not have on their library shelves, as de Maistre said when speaking of Voltaire's book collection, any of the great books of human destiny. Must one not say, like Saint Augustine, when he answered Dioscuros, who consulted him on several obscure passages of Cicero: "Themistocles was not afraid of appearing awkward when he excused himself from playing a certain instrument at a feast, by declaring that he did not know how to play it, and, when asked what he did know, answered: 'I know how to make a small republic great!' " Well, where are there republics more

[10] Charles François Dupuis (1742-1809), author of *Origine de tous les Cultes, ou la Religion universelle,* published in 1794, and an early student of Egyptian religion.

[11] Constantin François Chasseboeuf, Comte de Volney (1757-1820), a materialist thinker who saw the source of all evil in society in man's ignorance and covetousness, and in religion an illusion which has hitherto restrained man's capacity for perfection.

[12] "Jacques Antoine Dulaure (1755-1835), engineer, scholar, member of the Convention and of the Council of the Five Hundred. A friend of Dupuis . . . he had, among other works, published in 1825 a *Histoire abrégée de tous les Cultes.*" B331.

firmly established than that of Moses and more extensive than that conceived by Christ and made a reality by the works of the Church? Show us among the innumerable constitutions collected by Aristotle, in the political utopias of Plato and Cicero, dogmas which were able to command enthusiasm and devotion not for a few days or a few years, and not merely among a handful of studious men, hermits retired from the world, but for a long chain of centuries and everywhere, as the prayers of the Church were able to do wherever they were heard.

Poor physicians of mankind, you have never seen man healthy and wish to cure him! You are studying man deprived of warmth, crying in despair with the last chords of genius. But you are deaf; you are blind when mankind, full of vigor and endowed with a future, shows you the sources of life, hope, and love.

Your brother, you tell me, has just made a stupendous effort. He has consented to look at de Maistre. He has promised you to read Lamennais,[13] and in the invervals between his occupations with departmental law and the budget, which absorb him, he has dedicated a few moments to leafing through Ballanche.[14] That is a great deal, and I congratulate you upon it; but I shall be wrong if this first reading leaves anything more than weak traces on his mind. His prejudices will preserve almost their

[13] "Auguste Comte borrowed from Lamennais in his *Système de Politique positive* the idea of the critique of the two related dogmas of liberty of conscience and of popular sovereignty. Lamennais, on the other hand, expressed his satisfaction with the adherence of the Saint-Simonians to the theory of a society founded on religion." B335.

[14] "With regard to the influence which Ballanche's doctrine exerted on the Saint-Simonians, see index for references to Ballanche. And indeed Ballanche's doctrine constituted a sort of transaction between the theocratic doctrine proper and the prophetic character of the Saint-Simonian 'New Christianity.' (See the letters exchanged in March, 1829 between Ballanche and Enfantin.) Upon Enfantin's request, Ballanche transmitted to him for distribution among the Saint-Simonians copies of the *Palingénésie sociale,* which was being published one volume at a time but was not yet on the market. *Oeuvres de Saint-Simon et d'Enfantin,* XI, 39.) See Sainte-Beuve, *Portraits contemporains,* 1846, ed., I, 329 (essay on Ballanche): 'His lecture on his Prolegomena, about 1828, contributed much to the religious inspiration of the Saint-Simonian school, which was then still materialistic. Having been a witness to the effect of this lecture on some of the strongest minds of the school, I can testify to its directness and promptness.' " B336.

full strength if you do not assist him with a few explanations in
a work which he is undertaking with repugnance and which you
know can only be preparatory, since the view of the future is
almost entirely lacking among these writers whom I have just
named. May you see to it that the spirit of Saint-Simon, our
master, is always between the author and him. More than once
already have you seen how grossly we have been misunderstood.
You have seen how people, hearing us speak as we do of religious
ideas and of Christianity, have taken us for Christians of the
thirteenth century because we can appreciate the magnificent
founders of the Roman church and its more recent defenders.
Not much was needed for us to be called papists, ultramontanes,
and Jesuits. This misunderstanding seems inevitable, to be sure,
if we judge by the experiences of the past, for the disciples of
Christ and those of the apostles were called Jews for a long time
before being designated as Christians. We must, however, anticipate this mistake, because it comes from an incorrect way of
viewing Christianity[15] and the Saint-Simonian future. Try to
keep your brother from falling into this fallacy by fixing his
attention on some of the main points which differentiate the two
doctrines. Make him feel it. But I am getting away from the
goal which I set myself when I began writing you; or rather I
inverted the order which I should have followed in order to tell
you of the struggle I had to undergo against the old man in
order to be regenerated. I shall return to your brother's readings
and, above all, to the misunderstanding which I just pointed out,
to the confusion between the doctrine of the future and that of
the Middle Ages, because I myself was several times almost the
victim of this error.

Let us resume at the point when I recognized the nullity
of scientific verifications for or against the idea of God.

[15] "The Saint-Simonians have often tried to specify the reasons why, while
paying homage to the great historical role of Christianity, they consider it
about to be surpassed and completed. The main reasons are that Christianity
separates religion from politics and deprecates matter—which is contrary to
the synthetic, unitarian spirit of the Saint-Simonian doctrine. And also for
this reason the sympathies of the Saint-Simonians tend more toward Catholicism, a hierarchical organization, than toward Protestantism, which seemed
to them dangerously favorable to the spirit of individualism." B338.

Then I began to reflect about myself. I asked myself whether I had just been given a new faculty or whether I had simply been torn from my lethargy by Saint-Simon. I wished to know whether at the moment when I was waging an embittered war against religious ideas, I had not been religious unwittingly; whether I had not been as absurd as those seemed to me who in their simplicity believed in immortality and in an indestructible and eternal principle of order, life, and love. Soon all those great words which so often made my heart beat faster appeared to my mind: liberty, duty, fatherland, conscience, glory, and humanity.

Humanity! How did it happen that my hand shook and my heart burned with the desire to act when I pronounced the name of this collective being, thought of its happy future, saw its past suffering, and considered the chains in which it still struggles? I became filled with passion for a being which lived in time and eternity, whose origin and end were unknown to me, which resides everywhere and nowhere, for a being which has an inexhaustible store of rewards for the good (that is, for those who love it) and which punishes the wicked, the egoists, by the curse of all the ages. How could the man who believed in the nothing, in the eternal return to the earth, in sleep without reawakening, feel his heart palpitate when thinking of the way in which posterity might some day pronounce his name? What then would glory mean to him? Why would he have wanted to die like Socrates? Why would the fate of Christ, crucified for the salvation of barbarous mankind and for the emancipation of the slave, make him weep? Should he blush for his weakness and hide his tears? Should he fear the smile of the skeptic and of the atheist? No, my friend, the atheist did not smile at seeing this warmth, the love for the divinity which I adored. But the truly religious man smiled. He looked almost in pity at the pettiness of our sentiments, at the mediocre altar of philanthropy.

"Open your eyes," he will tell you. "Look how narrowly confined your God is. Lo! You have an immense, infinite world before you, and your view remains fixed on the earth? Why am I saying on the earth? It is rather on one organic species inhabiting it. Oh, yes, certainly the noble creature to whose worship you are dedicated is worthy of your love. You doubtlessly love it because you experience holy admiration in seeing the generosity of the sentiments which animate it, the orderliness of its progressive march, and the greatness of its deeds. You love it because you find in it love, science, and strength. Well, examine how it exercises this threefold power. It uses science to discover from century to century some of the world's laws; and with every step on this endless road, mankind increasingly realizes the immensity of the field which remains open. It uses its strength to change, combine, and transport matters; and here, too, the further it advances, that is the closer it seems to approach the impenetrable secret of creation, the more it senses its inability to discover this secret. Its love, science, and industry have just shown what should inevitably be the object of man's efforts. Yes, eternal wisdom possesses the secret of the world and calls ceaselessly upon us to know it. Perfect beauty reveals itself to us by giving man the strength to embellish the world and by giving the world the capacity for embellishing man. Being through its infinite goodness brings us closer to itself by making us love more and more all that is. Finally, it is sovereign science, sovereign creative force, and sovereign love which your God himself, which mankind worships. Prostrate yourselves with mankind before its God's feet; he is also your God. Sing with mankind the praises of the master whose laws mankind lovingly obeys."

How weak my speech is when I wish to make the religious man speak! I feel that my speech is no longer saturated with the poisonous vapors of criticism. But the fear of an audience made narrow minded by cold syllogisms always takes the warmth out of my words. For a long time yet we shall have to translate what I have just told you into a more vulgar language, into so-called scientific speech. For a long time yet when we wish to pronounce the name which for several thousands of years has made all mankind tremble with joy, fear, and hope, this name which Newton heard only in awe, we shall be forced, in order to avoid the laughter of our age of mockery, to prove mathematically, so to say, and by a cold calculus of probability, that our beliefs are those which the future will profess.

Keep from repeating to your brother what I have just said

about philanthropy, or at least use another form better suited
to his intellectual habits, which will be at the same time merely
another expression of the same idea. Have him compare fetishism, polytheism, the Jewish and the Christian religions. Show
him at last that the God of the philanthropists, mankind, has
always recognized and worshipped a God superior to it.

Let him for one moment reflect in good faith and conscientiously about the kind of emotion which his sincere love
for mankind makes him feel. You may rest assured that it will
be impossible for him not to recognize that they are as hypothetical as, and yet less broad than, the so-called religious emotions. The philanthropist will then appear to him as he is, a
second-class religious person, devoid of and deprived of a feeling
for the fine arts and above all of the sympathetic word which
electrifies mankind.

No, my friend, your brother will not resist. Overwhelm him
with examples which he himself cannot challenge, because he
loves poetry, music, painting, and architecture. The theater
moves him; and the popular platform, animated by Demosthe-
nes, Cicero, Fox, Mirabeau, and Foy, is the most beautiful spectacle of which his imagination can conceive. Overwhelm him
with examples, I tell you. They will not be lacking. Ask him
what Virgil, Ovid, and Lucretius have done for the welfare of
the world; what have been the subjects that have inspired Han-
del, Mozart, Haydn, Cherubini, and even Rossini, when they
composed their most beautiful works; and what have been the
subjects for which Raphael and Michelangelo found their most
beautiful colors. Let him show you a single worldly monument
which is not eclipsed by our pious basilicas. And if he dares to
take refuge in the theater, if he names Talma,[16] with Cicero's
enthusiasm for Roscius, handle him with care: do not overcome
him by confronting him with those sublime actors, those great
masters of the world, those divine orators who revealed Christian
hopes to the barbarian peoples; do not profane the names of the

[16] "Talma, the great tragic actor (1769-1828), after having had the
Emperor for his patron, became under the Restoration the object of a cult
by the parties of the opposition. When he died repeating the words 'Voltaire
. . . like Voltaire' and after having refused religious rites, his funeral took
on the proportion of a great national and political manifestation." B341.

Saint Pauls, the Saint Augustines, and the Saint Chrysostoms. Take the most obscure village priest, filled with evangelical morality and speaking to believers like him. Then, together with your brother, count the moral deeds brought about through the influence of the pulpit and of the decorated stage.

Indeed, my friend, this last idea pains me deeply, or rather it moves me to regrets and above all to desires. Like your brother, I also weep, moved, trembling and troubled at the voices of Desdemona, Tancred, or Arsace. But tears still flow from my eyes when your brother's have dried up. What do all the women sitting around me do at this point? Do they, dressed as for a holiday, come into this brilliant hall to witness the triumph of one of them? Will she be crowned who feels the deepest love? Yes, the most loving, the most passionate of all the women has the greatest power over our hearts. She is the sibyl of our days. She is the being who has the secret of noble inspiration. A Christian might ask, "Is it the immaculate Virgin whom you worship? Good God! In what temple have you placed her?"

Let us leave this subject; it is sickening.

Moreover, you will not have the most difficult struggle on this sad plane. I have spoken to you of the plebeian tribune and of the orators whose powerful voices animate a numerous audience or spread afar to stir the peoples. Your brother, confident of victory, will defend himself most ardently here. Here he believes himself to have overwhelmed all our legions by confronting Bossuet, Bourdaloue, or Massillon, noble but powerless rear guards of Catholicism in rout, with the colossus of the eighteenth century, Mirabeau. But continue making him shamefully aware of the poisoned weapon he uses against you. Do not attack persons first. Later your brother will understand that there exists a connection between the morality of deeds and that of doctrines. Go, therefore, straight to the latter, and place yourself fearlessly on your opponent's plane.

Well, what are the works of Mirabeau? What are the works of his age which he represents so well in all its aspects? They have broken the yoke of the past and destroyed the empire of Christian theology and feudalism. What passion did they excite in men to accomplish such a task? Distrust, hatred, vengeance

and even bloodthirstiness. These slogans were repeated by the
orators until the shouts of "liberty, equality, fraternity, or death"
were echoed instead.

Let us now look at the Christians. They also had a past to
destroy. They also had to apply bitter criticism to an ancient
theology and to the powers of the earth. Did the work they
accomplished require less strength and less genius? Was it easier
for the heirs of Augustus' century than for those of the age of
Louis XIV to destroy the old structure?

Indeed, the apostles had many more enemies to fight. All
the innumerable philosophic sects which disputed among themselves the rule of the world, and of which only one reached the
threshold of the future, were to disappear at their voice. All
were to lose their names in order to rally under the name of
Christ, although preserving in the heresies the marks of their
origin until the sole chair of Saint Peter was raised on the ruins
of the Lyceum, the Portico, and the Academy.

Hear those rebellious citizens and ardent revolutionaries!
The Christians also want "peace for the cottages," but they built
the palace of the Lord to obtain it. They also preach struggle
and war. But which enemy do they teach man to suspect and
fight? Man himself, and his egoism. The weapons they give us
to defeat egoism are not distrust and hatred; they do not incite
us to vengeance, but teach us to find our strength in faith, hope,
and love.

Let us stop here, my friend. We have just discovered the
secret of Christian strength and the cause for the impermanence
of criticism. We know why the atheist orators were destined to
pass from the Capitol to the Tarpeian rock, from the mountain
to the scaffold, from apotheosis to oblivion. We know the real
cause for the admitted and little-understood ingratitude of republics and why they sacrifice so many victims from among those
who are still in popular favor. But we also understand why the
Christian's day of glory, the day when he was assured of immortality for his name and when he won the love of posterity,
was also the day of his martyrdom.

"What?" they will exclaim. "Does one overthrow a detested
power and a despotic authority by preaching faith and blind

obedience? Does one claim to be able to free the weak by pro-
fessing doctrines so favorable to the strong? Can one arrive at
freedom through slavery?"

This is an incomprehensible mystery for our philosophers
who study men so conscientiously and who do not hear the voice
of human conscience. It is a monstrous paradox for our publicists, the apostles of independence,[17] who forget that man as a
social being necessarily depends on the society of which he is a
part. It is a miracle for all, since all know beyond doubt that
the submissive, humble, and peaceful words of Christ really broke
the slave's chain.

For us, on the other hand, there is no longer any miracle or
mystery in this sublime manifestation of divine goodness. We
go back to the pure source from which Christian philosophy and
politics drew their superiority over those of Greece and Rome, to
the source at which Saint-Simon was able to find new waters
hidden even to the Christians; waters which gave us the power
and the right to condemn all the doctrines of our day as well as
those of the past.

Yes, my friend, by preaching obedience, but obedience to the
will of a God of love, one simultaneously destroys anarchy and
despotism; that is to say, the egoism of ignorance as well as the
egoism of science, the impotent yet destructive desires of weakness as well as the proud pretensions of force. Any philosophical
doctrine which attempts to attain only one of these two goals is
false, incomplete, and not applicable to the organic state of mankind. It is Epicureanism or Stoicism, materialistic or spiritualistic egoism, but I have already said it still is egoism. Spiritual
egoism never grips the masses, but is reserved for a few self-
centered individuals whose solitary contemplations it beguiles.
Materialistic egoism comes like a flood upon sick mankind at
those epochs of crisis when man, tired of a senescent existence,
without faith in a better life, seems to ask even for death as a
remedy for his ills.

You recall the joy which we experienced the day we dis-

<hr>

[17] Here the Saint-Simonians have in mind Benjamin Constant, who had
called early during the Restoration for the formation of a Constitutional or
Independent Party dedicated to the defense of individual liberty. Cf. B345.

covered the emptiness of these two philosophies and their inability to govern the world. Then Saint-Simon had not yet
enlightened us; and like servile imitators of the Greeks and
Romans who, when disgusted with Epicurus and Zeno, flew to
Alexandria to practice éclecticism with the Neo-Platonists, we
left Helvétius and Rousseau for Stewart, Reid, and Laromiguière.[18]

Certainly, we made great progress, for we were seeking to
free ourselves from egoism, and yet, we were still walking in its
ways. Indeed, by taking some bits of debris from all doctrines,
without any principle of selection, we both had gradually heaped
together formless compilations which we called doctrines. And
they were not those of Descartes, Malebranche, Locke, Condillac,
or Kant. These great philosophers were no longer our teachers.
You were the student of your conscience, I of mine, and we
could use the expression so dear to egoism, "my doctrine."

Indeed, we did then as the school of Alexandria had done.
We, too, had long fought the Epicureans and the Stoics of our
day, and like the Platonists, to use an expression of Saint-
Augustine, had despised the noise of the false philosophers who
were barking at us. We passed lovingly under the standards of
the man through whom divine will manifested itself to us. Our
philosophic personality became obliterated before genius. We
no longer feared to acknowledge a leader, a guide, and a master.
And what a master! The man whom his age ignored, forsook,
and mistook; whose life, full of devotion, had to be a mystery for

---

[18] "This sentence defines well the two tendencies, the one more metaphysical, the other more psychological, expressed in the new doctrine of the
liberal spiritualists. 'To be eclectic with the Neoplatonists': Enfantin was
thinking of Victor Cousin, the editor of Plato and of Proclus. 'We left
Helvétius and Rousseau for Stewart, Reid and Laromiguière': Jouffroy had
undertaken, in 1828, his big French edition of the complete works of Thomas
Reid, with fragments by M. Royer-Collard. He had just started a course at
the Sorbonne in January 1829. He was the new name, the young hope of the
spiritualist school; and being more psychological than Victor Cousin, he
thought less of importing something of the teachings of Hegel and Schelling
than of continuing the more modest tradition of the so-called Scottish
philosophy which had been introduced into France before him by Laromiguière and Royer-Collard." B346.

egoism; who at the edge of his grave, at the point when the happy men of the age were abandoning themselves to despair and calling for consolation, when the men tired by useless lives gave evidence of the most Stoic indifference, filled us with ardor by revealing to us the hopes of mankind, and by his example imposed upon us the duty to sacrifice all for the realization of these hopes. He could finally say, like Simeon: "Nothing, O great God, prevents me any longer from walking in peace since my eyes have seen the instrument by which you have resolved to save the world." [19]

The beloved disciple of Jesus has said this, my friend. We no longer fear when we love. Obedience is sweet and faith easy when the master who commands orders us to believe in the noble destiny of the human species, when he forces us to guide all our thoughts and acts towards a goal which delights our hearts so greatly.

Apostles of liberty, will you yet long repeat that revolt is the holiest duty? Are you not afraid that this terrible weapon—which you have used blindly because you wanted only to destroy—will one day turn against you? Do you not tremble when you worry that soon perhaps mankind, taught by you, will rise in revolt against the heavy yoke which your doctrines have imposed on man for two centuries. You who constantly speak of the early Christians' fury against the enemies of the Church and of their cruel acts of vengeance, while forgetting that it was in the schools where your principles were professed that they had learned to seek vengeance; you who know that they acted not as Christians but as barbarians, since Christ had commanded them to pardon offenses; do you believe that human societies will never be led by men whose power they will cherish and whose authority they will defend? What! Hated leaders, masters who plot our ruin, who idly fatten themselves on our work and our sweat, monsters who live from our suffering and our tears! Is hell then your future? And you want your path to be followed! No, no, the sound of the alarm bell, the sinister cry "To arms!" must no longer be heard. Blood must no longer moisten our furrows.

[19] Apparently a paraphrase of Luke, II, 29-30.

Arson and war have long enough devoured the world. Stop intoxicating us with distrust and hate. The time has come for mankind to exclaim like Solomon: "Withdraw furious north wind; come gentle southern winds!" [20]

[20] Evidently a misquotation of the Song of Songs, IV, 16.

The Religious Development of Mankind: Fetishism, Polytheism, Jewish and Christian Monotheism

The religious problem to which we have called your attention is as great as it is unlooked-for. The solution we have given you dogmatically has inspired more repugnance and provoked more opposition than any of our other predictions concerning the future of mankind. Often the views presented by us up to that point, however radically opposed to the accepted ideas, were received with marked favor from the start. This has not been the fate of our religious predictions. Here, from the very first words on, we have seen the eighteenth century, whose reputation we had possibly shattered on many important points, suddenly regain its strength and rise up against us with all its antipathies, terror, and its entire disintegrating dialectic.

This reaction, gentlemen, was not unforeseen by us. If you recall some of the ideas we repeatedly presented to you on the essential characteristics of critical epochs, you will see that we must have expected it. It would be superfluous to return to what we have said about this subject. We shall merely remind you of this important point, that the great object of the epochs of criticism or of destruction—and our age will give you the necessary means to observe what we are pointing out—is the annihilation of religious ideas. This is the result and final end to which all efforts are directed in a thousand different forms and in all possible ways. Indeed, look at the bottom of the most profound scientific discussions and the most weighty literary debates carried on in these epochs. Consider carefully the nature of the attempts at political reorganization and of the social theories formulated in such ages, and you will see that everywhere the principal aim is to exclude God from the government of the world and from human thought. It will be easily understood that it cannot be otherwise, since man's idea of God is only his way of viewing unity, order, and harmony, of being aware of a destiny and explaining it to himself; and in the critical epochs, there exists for man neither unity, harmony, order nor destiny. Irreligion is, therefore, the moral trait characteristic of generations which prepare the critical epochs as it is the sum total of the education of these generations born and developed in their course.

Having reached, as we have today, the utmost limits of criticism, when so many calculations have been mistaken and so many hopes deceived, the critical faith might very easily have begun to waver about some of the dogmas holy to it. Thus one might easily imagine that men whose minds have been deprived of their former fervor might be persuaded by an organic idea of the future, whose character and import escapes them, to agree with us on some particular question. But on the question of religion, this attitude is impossible. Just as religion has always been debated in the development of critical ideas, and just as the negative solution of the problem of religion has been the basis and the sanction of all other negations, so it follows that as soon as this solution is attacked, everyone becomes immediately and instinctively aware that his entire system of ideas and preferences is at stake. It is hence inevitable, as we have just said, that the critical genius awakens in all its strength, because at this stage this question becomes a matter of life and death for it. The experience of all ages proves that mankind cannot be dispossessed so easily, and that it undergoes a complete transformation only after a long and painful struggle.

We have not been afraid of provoking this struggle. We knew that this meant taking the risk of losing the favor our previously expressed ideas had gained. But such a consideration could not stop us. For as long as our solution of the religious problem is not accepted, the ideas which we have expounded will not have been definitely established because they can be understood in their full scope only in relation to this solution, which forms their connective and their sanction.

The discussion is now under way; it must be continued. Today when the initial astonishment which this discussion inevitably aroused has passed and the explanations already given suffice to dispel the strangeness of our propositions, we hope to be heard more attentively and with less bias than we were at first.

While proclaiming that religion is destined to reassert its rule over society, we certainly are as far from holding that any of the religious institutions of the past should be re-established as we are from claiming to lead society back to the old state of war or slavery. We proclaim a new moral and political state. This is just as thoroughly a new religious state: for to us religion, politics, and morals are merely different names for the same fact. Although this problem is wider in scope than any other because it includes them all, and although it is likely to arouse men's emotions, since the fate of the entire system of ideas, pre-dominant preferences, and general interests of mankind must depend on its solution, it is, nevertheless, not less susceptible to being posed and resolved in terms which are both simple and clear. The method of investigation to be followed and the means of demonstration to be used in this connection are the same as for all problems that have occupied us before. In this respect we have not strayed from the rules we outlined at the beginning of this exposition, but we have rather advanced.

Before going further, we consider it necessary to recall the general, preparatory terms by which we have already presented the solution of this problem and to return briefly to the discus-sions in which we have engaged to prepare the public for this solution.

Mankind has a religious future, we have said. The religion of the future must not be viewed as being merely the outcome of inner and purely individual contemplation for each man, as mere sentiment, as as idea isolated from the totality of each individual's sentiments. It must be the expression of mankind's collective thought, the synthesis of all of man's conceptions, and the rule for all of his acts. The religion of the future is called upon to take its place in the political order; but to be exact, when considered in its totality, the political institution of the future must be a religious institution.

These were the important propositions which we had to

prove, but we first had to struggle against arguments and against critical axioms which barred even the examination of the problems proposed by us.

These arguments were drawn principally from the progress of the sciences, from a consideration of the mysteries illuminated by the sciences, from the positivistic habits (*habitudes de positivisme*)[1] which they had inculcated in men's minds, and from the disgust for hypotheses inspired by them.

We had to weigh the value of these arguments. First of all, when we enumerated the sciences we found none which by its subject matter or by its proper method of investigation could prove anything against the two fundamental ideas of all religions: providence and destiny. We have shown that if the scientists co-operated in the destruction of religious beliefs, they did so above all as fervent disciples of the critical philosophy and of its beliefs. To find in those facts by which they were contesting the existence of God the proofs of his nonexistence which they believed these facts had to provide, they needed nothing less than the strong faith inspired in them by this philosophy, or rather by a hypothesis about man, the world, and the relation between the two.

In next examining the sciences as to their subject matter and method, we established that these sciences did not only not prove anything against religion, but, moreover, that they themselves were rooted in and took their strength from an essentially religious idea, namely that there is constancy, order, and regularity in the chain of phenomena. Departing from this idea, we foresaw a time, no longer distant, when the sciences, freed from the influence of the dogmas of criticism and viewed in a much broader and general fashion than they are today, would no longer be considered antagonistic to religion, but rather as the means given to the human mind to know the laws by which God governs the world; the providential plan. Thus we summoned the sciences to spread, support, and strengthen the religious sentiment in the future, since each of their discoveries would

---

[1] "First appearance of this word (*positivisme*). In the spirit of the 'New Christians' which the Saint-Simonians claim to be it has a pejorative meaning." B353.

present the providential plan more broadly, and thus increase, confirm, and strengthen the love which man can conceive for the supreme intelligence that ceaselessly leads him to ever better destinies.

On the other hand, we pointed out that scientific procedure or method always presupposed axioms and beliefs before application; that its aim was merely to classify and arrange facts according to the hypothetical conception of a relation or link existing between them, and thus to confirm this conception. In other words, we said that, strictly speaking, there existed no method for discovery, imagination, conception, or creation, and that sentiment always formed the basis of science, limited its sphere, guided it in its research, and determined the order of the classifications by furnishing science with a criterion for the differences or analogies among phenomena.

We then considered all those sciences which are called "positive" today and are alone regarded favorable and spoken of when support on scientific grounds is sought. We pointed out that in their investigations they embrace only a very limited part of the universal phenomenal order. Man's moral or social existence remains outside their framework. They do not even consider these phenomena capable of being related to simple, regular, and positive laws and consequently offer no general explanation for them. Even those facts with which the present day sciences deal can be understood only incompletely because of the scientists' ignorance of the other important portion of science which deals with men's moral relations among themselves and the sympathetic bonds uniting mankind with the world. And, indeed, man cannot successfully explain and define the universe, whose infinite unity he feels, except by placing himself alternately and by abstraction now at the center, now at the circumference of this one, multiple phenomenon; now relating the All to his own existence, and then considering himself essentially dependent on the All, in relation to which his individuality is only a point. Or in other words, to explain and define the universe to himself, man, as Saint-Simon told us, must alternately experience man himself and what is not man, the little world and the great world, and must constantly link these two points of view with a conception of the sympathy between them, a conception which for man is the revelation of God himself. Only if the so-called positive sciences comprised all classes of phenomena which we encounter, could they claim to pronounce judgment on the existence of God, since by definition God is the infinite and universal being.

While evaluating the repugnance of our age for hypotheses, we have shown that all discoveries and all progress of the human mind up to this day have had hypotheses as their source, and that it must always be so; that all science, the most positive not excepted, rests on a hypothetical conception which delineates its scope, guides its research, and determines its classifications; that the noblest inspirations of man have no other foundations; that the critical faith which has been so strong and which still demonstrates its strength when attacked rested entirely on a series of hypotheses like the following: that no superior intelligence presides over the order of the universe; that human events are abandoned to the caprice of chance; that man has no existence beyond the limited manifestation we call life; and that he is born free. And finally, we have shown that despite its claims to the contrary our century has renounced the general hypotheses of providence, order, good, and immortality only to abandon itself unreservedly to the hypotheses of fatalism, chance, disorder, evil and nothingness.

Moreover, the arguments we have just briefly reproduced have been the subject of very extensive digressions which were necessary during the preceding sessions to save us from having to deal with them later. We hope now to have sufficiently defeated the unwillingness even to examine our position. We shall go directly to the heart of the matter and undertake to justify the truth of the propositions by which we have offered to solve the religious problem through the use of the historical method, the mechanism of which we have described at length at the beginning of this exposition.

Indeed, we shall rapidly trace the religious development of mankind, and show that the religious sentiments, far from having grown constantly weaker, as seems generally to be believed, have, on the contrary, constantly grown and acquired greater importance.

The religious development of man up to this day comprises three successive general states:

Fetishism, in which man deifies nature in each of its creations, forms, and accidents, without establishing any general link between himself and his environment or among the numerous beings whom he distinguishes in this environment.

Polytheism, in which, after having raised himself to more general abstractions about the world around him and about his own existence, man deifies these abstractions and thus connects them to previously isolated phenomena. At this epoch, man does not yet perceive a common link among all beings but supposes the existence of this link and gives witness to his inclination to grasp it by the kind of hierarchy he establishes among the different personifications worshipped by him.

Monotheism, in which, although he does not yet conceive of the living and absolute unity of being, man establishes a general link among its various manifestations by relating them to a single cause, external to the universe to be sure, but whose will as understood by him justifies and sums up all the facts he encounters.

The progress of religious feeling from each of these general states to the following is evident.* This progress can be viewed from several standpoints. If it were generally recognized and we merely had to show the direction it took, we would doubtless have to trace progress among the phenomena directly related to the triple moral, intellectual, and physical aspect under which we have always considered human activity. But at this point we are trying to prove the very existence of this progress. We must, therefore, take into account the attempts to deny it.

It is generally claimed today that religion has not ceased to lose in importance in individual as well as in social life.

This opinion has been expressed in the following terms as regards individual life: since man first conceived of the deity's

---

* Each of these religious states comprises several nuances or important phases, but we shall deal only with those of the last state.

existence, he has felt less and less love and veneration for it and has, by the weakening of his belief in a future life, gradually been withdrawing from domination by religious law.

But it is easy to prove that exactly the opposite has taken place.

In fetishism, that is to say in the least advanced state of civilization, fear is almost the only sentiment binding man to the deity conceived by him. The only object of the entire worship seems to be to avert the wrath of powerful enemies. And if, perhaps, love does appear in this worship, this expression of religious feeling is always too weak and too exceptional to determine its character.

If one considers the narrow scope within which the divinity is thought of and imagines in this epoch, it will easily be understood that it cannot inspire deep veneration. Thus we see the fetishist bargain with his idol for one power after another and believe that he has the right to punish the idol when he does not receive what he asked for.

Man in this state, living from day to day without tradition or future, entirely occupied with providing for his rarely satisfied primary needs, has little time for the contemplation of a future life. The awareness of immortality was doubtless not alien to him, since it is inherent in the very nature of man. But according to the kind of needs he has developed and according to his narrow way of understanding the world and his own existence, the future life, in the short moments when it occupies his thinking, appears to him almost as the mere prolongation of his state. Thus this belief remains almost sterile in regard to its influence on his decisions.

Polytheism offers noticeable progress from this threefold point of view. Love is no longer an expression alien to this religious state of man. The word "pity" was known among the pagans. But at this epoch, the feeling of fear remains dominant; and the religious man par excellence, the righteous man, is still portrayed as fearing the gods.

The polytheist's veneration for his deities is quite superior to the fetishist's. He believes, to be sure, that he can make them favorable to him by offering them rewards, but he does not feel that he has the right or the power to punish them.

Belief in a future life then takes on a greater importance, mainly as a penal sanction through the depiction of the punishments with which the guilty are threatened. The only reward offered the righteous which can attract them as effectively to another life can be acquired only in exceptional cases and is limited to the rare apotheoses of a few illustrious men who, as heroes or demigods, will take their places on Olympus. The immortality reserved to common virtues evidently has meaning only by contrast to the terrors of Tartarus; this view is sufficiently illustrated by the ancient traditions preserved for us in poetry depicting the inhabitants of Elysium, who in this state are but shadows perpetually wishing for even the humblest life on earth.

Monotheism constitutes two phases: Judaism and Christianity.

Judaism offers an important advance over polytheism. The feeling of fear doubtless still holds an important place in the heart of the people of Moses, and the terrible epithets with which he constantly describes the God whom he serves and the law of extermination which he executes in His name testify to the intensity of this feeling. But the living poetry that contains vigorous expression of this sentiment shows us that it had already ceased to be dominant and that the feeling of love was beginning to play at least an equal role.

Veneration for the deity then assumes a remarkable development. The Jew still sometimes dares to question God's justice, but he senses Him too far above himself to think of punishing his God or even of trying to tempt Him with the promise of rewards.

As the critical philosophers have liked to point out, the dogma of immortality is, to be sure, not formally expressed in the first books of the Hebraic tradition. But it is at least implicitly and quite clearly contained in several pages of these books.* It would thus be impossible not to recognize its existence

* As, for example, in the phrase used several times at the occasion of the death of the patriarchs: "And (he) was gathered unto his people."

in the promises made to God's people, promises which link the people's entire history and which appear both as the deepest reason for its undertakings and as the most general and powerful sanction of the law given to it. Moreover, in the development of Jewish doctrine and society, the dogma of immortality gradually wins its own identity and grows continuously towards Christianity. As the direct heir of the revelation of Moses, Christianity, by assigning immortality an important place among its beliefs, clearly illustrates the increasing role which this idea had played in the Jewish doctrine whose rule had just ended.

Christianity finally opens a new and tremendous path for all the advances we have just pointed out. If God at this epoch still reveals himself to men by awakening fear in their hearts (the inevitable consequence of the dogmas of the fall of man, of predestined damnation, and of stern punishments), this fear is, however, so subordinated, and love expresses itself so strongly and dominantly in the hearts of the new religious society, that if one cannot admit that Christianity is entirely a law of love, one can at least understand the reasons for this illusion in the past which made this expression so familiar.

The Christian's veneration for the God whom he adores raises him to the level of His love. However irreconcilable reality may seem to him with the notions of divine justice and providence which he has formed, he does not hesitate to subject his reason to the profundity of God's plan. Whatever his fortune may be, he neither claims the right to complain against his creator nor to censure Him. In all the situations in which he finds himself, he adores and respects His decree and accuses only himself. And yet, since he prays, unwittingly he still doubts divine goodness and wisdom.[2]

For the Christian the present life is only a preparation for

[2] Enfantin added this note in the edition of the *Doctrine* in the *Oeuvres de Saint-Simon et d'Enfantin* (XLII, 141): "It would be a mistake to take as an absolute condemnation what is meant here only as a relative evaluation of prayer and of the predominant role which it has played in Christian or rather in Catholic worship. The further developments of the doctrine, in unveiling the theoretical meaning, the practical value, and the religious prerogative of this sublime expression of human life, will show how, far from being destined to disappear, prayer will grow ceaselessly while being contained within the limits which the new dogma will assign it."

the future life. The idea of immortality, revealed in the fear of punishments or in the no less powerful desire for closer union with God, is habitual to him and often dominant. Moreover, it would be useless to dwell any longer on the importance the dogma of the future life has had in Christianity. If this doctrine has lost its hold on men's hearts in our time, what has come about is still close enough to remain in our memory.

The progress of the religious sentiment in terms of the place it occupies in individual existence is clearly shown in the succession of the three general states we have just examined, as well as in the two phases of which the last is composed. In this succession, we see the religious bond continually strengthened by the development of man's love and veneration for God and by the ever growing importance of the dogma of immortality.

There still remains for us to demonstrate the equally evident progress of the social importance of religion and of its power to unite men.

Just as in the world around him, the fetishist sees only isolated beings in the human family. The principle of association hardly extends beyond the immediate ties of the family, which to him is the final stage of individuality, since it is impossible to conceive of absolutely isolated individuals. If, however, there is agreement among a larger number of men, it is only for an exceptional situation, such as for a hunt or for offensive or defensive war. But after such temporary and accidental alliances, every one hastens to return to the bosom of his family. Worship, so to say, is then entirely individual. Like God himself, it is confined to the home, where the head of the family is the pontiff.

Just as the polytheist attributes the government of the world to causes as numerous as the abstractions which his mind can grasp, so he also divides the government of man among as many distinct gods as there are different associations on the surface of the globe. Here the religious conception first begins to assume a social character. Family cult still preserves great importance, but the city-wide cult prevails. However, at this stage the social value of the religious dogma is still very limited. First, it is only the city that this dogma unites, and even there not all men. The religion of the patrician and that of the plebeian are not the same, and the slave remains outside of any religious, and hence social, existence.

The monotheistic dogma of Judaism virtually calls upon mankind to form a universal association. By recognizing the unity of God, this people proclaims the unity of the human race. True, Judaism escapes the full social consequences of this general conception by the idea "that God has chosen a single people and has excluded the others from his alliance." But in contrast to the polytheistic city, the religious belief of the Jewish nation is common to all classes and binds them to society. We do, to be sure, find slaves among the Jews, but if we may say so, this is only an inconsistency—partly removed by the slaves' right to embrace and profess the religious faith of their masters, by their mild treatment, and by the very time limit placed on slavery.

Finally Christianity appears. Like Hebrew monotheism, it recognizes the unity of God and the unity of the human family. But it no longer assumes the exclusive election of a single people; nor does it admit that a portion of mankind may be denied the knowledge of God and the hope in his promises. On the contrary, it calls upon all men to share the same belief, to unite in the same association, and to form but one Church. True, after the establishment of Christianity slavery perseveres for some time. But from then on slavery is under direct attack in all its forms from the Christians and finally is abolished by their efforts. Christian monotheism at first has this disadvantage as compared with Jewish monotheism; that it does not contain a political law embracing and regulating all human activity, individual as well as social, or, from a different aspect, spiritual and material. We shall later have to show the reason for this phenomenon. And yet we shall observe now already that while Christianity still merely presents, properly speaking, a collection of individual precepts, Christianity, through the potential power of aggregation contained in the very enunciation of its moral dogma, has under the sway of Catholicism given birth to the greatest political association that ever existed.

From the preceding it may be concluded, as we said at the beginning, that religion has assumed increasing importance in its successive stages represented by fetishism, polytheism, and the two phases of monotheism, and that it has acquired this importance from the twofold standpoint of its social significance and of the ever increasing role it has played in man's individual existence. As we have said, religion is called upon today to make one tremendous new forward step. We shall constantly show in what this progress will consist and what changes it will bring to the world.

In the brief sketch which we just drew, we did not claim to instill religious conviction in our listeners or to prove to them what cannot be proven, namely the existence of God. We merely wished to establish with the help of the historical method, which has generally received their approval, that religious beliefs, far from growing weaker as it generally held, have pursued a clearly progressive course.[3]

The scientific language we have used until now is, as we know, little suited to forming religious convictions. Conversions

[3] "The positivistic philosophy of the Saint-Simonians thus culminates in a religion, a metaphysics. This metaphysics is a metaphysics of feeling. The need which this religion wishes to satisfy is the demand for unity. For neither science, which always opposes subject to object, one term to another, nor action, which sets a will against matter which the will wishes to exploit or one individual against another, can satisfy this demand. It is rather in the essence of feeling to associate or unite. Feeling is to all intents a 'synthesis.' It suppresses and 'transcends' any dualism, particularly the dualism of spirit and matter which Christianity, the sentimental expression of the last great organic epoch, permitted to exist. Having reached a higher and final stage of the 'synthesis,' the Saint-Simonians proclaim the 'rehabilitation of matter.' (*Doctrine de Saint-Simon. Deuxième Année,* Session VII.) In the final analysis, Saint-Simonism thus is pantheistic (*Ibid.,* Session VIII; *Oeuvres de Saint-Simon et d'Enfantin,* XLII, 305n)." B361.

Further in the same note, Bouglé and Halévy raise the question of Schelling's and Hegel's influence on Saint-Simonian theology. Pierre Leroux later held that "Enfantin's metaphysics is positively that of Hegel" and pointed out the close acquaintance of three of the Saint-Simonians—apparently Jules Chevalier, who had studied in Germany; Eugène Rodrigues, who in 1832 published a translation of Lessing's *Education of the Human Race* with an elaboration of Saint-Simonian theology in his *Letters;* and Charles Duveyrier, who helped Enfantin in the formulation of the dogma of eternal life—with Hegelian philosophy. Bouglé and Halévy, however, conclude that similarities between Hegelian and Saint-Simonian thought are a matter of "parallelism rather than of influence."

For a Saint-Simonian interpretation of Hegel, see the article on Prussia in the *Globe,* April 7, 1832.

of this nature are brought about by the language of inspired men, of prophets, a language which God does not permit anyone to use today, doubtless because no one would be able to understand it. The only result we wish to obtain for the moment is to pave the way for this language of sympathy by rejecting the sophism which the critical philosophy has implanted in the minds of men, by combatting the prejudices of atheism, and by destroying the disheartening hypotheses of egoism.

BIBLIOGRAPHICAL NOTE

There is an immense literature on Saint-Simon and on the Saint-Simonians. Extensive bibliographies are contained in Sébastien Charléty, *Histoire du Saint-Simonisme*(Paris, 1931; the 1965 edition does not contain the bibliography), and in Jean Walch, *Bibliographie du Saint-Simonisme* (Paris, 1967). Additional entries are found in Georg G. Iggers, *The Cult of Authority: The Political Philosophy of the Saint-Simonians,* 2nd edn. (The Hague, 1970).

The writings of Saint-Simon and some of the Saint-Simonians have been published in the 47-volume edition of *Oeuvres de Saint-Simon et d'Enfantin* (Paris, 1865–1878), recently reprinted. Very few of Saint-Simon's writings are available in English. The 1834 translation of the *New Christianity* has long been unavailable. Selections from Saint-Simon's writings were published as *Selected Writings,* ed. F. M. H. Markham (New York, 1953). The best biography and study of Saint-Simon in English is Frank Manuel, *The New World of Henri Saint-Simon* (Cambridge, Mass., 1956); an excellent study in French is contained in volumes 2 and 3 of Henri Gouhier, *La Jeunesse d'Auguste Comte* (Paris, Lille, 1933–1941).

On the history of the Saint-Simonian movement, there is the study by Sébastien Charléty mentioned above (reprinted without bibliography in 1965); on the political thought of the Saint-Simonians, see the work by Georg G. Iggers mentioned above. Interesting interpretations of Saint-Simonian thought from differing perspectives are contained in F. A. Hayek, *The Counter-Revolution of Science: Studies in the Abuse of Reason* (Glencoe, Ill., 1952); G. D. H. Cole, *A History of Socialist Thought,* vol. I; *The Forerunners* (London, 1953); J. L. Talmon, *Political Messianism: The Romantic Phase* (London, 1960); and Frank Manuel, *The Prophets of Paris* (Cambridge, Mass., 1962).

Index